Choosing your A levels

And other academic options

4th Edition

Cerys Evans

Other titles in the series

Choosing Your Apprenticeship
Choosing Your Diploma
Choosing Your GCSEs, 11th edition

Choosing your A levels and other academic options

This fourth edition published in 2012 by Trotman Publishing, an imprint of Crimson Publishing Ltd, Westminster House, Kew Road, Richmond, Surrey TW9 2ND

First and second editions published by Trotman and Co. Ltd in 2005, 2006
Third edition published by Trotman Publishing in 2008

© Trotman Publishing 2012, 2008

Author: Cerys Evans
Author of editions 1–3: Gary Woodward

British Library Cataloguing in Publication Data
A catalogue record for this book is available from the British Library

ISBN 978 1 84455 426 3

Typeset by IDSUK (DataConnection) Ltd
Printed and bound in Great Britain by Ashford Colour Press, Gosport, Hants

Contents

Acknowledgements

Thanks to all the students who shared their experiences of advanced level study; a particular mention goes to the staff and students of Hillsborough College (part of Sheffield College). David Shaw, International Baccalaureate Co-ordinator at Bilborough College, was a great help, providing insight into the IB Diploma. Thank you to University of Cambridge International Examinations for permitting the use of quotes from students on the Cambridge Pre-U Diploma.

A special thank you goes to my family and friends who have, as ever, been unwaveringly supportive.

Introduction

What next? You will probably ask yourself this question at various points in your life, but one of the most crucial times is when you are thinking about your options at the age of 16. Many of you will be considering further study after your GCSEs, and this book gives you details of the most popular options so you can make an informed choice. As university applications and the job market have become more competitive, the decisions you make now can determine your future path. It is now more important than ever to get things right.

The book is primarily aimed at students who may be considering university. We'll explore the best course of action to help you reach your goals and explain how to keep your options open if you haven't decided on your future plans yet. We'll concentrate on A levels, but you'll also find plenty of information about alternative qualifications, such as Scottish Highers and Advanced Highers, the International Baccalaureate Diploma and the Cambridge Pre-U.

This book will help you to find answers to questions such as those listed below.

- What subjects are available?
- What's the difference between qualifications at this level?
- Which subjects are 'soft'?
- What should I choose if I want to get into a top university?
- Which combinations are preferred for certain degrees?
- Is that subject right for me?

Whatever your situation, it is clear that getting the right answers to these questions is very important: snap decisions at this stage can have significant consequences later on in life. Hopefully, though, with the aid of this book, you will be able to navigate your way successfully through the qualifications maze and make the best choices for you.

'What do I need to think about when deciding what to study?'
See *How to choose* on page 3 and *Planning for the future* on page 34.

'I want to do further study after my GCSEs (or equivalent), but I'm not sure whether A levels are the best option.'
See *Qualifications on offer* on page 19.

'I know what I want to study at university but I'm not sure which subjects I should choose.'
See *Planning for the future* on page 44.

'What are the practical considerations when choosing my subjects?'
See *How to choose* on page 3.

'How do I find out about individual subjects at advanced level?'

See the Subject Directory from page 55.

'I haven't decided on my future plans. How can I make the right decisions?'

See *Planning for the future* on page 40.

'I want to go straight into work after I finish sixth form or college.'

See the Subject Directory (non-graduate jobs) for each
subject you are interested in, from page 55.

PART ONE

OPTIONS AND DECISIONS

CHAPTER ONE

How to choose

You may not have had to make a decision quite like this before. While your subject choices will not necessarily map out your entire future, they will have a dramatic impact on your direction for some time. It is important that you take your time with the process, gathering all the necessary material and getting all the assistance you need. First of all, you need to be sure that you have enough information at your fingertips. This chapter introduces you to some of the key aspects to consider as you decide on your options.

Getting started

Before you even start to consider what subjects to take, there are a few basic (but crucial) questions you should ask yourself.

- Do I *want* to continue with academic study?
- *Should* I continue with academic study?
- Are A levels right for me?

If you already know that academic study is the right choice for you, just jump straight to *Are A levels getting easier?* on page 5.

Do I want to continue with academic study?

Think about how much you have enjoyed your GCSE (or Standard Grade) study so far. Ask yourself whether you are ready to commit to another two years of challenging academic work. Will you be a motivated and interested student, willing to read around the subject and keen to learn more? If not, then you may find academic advanced level study a struggle.

Should I continue with academic study?

Consider how you approach your studies. Do you cope well with the stresses and strains of exams and schoolwork? Do you meet your deadlines or are you the last to remember that a piece of coursework is due in on Wednesday? Ask your teachers for their opinion, or look at your school reports or progress file for some evidence of how you manage. Your parents will be able to reflect on the approach you take and how you are affected by academic pressures. Bear in mind that poor organisation can be improved upon and revision techniques can be developed, but make sure you are motivated enough to do so.

How good are you at academic study? It is essential to be realistic about your academic ability. Consider your grades and predicted grades so far; are these grades a good indicator of success at a higher level? Scraping through your GCSE qualifications is unlikely to stand you in good stead to achieve the highest grades at A level standard. In fact, lower achievement at GCSE level may limit the number of subjects you can take, the subjects you are able to choose from and whether you can study A levels at all. All of which brings us on to the final question...

Are A levels right for me?

Everyone is different, which means that A levels are not the right choice for everyone. It is often assumed that A levels must be the next step, when this is not always the case. Often, the weight of expectation from teachers, parents, friends (along with the pressure individuals put on themselves) can lead to the wrong choices being made. Plenty of students waste a year or two studying A levels, even though the qualification is not right for them; this often results in them achieving low grades or dropping out and therefore their confidence takes a knock, too. To avoid this scenario, it is important to spend some time finding out about A levels and their alternatives from a range of sources. For details of various post-16 options, see Chapter Two (page 19).

'A levels were an abrupt step up from GCSE: much more in-depth with a faster pace to learning. Far more work was needed out of the classroom than with GCSEs.'

Andrew Burnage

Do I need high GCSE grades to study A levels?

Some institutions ask for a bare minimum of five GCSEs at grade C or above, including English and mathematics, with additional requirements for particular subjects. At the other end of the scale, some selective or independent schools expect all As and A*s at GCSE, in addition to selection tests and interviews.

Requirements might depend on where you apply. If your school has a sixth form and you choose to study there, the staff will already know your abilities and potential so may offer a little flexibility in entry requirements. If you apply to another sixth form or college, then you are more likely to be starting from scratch, although a good reference (or explanation of your achievements) from your school may help.

Achieving the very minimum requirements to join an A level programme (without any extenuating circumstances) might be a reason to investigate whether other learning options would be more appropriate. Students who achieve Cs and Ds at GCSE are more likely to struggle with A levels, often failing to achieve the grades they need to progress.

Of course, some people buck the trend, flourishing at A levels with the help of new teachers or a new setting; however, this tends to be the exception rather than the rule. This is the time to be honest with yourself (and your parents) rather than getting caught up with the A level bandwagon. What are you capable of? If you didn't achieve to your full potential, what prevented you from doing so? How will things be different at A level?

For certain subjects there will be additional requirements, which are often based on the grades you would need at GCSE level to be successful at A level. For example, applicants to A level Maths courses are often asked to achieve a minimum grade B at GCSE from the higher tier.

'It would have been helpful to gain some advice regarding A level requirements during my GCSE period, as I had wanted to study biology at A level but hadn't known that I would need to take the higher paper to do it. Although I was in the top science class, I had decided to do a foundation paper due to stress levels and had thought so long as I got a C in it, it would be fine.'

Helen Jones

Top Tip

You will need strong grades to join an A level programme, but your GCSE grades will also be important when you apply to university; competitive courses, such as medicine and dentistry, and selective universities often require A grades at GCSE, in addition to the highest grades at A level.

Are A levels getting easier?

Every August, newspaper headlines proclaim the news that A levels are getting easier. But is this true? And how could this affect you?

Certainly, results have been improving for the past 20 years or so, with 27% of candidates achieving A or A* in 2011, according to figures produced by the Joint Council for Qualifications. But A levels today are very different from those on offer 20 years ago, when success or failure was mostly based on how well you did in your final exams at the end of two years of study. In the modular A level system in place at the moment, students are assessed and examined on separate modules of work, with the possibility to re-sit, if necessary. This gives students more opportunity to check their progress and step up a gear if they aren't achieving. It also gives them more chances to get things right.

Top Tip

If you start on a modular A level programme then the style of assessment will not change midway through your qualification.

The pressure on schools and colleges to produce great results may also have had an impact on grades. Today, schools and colleges may find themselves far more selective when choosing candidates for A level study. Entry requirements may be higher, with As and Bs required when grade Cs might have been acceptable in the past. In addition, students who don't succeed at AS level standard won't be offered the opportunity to continue to the second year, thus further improving the statistics.

But A levels look set to change over the coming years. Possible reforms include the involvement of universities in the development of qualifications and a shift away from the modular structure. The International Baccalaureate and the Cambridge Pre-U already offer qualifications based on final exams, and you may find a move back towards A level final exams in the next year or so.

Who can help me choose?

The good news when you start choosing your next steps after GCSE (or Standard Grades in Scotland) is that you are not alone. Your school will have a keen interest in supporting you to make the right choices and most institutions put on activities or events to help you to do so, whether you are staying at the same school or moving on.

The post-16 options evening is a key date in the calendar of most schools. This will give you and your parents a chance to find out what is on offer within your current school or within the local area. In addition to A levels (or Scottish Highers), this might include International Baccalaureate provision, vocational qualifications, apprenticeship opportunities, and so on.

'We had options evenings at school where we could go round and ask questions to the different departments about the course content and required grades, etc. I think we had an assembly on it as well.'

Ellie Wigg

Take advantage of these events and bring a list of questions along with you to make sure you get all the information you need. Talk to teachers, heads of year, careers advisers and current students to find out more about all aspects of the experience. Examples of what you should query are listed below.

- What questions do I need to ask?
- What are the entry requirements?
- When and how should I apply?
- How do you decide who gets a place?
- What will the syllabus cover?
- How will I be assessed?
- What kind of support can I expect?
- What grades have past students achieved?
- How can I find out how satisfied students are with their experience?
- Where have past students gone on to study?

You can go to open days at specific institutions to find out more about what they can offer you and see their facilities. If you miss these, see what you can discover online. Some sixth-form schools and colleges have great websites with students' profiles to help you get a student's perspective on things. Don't forget that these are edited by the school or college, though, and therefore tend to give a favourable impression.

Bear in mind that some staff may be keen to recruit students for under-subscribed courses, while others may try to sell their course to high-achievers who are likely to do well. These scenarios happen occasionally, so try not to be swayed by rhetoric and keep a focus on your own plans when considering the suggestions of others. It is always worth asking about success rates and grades from previous years.

Top Tip

Pay close attention to closing dates; you may need to apply from up to a year in advance. Late applicants may miss out on places, particularly for the most competitive institutions and the most popular subjects.

As with all research, it is important to gather information from a variety of different sources and consider the potential for bias; beware of out-of-date material and subjective views. Before coming to their own conclusions, most students discuss this decision with their parents and friends or talk to other students about their experiences. Ultimately, in order to succeed, remember that the choices you make need to be right for you.

If you have some idea about future educational plans, it is worth making enquiries with your preferred universities, either online or over the phone, to ensure that your choices meet their requirements. Likewise, if you have a chosen career in mind, you can talk to a careers adviser about the entry requirements. Chapter Three (page 34), explores this in more detail.

How do I know which subjects to choose?

In this section, you will come across some of the questions to consider when making your subject choices, whether you have clear plans for university or your career direction. Now is the time to take a long, hard look at yourself (metaphorically, at least). You will need to reflect on your own academic ability, your likes and dislikes, how you prefer to learn and which styles of assessment suit you best.

Don't use the answers to the following questions in isolation. For example, there is no point in choosing four subjects just because you are doing well in them if they aren't going to lead to your chosen course at university. You should consider all the questions in

Chapters One and Three before you start to narrow down your choices using the tips in *How can I decide?* on page 50.

> '*Maths was the wrong choice for me. I realised it was very different from GCSE and I knew I would not do well if I continued studying the subject. I was able to swap A level Maths for History. This was a very good decision as history is now my most enjoyable A level and the one I am doing best in.*'
>
> Mohammed Saleh

How many subjects should I take?

Many pupils start with four subjects at AS level, often choosing to drop their least favourite, least relevant or lowest graded choice before moving on to study three subjects at A level. This system allows you some flexibility and removes a little of the risk around making the wrong subject choice. If your GCSE grades are weaker, then you may find you are only allowed to choose three A levels.

In order to gain entry to the most selective universities, you will need three to four good grades at A level. Four AS levels followed by three A2s is a common combination, often welcomed by the more competitive institutions. In most cases, university offers are based on three – rather than four – A levels. If you decided to take four, a university might show you some flexibility in the final grades you will be asked to achieve.

The most academic and talented students might even take on five A level subjects; this helps to demonstrate exceptional skills but is not needed in most cases. If you are choosing to take on more than four A levels, be sure that you can achieve the high grades needed to meet any offers; it is better to gain three A*s than five Cs. Universities may prefer to see that you have read around a subject and that you are passionate about it, rather than be presented with a longer list of qualifications lacking any depth of understanding.

Top Tip

Remember to allow yourself enough time to gain any experience necessary for your chosen degree course; in some cases this will be more relevant than a fourth or fifth A level.

For Scottish Highers, most students take four or five subjects, with the possibility of taking two or three to Advanced Higher level. Cambridge Pre-U students choose three to four Principal subjects (or possibly fewer if they are mixing and matching with A levels). International Baccalaureate Diploma students have to focus on six subjects, although only three of these would be at higher level.

Top Tip

Questions to ask when choosing your subjects.

- Will I enjoy it?
- Will I do well in it?
- Where will it lead?

Should I choose the subjects I enjoy?

This is one of the most important points to consider. If you are intrigued by a subject and have a natural interest in it, then this inevitably makes studying it less of a chore and far more enjoyable. Learning for learning's sake might help to keep you motivated if the pressure of your studies starts to get too much.

It's possible that you can be good at a subject and not enjoy it, and vice versa. However, experience shows that those who go for subjects they are really interested in tend to do better. This is largely because they have a natural talent for that area but also because they are likely to have the motivation to do the reading around the subject, which is needed to get the top grades. One word of warning, though: if you are planning to go for subjects that you enjoy, check whether your selection could be ruling out any universities or career choices. See also *How do I know which combination of subjects is best for me?* on page 13.

'Biology and chemistry were the wrong choices for me because I have now realised that they have nothing to do with what I want to do in the future!'

Yumna Khan

A good starting point is to think carefully about precisely what it is that you enjoy about a subject. Reflect on the GCSE subjects, and also the individual modules, that really inspired you. What did you enjoy about them? The subject content, the way in which you were taught or perhaps the skills you had to use?

Likewise, think about the subjects and the individual modules that you didn't enjoy. Try to pinpoint the real reasons why. Did you find the subject uninteresting, too challenging or was it to do with the way that you were taught? Disliking part of the course doesn't necessarily mean that you will dislike the subject at the next level.

Focusing on subjects and modules you dislike can help to reduce the chances of making a poor choice. The key to success here is to uncover the real reason why the subject or module didn't work for you and to take this into account when making your choices.

Top Tip

- Remember that the advanced level syllabus may offer quite different subject content from GCSE or Standard level. Don't be too quick to rule out History, for example, just because you didn't enjoy the historical period you studied at GCSE.
- On the flip side, loving a subject at GCSE doesn't guarantee that you will love it at A level.
- Don't forget the new subjects available at this level. Maybe you didn't enjoy all of your Maths GCSE but would find economics and its relevance to world events fascinating.

'I've always enjoyed ancient history and thought a History A level would include elements of it at least, but when it didn't, I grew bored and ended up not doing very well.'

Helen Jones

Should I choose the subjects I am best at?

Strength in a subject is a good starting point and would certainly suggest that you have a better chance of achieving high grades. Think about the subjects you have studied so far at GCSE and which ones you have had the best results in. This should give you the confidence that you could study them at a higher level, but don't forget that there can be quite a jump in difficulty between GCSE and A level qualifications. Aptitude in a subject is just one factor to consider, alongside interest and future plans.

'I was good at GCSE Maths so was persuaded by my teacher to do it at A level, but it was hard, tedious and boring. I ended up with DEU in the exams and E overall. Plus, trying to understand and do the C2 unit meant my other work suffered.'

Nicky Craig

'Chemistry was the wrong choice for me – I got an A* at GCSE so I thought I would be fine despite whatever anyone said about how difficult it was. I was wrong and came out with a C at AS even though I put at least twice as much effort into chemistry than geography (I got an A in that, so unfair)! Looking back, I should have listened to those who had done Chemistry A level and found it difficult. I didn't know how much of it would be maths based. I dropped it after AS and haven't looked back since; it was definitely the right decision as now I can fully concentrate on my other A levels.'

Claire Perry

How can understanding my skills help me to choose the right subjects?

Finding a subject that is interesting, enjoyable and suits your strengths and skills is ideal. For this reason, you need to have an understanding of your own skills or those you feel you can develop. However, perhaps your natural skills and those you enjoy using aren't compatible with the ones required for the study of this subject. So let's find out more about the skills needed by the various disciplines.

Skills	Relevant subjects
Communication Communication with others, reading, writing essays, learning languages	All subjects, but particularly arts, humanities and social sciences. English, history, sociology, languages; media and communication and culture
Attention to detail Good with small details, checking facts, figures, specifics, quantities	All sciences, along with geography, history, engineering, archaeology, IT, geology
Physical Making things, doing things, exercising, using your hands, carrying out experiments	PE, engineering, archaeology, IT, photography, art and design, design and technology
Creative Making things, writing, drawing, performing	Art and design, design and technology, English literature, drama, performing arts, music
Memory and recall Memorising facts, words, vocabulary, theories	Many subjects, but particularly history, maths, sciences, philosophy, languages
IT and computing Use and understanding of hardware, software or systems	IT, archaeology, design and technology, music technology, engineering, physics, technology, geology
Mathematical Using figures and statistics to investigate and draw conclusions, doing mental calculations	Maths and all sciences, particularly physics, also engineering, psychology, design and technology, geography, geology
Emotional intelligence Empathising, intuition, vision, creativity, tact, interpersonal skills	Religious studies, English literature, history of art, communication and culture, psychology, history, classical civilisation, music, health and social care
Spatial awareness and mechanical The ability to see where objects are in relation to one another, making and working with mechanical objects	Engineering, physics, art and design, design and technology, IT, construction and the built environment
Business Understanding business, finance and economics, and specific sectors of work	Accounting, business studies, economics, law, travel and tourism, leisure and recreation
Citizenship Social, political and environmental issues of the past and present	Ancient history, classical civilisation, geography, history, environmental science, government and politics, law, philosophy, Latin/Greek, sociology, religious studies, English literature, media studies

Advanced level study itself will help you to develop a range of skills, including research, analysis and study skills, along with independent thought.

'I lived overseas for my secondary education so did a range of GCSEs and IGCSEs. I found there wasn't a huge jump between IGCSEs and A level, and whilst the work was definitely harder, the work was still doable.'

Becky Whitehead

Why is it important to know how I learn best and how I prefer to be assessed?

Choosing the right qualification and subjects requires some self-awareness. Just as you need to understand your strengths and skills, you also need to recognise how you learn best and how you prefer to be assessed.

A levels are based on academic and theoretical study, giving you the chance to learn about a subject in detail; if you prefer practical activities and learning by doing, then you may need to look at alternatives (see Chapter Two page 19). On the other hand, if you are interested in theory but like to see how you might apply that to practical situations, then an Applied A level might suit you.

If you have a fear of exams, then A levels might not be the best option, as written exams are an important method of assessment. However, A levels tend to be assessed by a combination of activities which also include coursework (essays, projects or case studies), completed during the course in your own time, and practical exams (especially for sciences or other subjects where practical skills are essential). Not only is there variation between subjects in terms of the type of assessment, but there also will be some variation between different examination boards offering the same subject. So try to work out whether you are better at exams, coursework or practical work and bear that in mind when choosing your subjects.

To find out more about the methods of assessment for the International Baccalaureate, Cambridge Pre-U and Scottish Highers and Advanced Highers, see *Qualifications on offer* (page 19) and the Subject Directory (from page 55).

'At this level, there is greater emphasis on independent learning and independent thought. Also, although this may have been a product of the type of subjects I chose, there was much more debate in class.

'I think it will be the transferable skills rather than knowledge gained that will help me with my future career plans. My A levels introduced me to a variety of thinking and analysis styles, and to approaching topics from different perspectives.'

Sarah Hembrough

Are all A level subjects seen as equal?

The answer to this question depends on who you ask and on what you intend to do in the future.

The exam boards might well tell you that all A levels are assessed in an equally stringent way, so that all should be equally challenging. Other people might think that differences in marking schemes mean that it is easier to do well in some A levels than others. These discussions have been rumbling on for many years but, essentially, there are no easy options at A level standard.

The key question is whether your subjects will lead you to your chosen destination; if you are aiming for top universities and employers, will they approve of your choice? If you hope to attend one of the UK's leading universities, then you will need to choose your subjects wisely. Some of the most selective institutions have lists of acceptable subjects or acceptable combinations of subjects, so look carefully on their websites for more information. As a general rule of thumb, the most traditional and academic subjects are accepted more widely, whereas the newer or applied subjects are sometimes less favoured, but there are some surprising exceptions. You can find out more in Chapter Three (page 42) and in the Subject Directory (from page 55).

Top Tip

General Studies and Critical Thinking A levels are rarely included in university offers. You might choose one of these subjects as a fourth (or even fifth) A level, but you could limit your options if you made one of these subjects your third choice and relied on it to get into university.

Don't forget that there are plenty of universities out there that will consider most subjects at advanced level standard. In addition, plenty of courses do not require previous study of a specific subject. If you aren't aspiring to one of the top universities or a highly competitive subject, you may be able to concentrate on other factors when choosing your subjects, rather than the contentious issue of what is 'hard' and what is 'soft'.

How do I know which combination of subjects is best for me?

When deciding on your ideal combination of subjects, you need to consider your future plans for university or work and any specific subject requirements. It might seem like jumping ahead of yourself, but what you don't want is to be stuck wanting to do medicine in two years' time and all you've got is a handful of arts subjects.

Some universities publish quite complex lists indicating how the different subjects are accepted in combination. For example, Trinity College, Cambridge, will accept only as a fourth subject A levels such as Environmental Science, ICT or World Development as a fourth subject; other A levels are considered to have limited suitability in certain cases, including Archaeology, English Language and Psychology (www.trin.cam.ac.uk/index.php?pageid=604). Find out more on the undergraduate admissions pages of your chosen university's website.

If you don't know what you want to do next (which is the case for many students), then you might like to consider combinations that allow you to keep your options open (find out more on page 40).

Perhaps you want to try out something new and decide to pick a complementary or a 'contrasting' subject. A contrasting subject can show the breadth of your academic ability or provide a welcome alternative by challenging you in a different way. Consider, for example, how a language or an arts subject might give you a much-needed break from three maths and science A levels. Picking a different subject will also provide more balance to your academic knowledge, to the breadth of skills you develop, and to the range of teaching and assessment methods you encounter.

'In the case of geography, we covered similar things as IGCSE, only the A level was far more in-depth, so it was good to have the base knowledge. In the case of English and Psychology, the contents of the courses were entirely new.'

Becky Whitehead

Subjects that complement one another can allow you to specialise; some naturally go hand in hand, each enhancing your learning in the other. For example, maths can be directly applied to physics, so the two work very well in combination. If your strengths lie very clearly in one area, then complementary subjects allow you to concentrate your knowledge. As you would expect, choosing all arts or all science subjects will lead you in a particular educational or career direction. Make sure there is not too much overlap between subjects, otherwise it might restrict your university choices. For example, Economics and Business A levels are not always accepted in combination.

If it is feasible, try to consider the balance of subjects you choose. All exams might mean a lot of pressure at certain times of the year, whereas too much coursework could overload you.

'I started off studying English, history, French and art. I really loved art, but I knew that I wasn't going to study anything creative at university I found that the amount of time I needed for art homework was making my other subjects suffer, so I dropped it at the end of the first year.'

Charlie Smith

What if I want to study a subject at A level that I didn't choose for GCSE?

If you can convince your tutors or teachers that you have the right academic potential (as well as the right attitude) then it may be possible to pick up a subject at A level that you didn't study at GCSE. However, some subjects really build on the knowledge you've learned at GCSE. These include:

- languages
- maths
- sciences.

It would be very difficult to pick these subjects up at advanced level without any prior learning, and you probably wouldn't want to attempt it!

Research any new choices carefully to make sure you fully understand what the subject involves and what the syllabus covers at this level; you need to know what you're letting yourself in for.

Top Tip

Sometimes even familiar subjects feel new and exciting when you study a new syllabus or are taught by a new teacher.

'I love science and languages and had never done a subject involving essay writing and evaluative skills before. I chose to study economics because there was a Spanish trip with it and I liked the idea of it being an 'easy' subject . . . certainly learned my lesson there.

'With hindsight, I wish I'd been fully informed about what the subject actually involves. I wish I'd thought about whether I'd be better suited to a subject I know I enjoy and am good at. Also, I could not care less what is in the news, anything finance/business/politics related . . . this should have been a good indicator to the fact that I was never going to enjoy a subject about it at all!'

Harriet Glossop

What do I need to know about taking a new subject at A level?

There are a range of subjects that are not studied at GCSE level that most people encounter for the first time at A level and they assume no prior knowledge. These include:

- government and politics
- law
- philosophy
- sociology.

Subjects that are new to you at A level standard can be very tempting but should be considered very carefully. There may be a certain glamour or excitement around new choices, such as philosophy, economics or psychology, but it is essential that they live up to your expectations, so do your research. Talk to subject teachers or students who have studied those subjects. Find out the kinds of skills you might need to use on a course like this, along with any prior subject knowledge that would be beneficial. Many students don't expect to find maths content in psychology, for example.

Remember that with new areas of study (for A levels, at least) there is limited time to adjust before you start being assessed on your work, so you don't want to get any nasty shocks with the subject, the syllabus or the way in which it is taught. A common reason for dropping out of a subject is that it didn't live up to expectations; you can reduce the risk of this happening to you by investigating thoroughly before you start.

There are plenty of benefits to studying something entirely new. Many students relish the chance and the challenge of a different subject. Consider how rewarding and enjoyable it can be to learn something fresh and stimulating.

How do subjects at A level differ from those at GCSEs?

'A level is so much harder! But A levels are your own choice and so ultimately something you should enjoy studying. You take fewer subjects so you have more time to focus your attention.'

Melissa Handley

There can be some big adjustments to make when moving from GCSE to advanced level. Class sizes get smaller, and there will be more independent study, longer assignments and the possibility of being treated as an adult. There can also be big differences in the syllabus, for which you need to be prepared; for example, an A level in a modern language requires the study of literature and current affairs. The Subject Directory gives more details of the changes at advanced level (from page 55).

'I underestimated how difficult A level Spanish really is. The jump from GCSE to A level was not explained well at all. I was aware that with any subject it would be much more difficult and require a great deal of work, but doing Spanish was killing me.'

Zachary Bickford-Jones

'A levels were a lot more demanding, particularly in the transition from RE to theology. I was trying to understand abstract concepts and debate ethics; however, this also made it more enjoyable.'

Ellie Wigg

Of course, we are all individuals, so the transition from GCSE to advanced level is experienced in different ways; some don't find it such a jump after all.

'I didn't really find much difference between my GCSEs and A levels (Biology, Physics, Chemistry and English Language).'

Rebecca Ferris

Practical considerations

Once you have considered your choices, there will be additional practical concerns that determine whether you want to study a subject or whether you are able to do so. These might include:

- timetabling issues
- permitted subject combinations
- local availability of subjects
- the syllabus on offer
- success rates
- strength of the teacher.

In an ideal world, your choices would be entirely based on your own strengths, interests and future plans, but in real life you will need to consider other factors.

'I needed three sciences to progress to a medicine course, so I chose biology, chemistry and physics. I wanted to do French, but it didn't fit with chemistry on the timetable so I was limited in my fourth choice. I chose English language as I wanted something different to the sciences.'

Rebecca Ferris

'I wanted to choose Spanish A level, but they had to discontinue the A level as not enough people chose it.'

Annabel Weeden

If you can't take your chosen combination because of timetable or subject restrictions at school or college, talk to the staff to see whether anything can be done. If not, look into whether other complementary courses would suit you and your plans. Check out whether it is essential for you to study a particular subject at A level standard, as sometimes this is not necessary in order to pick it up at degree level; in fact, in some cases it might even be preferable if you haven't. (Find out more on page 42.)

If you are asked to make a compromise, you need to consider whether this is right for you, as you could choose to study at another sixth form or college rather than give up your chosen subject. You might have to ask yourself similar questions if the syllabus on offer doesn't match your interests and strengths.

Perhaps your ideal subject has poor success rates, is taught by an uninspiring teacher or one you don't get along with. These factors are likely to impinge on your potential grade, as well as on your enjoyment and motivation for your studies. Remember that things change; you might end up with a different teacher, and success rates can change considerably, along with staff and syllabus. Think about whether there is room for compromise on any of these factors or whether you need to look elsewhere.

Top Tip

One aspect that shouldn't play a part in your decision making is whether your friends are studying that subject.

What if I choose the wrong subjects?

If you realise that you have made the wrong decision, then you should talk to your teacher or tutor as soon as possible. Discuss with them whether this is a short-term issue that can be resolved with some extra work or additional support. However, if you decide that you cannot continue, you may be able to change subject, depending on whether it is early enough and availability. Have a good think about the reasons why the choice you made is not right to make sure that you don't make the same mistake again.

At some point in the year, it will be too late to change subject and you may decide to continue with what you have chosen, at least until the end of your AS level. If you feel that a number of your subjects aren't right (or if your AS results are disappointing), then things become slightly more complicated. Discuss the situation with the staff and with your parents. If the subject is the issue, rather than your academic ability or aptitude, you may choose to start the year afresh with new choices. If you are struggling with the level of work, rather than the content, then you may need to look at alternative options (see page 19).

Find out more

Use some of the following sources to find out more:

- current teachers
- potential teachers or tutors
- careers advisers
- A level subject information from sixth forms and colleges
- sixth-form or college students
- UCAS (Universities and Colleges Admissions Service; www.ucas.com)
- university admissions departments
- exam boards for subject and syllabus information:
  - AQA: www.aqa.org.uk
  - Edexcel: www.edexcel.com
  - OCR: www.ocr.org.uk
  - WJEC: www.wjec.co.uk
  - CCEA: www.rewardinglearning.org.uk.

Top Tip

1. Study what you enjoy.
2. Consider your career plans.
3. Make an informed decision.

CHAPTER TWO

Qualifications on offer

This chapter will introduce you to the different academic qualifications available after GCSE or Standard Grade qualifications; the information will help you to start deciding which options suit you best.

You will also be able to see how each qualification fits onto the UCAS tariff: a points system which helps universities to compare applicants with different qualifications. Many institutions ask for a certain number of points to allow you to study there, although the top universities still tend to make offers using grades.

Learning at advanced level (sometimes known as level 3 in England, Wales and Northern Ireland) involves obtaining detailed knowledge and skills. Depending on the type of qualification you choose, advanced level study can be appropriate for people wishing to go to university, those who are moving to skilled jobs or for those supervising and training others in their field of work. It includes academic options, such as A levels, and more vocational study, including a selection of diplomas and work-based NVQ Diplomas.

The qualifications explained in this chapter are those that tend to be preferred if you intend to apply to university, although they also build up some of the skills that are needed by employers. Although A levels (or Highers in Scotland) might be the traditional choice, there are now some alternatives that will stretch you in different ways and might even suit your style of learning better.

Alternatives to academic qualifications

Academic options don't suit everyone. A range of more vocational qualifications are available, some of which will still get you into university but are not always favoured by the top institutions in the country. If you prefer to be assessed by coursework, rather than exams, or if you thrive on a more applied, hands-on style of learning, qualifications such as BTEC Diplomas, Advanced Diplomas, CACHE Diplomas or NVQ Diplomas might be more appropriate. Most of the diploma courses are related to a broad job area, such as manufacturing engineering or animal management. They tend to offer a combination of classroom-based theory, coursework, presentations and work placements. Alternatively, NVQ Diploma qualifications focus more on learning by doing the job. In these qualifications, you build up a portfolio of evidence and will be observed carrying out work duties to prove you have the necessary skills. To find out more, talk to your careers adviser at school or take a look at these websites:

- BTEC Diploma: www.edexcel.com/quals/nationals10/Pages/default.aspx
- Advanced Diploma: www.direct.gov.uk/en/EducationAndLearning/QualificationsExplained/DG_070676
- CACHE Diploma: www.cache.org.uk/Qualifications/CYP/CYPL3/Pages/Home.aspx
- NVQ Diploma: www.direct.gov.uk/en/EducationAndLearning/QualificationsExplained/DG_10039029.

Top Tip

Make sure you know which diploma you are interested in. There are many diploma options available, at a wide range of different levels and varying in their breadth, too. You need to know exactly which course you are signing up for.

GCE AS and A levels

A levels are probably the most widely known post-16 qualification and are still seen as the traditional gateway to higher education. One of the benefits of taking a well-known qualification such as A levels is that they are clearly understood by universities and employers.

Amendments to A levels are being discussed, which means that their format might be quite different from September 2014. Possible changes include methods of assessment, options around re-sits and a more linear system of examination, although nothing has been finalised yet.

The A level currently consists of two parts: the one-year AS and the one-year A2. Each part has its own separate syllabus and assessment, with exams taking place in January and June of each year (although some sixth forms concentrate on June exams).

The Advanced Subsidiary (AS) is a stand-alone qualification and is valued as half an A level. It tends to have two (or sometimes three) units that contribute 50% of the full A level.

The A2 is the second half of an A level qualification and very often builds on the knowledge and skills gained at AS level; for that reason, the A2 is not available as a separate qualification and it cannot be taken without the AS. The A2 covers the more demanding material, combining knowledge, understanding and skills from across the A level course. For example, in the A2 students might:

- specialise in an area they studied at AS level
- extend their knowledge and understanding of the subject by studying new topics
- improve their skills.

Top Tip

Considering a one-year A level programme? This is possible in some cases, but you will need to be academically ready and choose your subjects wisely. Science subjects can be problematic, as A2 tends to build on AS, but may still be possible. Other subjects are more achievable. Your selected sixth form or college will be able to help you make the right decision.

At AS and A2, most units are assessed by examination, although some subject specifications also feature coursework when it is considered to be the best method of assessment. Subjects such as art and design and the sciences will require practical work, too.

You may come across something known as 'stretch and challenge' as part of your course or assessment, where you should be given more opportunity to demonstrate your full potential. For example, certain exam questions are now more likely to be open-ended, thus allowing you to extend your writing and highlight your skills and knowledge. A levels are also synoptic in their methods, which simply means that links between different topics will be explored; this also means that areas of study from AS can crop up in A2 exams.

> *'At this level, there is a much bigger workload, more independence expected and you need to be committed (as you can't wing it through A levels); there are smaller and more focused classes, as students want to be there.'*
>
> Michael Hall

Grades

Your first exams might take place in the January after you start the course, so the pace is fast and doesn't allow much time to adjust to advanced level study. If you're not happy with your grades, there are opportunities to retake parts of your qualification, but this isn't an easy option; there are restrictions, and any additional work is likely to increase the pressure on the rest of your studies. Once you are satisfied with your result, you can cash it in with the exam board, thereby accepting the grade.

AS levels are graded A to E, with A levels graded A* to E. The coveted A* grade is only awarded to students who have achieved a grade A at A level (which requires 80% overall), along with an average of at least 90% on all A2 units for the subject. Some students achieve B grade at AS level, yet do well enough at A2 to gain A* grade at A level.

Grading is based on the uniform mark scale (or UMS). Some universities, including the University of Cambridge, are keen to know your UMS scores; it provides them with consistent information about candidates, helping them to make a decision about your capabilities and therefore your suitability for their courses.

On the UCAS tariff for university applications, at A level you can achieve a maximum of 140 points for an A* grade, 120 for an A, 100 for a B, etc. down to 40 tariff points for a grade E. AS levels score exactly half of the A level points, from 60 at grade A (remember there is no A* at AS level) to 20 at grade E. The tariff may well change or even disappear, as it is being reviewed at the time of writing.

Top Tip

Most students start off with four AS levels but then drop one subject at the end of the first year to focus on three A levels.

Extended Project

For students who wish to demonstrate more than just academic prowess, the Extended Project (EP) can be a useful addition to A level studies. You get the chance to complete an independent piece of work of up to 5,000 words on your own choice of subject. Your skills in critical thinking, self-motivation, research and independent study will develop, standing you in good stead for university and beyond.

Although your work will be at A2 standard, the Extended Project is comparable to an AS level in the UCAS points it attracts, ranging from 70 tariff points if you achieve grade A* down to 20 points for grade E. Some universities will make a more favourable offer to applicants with the EP; others might be more flexible if you slightly miss your grades; while others might recognise the skills it develops, without including it as part of an offer.

'Where applicants have undertaken the Extended Project (EP), this will not be a condition of any offer but the University recognises that the EP will provide an applicant with the opportunity to develop research and academic skills relevant for study at Oxford. Candidates are encouraged to draw upon relevant EP experience when writing their personal statement.'
University of Oxford entrance requirements, www.ox.ac.uk/admissions/ undergraduate_courses/courses/courses_and_entrance_requirements/index.html

'I'm also doing an Extended Project at the moment and I think this has helped me to get offers on some of the courses I want, as it does show the extra effort.'
Becky Whitehead

AQA Baccalaureate

Three A levels and the Extended Project can be combined more formally through the AQA Baccalaureate, which helps students to demonstrate skills in leadership, independence, communication, time management, commitment and perseverance. The programme also includes enrichment activities (for example, community activities or work-related learning), alongside an AS in General Studies, Critical Thinking or Citizenship.

The AQA Baccalaureate is available at sixth forms and colleges in England, Wales and Northern Ireland. To find out what is on offer in your local area, check out yp.direct.gov. uk/14-19prospectus/.

Are A levels right for me?

If you're academically strong, if you want a well-established qualification, if you're looking for something that is understood by universities in this country and overseas and if you want a qualification that is recognised by employers, then A levels might be right for you.

Applied GCE AS and A levels

Applied A levels give students a broad introduction to a vocational area and the chance to put the knowledge they learn into practice. These applied (or work-related) options tend to be assessed by portfolios of coursework, with fewer exams. The increased coursework element means you will need to be motivated, organised and prepared to work as part of a team.

The qualifications are available in the following subjects:

- applied art and design
- applied business
- applied ICT
- applied science
- engineering
- health and social care
- leisure studies
- media
- performing arts
- travel and tourism.

Applied A levels are taught during a two-year programme. They are available at AS and full A level, and sometimes as a double award (the equivalent of two AS or A levels). On the UCAS tariff, you will gain the same number of points for both Applied and GCE A levels: from 40 points for an E at A level (single) to 140 points for an A*. You can mix and match Applied and traditional A levels.

Are Applied A levels right for me?

If you prefer to relate your studies to an area of work, if you perform better in coursework than in exams, if you're keen enough on a subject to study it as two A levels and if you don't plan on applying to the most competitive courses or to the most selective universities, then Applied A levels might be right for you.

Advanced Extension Award

Advanced Extension Awards (AEAs) were designed to challenge the most able advanced level students, ensuring that they were tested against standards comparable with the most demanding found in other countries. However, following changes to A levels, which brought in the A* grade, placed more emphasis on depth of study and encouraged candidates to make connections between the different topic areas, AEAs were no longer required; the qualification was withdrawn in 2009, with the exception of AEA Maths.

The AEA in Maths is well recognised by universities and is often included as an entry requirement by some of the top schools of mathematics; it can be used to help universities differentiate between the most able candidates. In addition, the style of questioning can be a better preparation for mathematical thinking at university level.

The AEA is designed to be accessible to all able students, whatever their school or college and whichever specification they are studying. The qualification requires no additional teaching, although preparation using past papers is highly recommended. You can achieve a distinction (attracting 40 UCAS tariff points) or a merit grade (which attracts 20); most of the top universities that require the AEA tend to ask for a specific grade rather than making a points-based offer.

To find out more see page 195.

Is AEA Maths right for me?

If you have strong maths skills, are intending to study maths at university and want to demonstrate your high level of ability, then the AEA in Mathematics might be right for you.

The International Baccalaureate (IB) Diploma

The International Baccalaureate Diploma was set up to establish a common curriculum and university entry qualification for students moving from one country to another.

It was thought that students should share an academic experience emphasising analytical thinking and intercultural understanding, and demanding an enquiring approach. The programme has earned a reputation for rigorous assessment, giving International Baccalaureate Diploma holders access to some of the world's leading universities. It is now offered by more than 200 sixth forms and colleges across the UK.

The programme is a comprehensive two-year international curriculum. It is assessed by coursework (which accounts for 20–100% of the marks, depending on what you study) and by exams in May of the second year. Unlike A levels, the IB is not studied as separate modules, which means that retakes are only available six months or one year after final exams; consequently, re-sits are not as common as in the A level courses.

Students study a broad curriculum of six subjects, specialising in three at Higher level (HL); the remaining three are studied at Standard level (SL). It is possible to opt for four HL subjects and two at SL, although this will be more challenging. The subject choices made at Higher level will determine which university courses are open to you. One subject is chosen from each of the following groups.

- **Group 1: studies in language and literature.** Students study language and literature in their first language (most often English for UK students).
- **Group 2: language acquisition.** Students study a modern or classical language. The languages on offer will vary between institutions. Modern languages can be studied from scratch (at Standard level) or can extend prior language learning.
- **Group 3: individuals and societies.** Students choose an option from business and management, economics, geography, history, IT in a global society, philosophy, psychology, social and cultural anthropology and world religions (SL).
- **Group 4: experimental sciences.** Options are biology, chemistry, physics, environmental systems and societies, and design technology.
- **Group 5: mathematics and computer science.** Maths is compulsory, although different types of mathematics courses are available, depending on your aptitude for the subject and your future plans. Computer science is optional.
- **Group 6: the arts.** Choose from visual arts, music, dance, film and theatre. If you do not wish to choose an arts subject, you can select an additional subject from groups one to five instead.

Top Tip

Biology, chemistry and physics can be a popular A level combination, but it is not possible to study all three sciences together at Higher level on the IB Diploma. If you're planning to study medicine, dentistry, pharmacy or veterinary science at university, you can still ensure you meet the entry requirements by combining two HL subjects from the science group with HL maths.

As well as the six compulsory subjects, there are three core components: the Extended Essay (4,000-word independent research), Theory of Knowledge (or ToK – interdisciplinary study which encourages critical thinking) and 150 hours of Creativity, Action, Service (or CAS), where students are required to take part in artistic pursuits, sports and community service work. These additional requirements mean that IB students tend to be well prepared for the independent study, time management and research skills needed to be successful at university. It also means that they get far more contact hours with their tutors (and fewer free periods) than students taking A levels.

Grades

Each of the six subjects is graded on a seven-point scale, with 7 representing the highest. The Theory of Knowledge and Extended Essay are worth a maximum of 3 points. Therefore, students can achieve up to a maximum score of 45, although only 0.24% of students achieved this in 2011. Anything above 39 should be considered a very strong performance.

If you want to compare the IB to A levels on the UCAS tariff, a 7 at HL gains 130 points, while an A* at A level equates to 140 points. A grade 7 at SL attracts 70 UCAS points, while AS level grade A gains 60 points on the UCAS tariff. At the time of writing, the UCAS tariff is undergoing a review, so things may change. Offers from the top universities tend to be based on grades anyway, rather than on the tariff.

The University of Oxford asks for 38–40 points (with 6s and 7s in HL subjects), while the University of Cambridge specifies 40–42 points (with 776 or 777 in HL subjects). One benefit of the qualification is that universities may find it easier to differentiate between top candidates on the IB Diploma. You should check with your selected university for the latest requirements. The IB is widely recognised by both universities and recruiters across the globe.

Is the IB right for me?

If you're a good all-rounder, if you don't want to narrow down your subject choices, if you're looking for a qualification with a global perspective, if you want to develop more than just academic skills and if you want to get involved in a range of extracurricular activities, then the IB might be right for you.

Cambridge International Exams Pre-University Diploma (Cambridge Pre-U)

This two-year programme is available in more than 130 schools, both state and independent. It is a new qualification (the first students completed the programme in 2010) and is aimed particularly at students who intend to go to university. The focus is very much on studying complex subjects in depth, thus preparing students for the independent, self-directed study needed at university. Exams are taken at the end of the second year, which means that students are allowed to grow into their subjects before being assessed; it also means that a lot rests on your final exam performance.

Subjects are predominantly academic and include classical heritage, comparative government and politics, and philosophy and theology, along with sciences, languages and arts subjects. Unlike the IB Diploma, which is a single qualification, each Cambridge Pre-U subject can be mixed and matched with other qualifications, such as A levels. There is no restriction on subject combinations either, but as there are only 27 Pre-U subjects on offer, opting for an A level or two would permit a wider subject choice. As each Pre-U Principal subject can be broadly compared to an A level, combining the two qualifications is fairly common and quite straightforward. Your sixth form or college will be able to advise you further.

In order to achieve the full Cambridge Pre-U Diploma, at least three (and up to four) Principal subjects and a core component – Global Perspectives and Research (GPR) – are required. Students who choose to replace one or two Principal subjects with an A level can still gain the full diploma. The final mark is based on the total score for the three Principal subjects (or A levels) and the GPR. Short Courses are available in modern languages and maths; they carry UCAS tariff points but are not part of the overall Pre-U Diploma.

Top Tip

The GPR component could be offered in place of a fourth subject at AS or A level.

The Global Perspectives element looks at ethics, economics, environment, and politics and culture; students are encouraged to debate and investigate in a critical but disciplined way. It is assessed by written exam, reflective essay and presentation. The Research element requires a 4,500–5,000-word report on a research project; you could investigate a particular subject in greater depth, choose an interdisciplinary topic or explore something entirely new.

'I enjoyed Cambridge Pre-U Global Perspectives and Research (GPR) because it gave me the opportunity to choose the topics that really interested me and study them in real depth. I found it interesting, challenging and incredibly valuable for my university study.'

Jacqueline Agate

Grades

Grades range from Distinction D1 down to Pass P3. Looking at how the grading compares with A levels, the grade D3 in a Cambridge Pre-U Principal subject is worth 130 points – a little over the 120 points received for a grade A at A level. Grades D2 and D3 exceed the UCAS tariff points awarded for A* at A level. The UCAS tariff points awarded to the GPR component are very closely matched to the equivalent grade at A level, although the highest grade of D1 is yet to be included on the tariff. The Cambridge Pre-U should make it easier for higher-achievers to be recognised and differentiated by the leading universities.

Is the Cambridge Pre-U right for me? ?

If you want to be challenged and encouraged to think for yourself, if you prefer exams as a means of assessment, if you'd rather be tested on your understanding after you've had time to study the subject in more depth, if you'd like to mix and match with A levels and if you want to prepare yourself for the style of learning used at university, then the Cambridge Pre-U might be right for you.

Scottish Highers and Advanced Highers

The Scottish Higher qualification is taken in S5 (or Y12), with some students choosing to go on to Advanced Highers in S6 (or Y13). The qualifications can lead to a job or entry to higher education. As you might expect, SQA Highers and Advanced Highers are offered mainly by schools and colleges in Scotland.

Highers

Whereas A levels are taken over two years, it only takes one year to study for a Higher and it's common to take between four and six Highers in any one academic year. In many

Scottish universities, Highers alone are sufficient for university entry. Most universities require four, although some of the more competitive institutions or courses require five.

Each qualification consists of three units, each of which is a qualification in its own right (called a National Unit). There is an exam in May or June on everything you have covered in the course, which is combined with coursework to give students a final grade.

Top Tip

Core Skills in communication, numeracy, problem solving, IT and working with others are incorporated into SQA qualifications; your certificate will come with a Core Skills Profile, listing what you have achieved.

Advanced Highers

An Advanced Higher takes a further year of study. You would tend to continue with some of the subjects taken at Higher level; typically, students go for two or three (occasionally four) Advanced Highers. You will be expected to undertake challenging, independent study in addition to your classroom learning. The assessment is based on coursework, unit tests or practicals, followed up with an end-of-year exam or project covering everything you have learned.

The Advanced Highers can bridge the gap between the class-based style of learning you get at Higher level and the independent study skills needed for university. You should develop skills in investigation, research and analysis, along with extended essay writing.

Should I study Advanced Highers?

S6 might be spent studying additional Highers, retaking some if necessary, or taking Advanced Highers; some students will do a combination of these options. Your choices in the sixth year will depend on your future plans.

The first year of a degree course in Scotland requires far more breadth of study than in the rest of the UK (most bachelor's degrees in Scotland take four years), so leading universities in Scotland are looking for a range of subjects and will accept Highers. Advanced Highers can sometimes be used to gain direct entry to the second year of a degree programme in Scotland.

Leading universities in the rest of the UK often require more specialisation (which reflects the style of degree), so offers tend to be based on Advanced Highers.

Scottish Baccalaureate

A Scottish Baccalaureate is available in languages or science. It incorporates two Advanced Highers and a Higher; candidates study maths or English (or Gaelic), two subjects from a relevant selection of languages or sciences and an interdisciplinary project.

Grading

Highers and Advanced Highers are graded A to D. Back in 2010, the UCAS tariff increased the points awarded for Advanced Highers at A, B and C, so they now gain slightly more than the equivalent A levels. For example, Advanced Higher grade A is 130 points, while A level grade A is 120.

Are SQA Advanced Highers right for me? ❓

If you're being educated in Scotland then it is more than likely that you'll be studying Highers, but why bother progressing to Advanced Higher? If you want to develop your independent study and research skills, if you want to study the subject in more depth in your sixth year, if you want to ease the transition to university, if you'd like to be considered for the second year at some Scottish universities and if you'll be applying to universities in the rest of the UK, then Advanced Highers might be right for you.

The Welsh Baccalaureate (WB) Advanced Diploma

The Welsh Baccalaureate provides a broad, diverse study curriculum for students aged 16–18 and, unsurprisingly, it is mainly offered by schools and colleges in Wales. WB students should develop a useful blend of skills and awareness, alongside a choice of academic (or vocational) studies. The emphasis is on a broader curriculum, including work and industrial experience, and the argument is that this breadth and balance will better prepare students for university or the workplace.

Unlike the IB, the WB is made up of separate existing academic qualifications (A levels, for example), with a common core comprising the following.

- **Key Skills.** They cover communication, ICT, application of number, problem solving, working with others and improving own learning and performance.
- **Wales, Europe and the world (WEW).** Students learn how political, economic, social and cultural issues affect Wales, and they consider the nation's relationship with Europe and the world. This component also includes a language module.
- **Work-Related Education (WRE).** This option involves working with an employer and taking part in a team enterprise activity. The module develops

a better knowledge of the world of work and business, as well as improving understanding of careers.

- **Personal and Social Education (PSE).** Students explore issues around citizenship, health, positive relationships and sustainable development. They carry out an activity within the local community.
- **Individual Investigation.** A piece of personal research into a subject you are studying within your academic studies or the core component. It will include a 2,500-word report or a 10-minute presentation (supported by substantial written notes).

The core is worth 120 UCAS points, comparable to a grade A at A level. Any academic qualifications and subjects you choose to study alongside this should reflect your interests, abilities and any future plans. Check whether any of the universities where you wish to apply will include the WB Core within any offers they make. A typical offer might require a pass in the core element alongside two specific A level subjects and grades. The University of Bristol, Cardiff University and the University of Manchester are among the universities that currently make offers including the WB Core.

'Two of my subjects weren't right for me at A level. I dropped one after AS, but the other wasn't so important because my university offers were only based on two A levels (alongside the Welsh Baccalaureate Core).'

Bethan Moseley

Is the Welsh Baccalaureate right for me?

If you want more breadth in your studies beyond pure A levels, if you're hoping to get to university with fewer traditional academic qualifications, if you'd like to build up skills that employers want too, if you like to learn by doing (alongside theoretical and academic subjects, if you prefer) and if you want to carry out a research project, then the Welsh Baccalaureate might be right for you.

Foundation Diploma in Art and Design

The routes that lead students to study art and design at university are different from those for most other subjects. Often, Art and Design A levels alone are not sufficient preparation for university, so students might choose to take an Art Foundation Course after A levels but before an undergraduate degree. You can attend an Art and Design Foundation Course at college or university, although it is classed as a further education course.

The main Art Foundation Course on offer is the BTEC Foundation Diploma in Art and Design, although other qualifications are available. Its aim is to enable students to make informed decisions which will help them progress to appropriate higher education courses in art and design. The qualification builds on the student's prior experience and skills gained at A level standard.

This one-year course is made up of nine units so that you have the opportunity to explore first and then to follow a specialist pathway, before confirming your direction. This structure supports the progression of the student towards independent and self-reliant learning.

Is the Foundation Diploma in Art and Design right for me?

?

If you want to explore various fields of art and design before specialising, if you'd like to try out options that weren't available at sixth form, if you want to enhance your practical techniques and ability, if you need a more substantial portfolio for university or if your chosen university demands that you attend a Foundation Course, then the Foundation Diploma in Art and Design might be right for you.

For more information on the Foundation Diploma in Art and Design, see page 68.

Find out more about each qualification

Find out what the awarding bodies have to say on the websites listed here:

- GCE A levels and GCE Applied A levels:
    - AQA: www.aqa.org.uk
    - Edexcel: www.edexcel.com
    - OCR: www.ocr.org.uk
    - WJEC: www.wjec.co.uk
    - CCEA: www.rewardinglearning.org.uk
    - AQA Baccalaureate: www.aqa.org.uk/qual/bacc.php
- International Baccalaureate Diploma (IBO): www.ibo.org
- Cambridge Pre-U (Cambridge International Exams): www.cie.org.uk
- Scottish Highers and Advanced Highers (SQA): www.sqa.org.uk
- Welsh Baccalaureate (WJEC/CBAC): www.welshbaccalaureate.org.uk
- Foundation Diploma in Art and Design (Edexcel): www.edexcel.com.

To discover some of the subject options available for these qualifications, see the Subject Directory starting on page 55.

To explore what is available in your local area, you could start with your local 14–19 prospectus at yp.direct.gov.uk/14-19prospectus/.

So by now you should have a fairly good idea of some of the most common post-16 options that will get you to university, but what difference will your choices make? And how can you decide between them? The next chapter will show you.

CHAPTER THREE

Planning for the future

Unless you know exactly which university you want to go to, what you plan to study there and your eventual career path, there will be some uncertainties about the choices that you make. This chapter explores how to choose so that you maximise your chances or keep your options open, if need be. We will look at the subjects that will extend (and those that might limit) your opportunities. However, if you have some clear ideas about your future, we'll also take a look at the subjects needed for certain degrees or jobs.

You will be getting lots of advice as you make these decisions — not all of it welcome. You will hear comments along the lines of: 'You shouldn't choose that; it's too hard' or 'That subject's a waste of time' and even 'It's impossible to get good grades in that.' You might see courses described as easy, 'soft' or 'Mickey Mouse'. You might be told to choose traditional subjects, academic subjects or hard subjects. So what should you do?

There is a lot of emphasis these days on choosing the right subjects, but you should not pick your subjects based solely on what the leading universities want or what you think will lead to a high-flying job. This can be a route to disaster. If you happen to be interested in what the leading universities want, then this is fine. But do not, under any circumstances, choose a subject purely on this basis. Remember that your grades are as important as the subject you study; you need to have an interest in the subject and an aptitude for it, otherwise you'll end up with the right subjects but the wrong grades.

'Physics and computing were the wrong choice for me. I didn't enjoy them but felt pressured to take them by parents and teachers who felt that a pure science background would afford me the best opportunities at university and beyond. This didn't work out, so I re-sat the year and dropped physics and computing, taking up geography in their place, whilst continuing with chemistry and biology.'

Luke Cox

'I don't think I'd have made the wrong choices if teachers had told me to study what I enjoy and feel motivated to study, rather than what I thought would lead to the best-paying career.'

Arron Clarke

Top Tip

It is worth remembering that many degrees and careers are open to students of any subject; some universities and employers are more focused on the idea that you have the ability to study at a higher level rather than on what you actually studied.

I want to get into a top university

What should you study if you're thinking of applying to Oxford, Cambridge, a Russell Group university (a group of 24 leading research universities, www.russellgroup.ac.uk), a 1994 Group university (www.1994group.ac.uk) or another respected university? In most cases, you'll need strong GCSE grades to start with (sometimes as many as eight A*s); the numbers of GCSEs required and the subjects specified will vary depending on your choice of course, but English, maths, separate sciences and a modern language are often needed.

If you want to get into a top university, at the very least two (or probably three) of the more academic subjects will help; your subjects should be seen to be challenging. In the majority of cases, Applied A levels are not considered to be relevant by the most selective universities. If you do end up taking an applied subject, you'll need to supplement it with some heavyweight subjects with brilliant grades to even have a fighting chance of success.

Non-preferred subjects

Subjects that focus on the development of applied or practical skills are not favoured by some of the leading research universities. The University of Sheffield, University College London, London School of Economics and Trinity College, Cambridge, publish lists of the subjects they favour (or of the subjects that they don't consider as adequate preparation for university). The list below features subjects that are *not* preferred by at least one (and often a number) of these universities:

- accounting
- art and design
- art and design (applied)
- business (applied)
- business studies
- communication and culture
- critical thinking
- dance
- design and technology
- drama and theatre studies
- electronics
- engineering

- film studies
- general studies
- health and social care
- home economics
- ICT
- ICT (applied)
- law
- leisure studies
- media studies
- music technology
- PE
- science (applied)
- travel and tourism
- use of maths.

This is not a subject blacklist; in most cases, even these subjects will still be considered if supplemented by two or three preferred subjects, such as physics, religious studies or geography.

Of course, many students make their A level choices to gain more insight into whether they should study something further. For example, an A level in Drama and Theatre Studies is a logical choice if you hope to study the subject at university. In some cases, you won't need to have studied the subject beforehand (English literature might be just as useful); however, it will help to confirm whether you want to continue with the subject and help to demonstrate that you have the right skills to cope with a degree. If you're looking at a top university that classes it as a non-preferred subject, consider combining drama and theatre studies with more academic choices, such as English literature, languages or music.

You should check admissions criteria and any acceptable combinations closely, as they vary so widely between universities, departments and courses. Often it is the combination of subjects that limits applications, rather than one specific subject not being accepted. Remember that admissions criteria will change, so speak to your chosen university or see their website for the latest information.

'I studied business, law and applied ICT (double award) without realising that subject choice had such a big effect on university applications.'

Thomas Priday

'Media studies was the wrong choice for me. I now know that it is considered very low in the eyes of admissions tutors and, for the course I want to do, that's going to make life difficult. I wish I'd had earlier advice. I was only ever told which subjects are deemed as academic and preferred after it was already too late to change. Unfortunately, I'm stuck now, so I just have to stick it out and try my best.'

Jack Clarke

Preferred or acceptable subjects

The same four universities mentioned previously (University of Sheffield, University College London, London School of Economics and Trinity College, Cambridge) all accept the following subjects to meet their general entry requirements:

- ancient history
- archaeology
- biology
- chemistry
- classical civilisation
- economics
- English language
- English literature
- further mathematics
- geography
- geology
- government and politics
- history
- history of art
- languages
- mathematics
- music
- philosophy
- physics
- psychology
- religious studies
- sociology
- statistics.

Please note that some of these subjects are more relevant to either arts or sciences at university, so Trinity College, Cambridge, considers them to have limited suitability. Psychology, sociology and English language, for example, are classed as having limited suitability, as they are suitable for arts degrees but not for science degree.

Top Tip

If English isn't your first language (perhaps you are a French or Arabic native speaker, for example) don't depend on taking an A level in your native language to boost your grades; an A level in your mother tongue might not be included in a university offer.

Don't forget that hundreds of universities across the UK will accept all advanced level subjects, including Applied A levels and some of the subjects with more practical content. Check websites for the latest admissions requirements.

Which A levels do leading universities favour?

It can be hard to tell which subjects some of the other leading universities favour, as this information is not widely published. In the Policy Exchange report *The Hard Truth about 'Soft' Subjects* (Fazackerley, A. and Chant, J., December 2008; available online at www.policyexchange.org.uk/publications/category/item/the-hard-truth-about-soft-subjects [accessed 16 March 2012]), the authors tried to find out which A levels were actually getting students places at the leading Russell Group and 1994 Group universities. The list of 'soft' subjects they were investigating included art and design, drama, film studies, media studies, business, accounting, law, sociology and psychology.

When considering which subjects to choose, it is worth thinking about some of their findings.

- At leading universities, such as Bristol and University College London, nearly half of all the A levels from the students they accepted came from biology, chemistry, physics, maths and further maths.
- Although A level Law is taken by far more pupils than A level French, the University of Warwick accepted around four times more A levels in French than in Law.
- The University of Oxford accepted more A levels in Latin than in Business Studies, Law, Psychology and Sociology put together.

They reported that, although some of the 'soft' subjects are very popular in schools, most research-intensive (leading) universities admit far more traditional A levels. They spoke to a number of heads of admissions who felt that some of the 'soft' subjects did not prepare students sufficiently for university or for certain university courses.

It is clear, therefore, that there can be difficulties with certain subjects: generally those that aren't seen to prepare students for degree level study. More information on this topic can be found on page 42. Some of the published university views on specific subjects can be found in the Subject Directory, starting from page 55.

What else are top universities looking for?

Your predicted grades, first year grades and your UMS (uniform mark scale) results are as important as the grades you achieve at the end of year two; indeed, without these, you'll struggle to get an offer. The most respected universities (and the most competitive professions) may also be looking for high achievement at the first sitting, so retakes at advanced level aren't always considered. Sitting A levels early doesn't always take the pressure off in the second year, either; in some cases three full A levels are required from Y13, even if you already have an A level.

You might have to sit additional tests in order to be considered; for maths at a top-rated department, you'll probably need to sit STEP or AEA (see page 195), while many departments now use admissions tests (UKCAT, BMAT or LNAT, for example) to differentiate between the best candidates. Find out about admissions tests at www.ucas. ac.uk/students/choosingcourses/admissions.

Take advantage of the opportunity to demonstrate your research, evaluation and writing skills through an Extended Project, Cambridge Pre-U GPR, the IB Extended Essay or the Welsh Baccalaureate Individual Investigation.

In addition to your strong academic profile, additional activities may be required. Here's where the International Baccalaureate CAS (Creativity, Action, Service) and the Welsh Baccalaureate WRE (Work-Related Education) and PSE (Personal and Social Education) come in handy. If not, activities such as the Duke of Edinburgh's Award can demonstrate some valuable traits. Don't forget practical experience; for courses including medicine and dentistry (and many more) some experience or insight into the profession is a must.

Top Tip

Can't find your IB, Cambridge Pre-U, Higher or Welsh Baccalaureate mentioned as an entry requirement on a university website? Don't worry; it doesn't mean that they won't consider it. Many universities are very clear about their A level requirements but may be less clear about alternatives.

You might need to hunt around the website a little or even speak to the admissions tutor at the university if you need further confirmation.

Find out more

- 'Informed Choices' (Russell Group): www.russellgroup.ac.uk/media/informed-choices/InformedChoices-latest.pdf
- 'The Subject Matters' (University of Cambridge): www.study.cam.ac.uk/undergraduate/events/docs/sminfopack.pdf
- University of Oxford entrance requirements: www.ox.ac.uk/admissions/undergraduate_courses/courses/courses_and_entrance_requirements/table.html

I know I want to go to university, but I don't know what I want to study. How can I keep my options open?

One of the hardest parts about choosing the right qualification and subjects at this level is that you might not know exactly what you want to study afterwards or what the next step on your career path should be. This is a common predicament: you know that you want to go to university, but you don't have a clear career plan or you need time to decide on your degree subject. In such competitive times, when the subjects you choose can make a big difference to your future success, how can you make sure you are not limiting your future options?

'A levels gave me time to consider my options whilst gaining qualifications that enhanced them.'

Samuel Plaxton

It might seem simple: choose an arts subject, a science and a humanities subject, for example, to demonstrate breadth of knowledge. Unfortunately, this isn't really a reliable solution. This combination might get you onto an arts or humanities degree, but could make you less of a contender for some top science courses.

Choose facilitating subjects

The Russell Group produces 'Informed Choices: a guide to making decisions about post-16 education'. It includes a list of what they describe as 'facilitating subjects'; when specific subjects are needed to get onto a degree, these are the ones most commonly required, often because degree level studies build upon the knowledge gained from these subjects at advanced level:

- biology
- chemistry
- English literature
- geography
- history
- languages
- maths and further maths
- physics.

Choosing these subjects is a way to keep your options open. Some students might choose all their subjects from this list, but that needn't be the case; including at least two or three might be helpful, but you will still need to be sensible about how you combine them.

Top Tip

Don't assume that any subjects not mentioned on this list are somehow less valid or are blacklisted in some way; there are plenty of well-respected subjects that are very rarely part of a university's entry criteria and therefore wouldn't be considered to be facilitating (religious studies is a fine example).

'I chose art, English, physics and PE. I knew it was a mistake from the beginning. A few friends went into the science route, language route and arts route. I had no idea what to study, so I just split my choices. No university course would accept me as I didn't have any complementary subjects.'

Akinhuwne Djembe

Make sure you don't make a decision based only on whether something is a facilitating subject; in many ways, it is just as important that you choose subjects that are right for you. Don't forget the other tips in Chapter One and this chapter about making the right choices for you.

'I studied biology, chemistry and maths, but should have picked subjects I actually enjoyed.'

Sophie Connor

Arts or sciences?

Keeping your options open is a bit easier if you see your future in either the arts or the sciences. The University of Cambridge guide, 'The Subject Matters', suggests the following.

'If you think you would like to study an arts or social sciences course at university but you are not sure which one, then English literature, history, languages and mathematics are good "keystone" subjects: choosing one or more of these will provide a good foundation for your subject combination. Other good choices to combine these subjects with include: an additional language, ancient history, classical civilisation, economics, further mathematics, geography, philosophy, religious studies and sciences (biology, chemistry or physics).'

If you see yourself with a future related to sciences, the following is recommended:

'If you think you would like to study a science course at university but you are not sure which one, then you are advised to take at least two, and ideally three, of biology, chemistry, mathematics and physics. Some pairings of these subjects are more natural than others. The most natural pairs are biology and chemistry, chemistry and physics, and mathematics and physics.

> *'In practice the vast majority of applicants for science courses at Cambridge take at least three of these subjects. Another useful combination is mathematics, further mathematics and physics. Many students take four of biology, chemistry, mathematics, further mathematics and physics.'*

If there are career areas or degree courses that you are considering, but you just haven't made up your mind yet, it is worth checking that the subjects you choose don't rule these possibilities out. See page 45 for some of the subjects that you need for specific degrees. For details of a wider range of degrees and their requirements try UCAS (www.ucas.com). You could also take a look at the job profiles at the National Careers Service (nationalcareersservice.direct.gov.uk/advice/planning/jobfamily/Pages/default. aspx#JobProfileSearch).

Which subjects are considered 'soft'?

From newspaper articles to The Student Room, it feels like the whole world has a view on the 'soft' subjects that might restrict your choices, but unfortunately there is no conclusive list. Certainly, applied and practical subjects are often considered to be 'soft'; many successful applicants to the leading research-based universities don't choose to study any of these.

Subjects such as media studies, travel and tourism, and health and social care can restrict your choice but so can accounting, psychology and law. The list of non-preferred subjects (page 35) reveals many of the subjects that may cause problems. General studies, critical thinking and citizenship should not be selected as a third A level choice, as they are rarely included within a university offer.

Making the situation even more confusing, many universities are not transparent about their views on certain subjects. So you might have heard a rumour that some institutions prefer it if you don't study law or psychology, but many don't say so on their website or in the prospectus; it can be hard to get a clear and definitive answer.

> *'All my choices were wrong the first time round. I could have done with better career advice, a better selection of choices and more advice on subjects. I feel that 16 is very young to make decisions about the rest of your life and a lot more help should be given. I chose subjects I enjoyed; however, it was not made clear that career options would be minimal and some subjects are not as highly regarded by universities and employers. Schools still tell students that an A level is an A level, but that just isn't true.'*
>
> Ed McBride

Some sixth forms and colleges use their past experience in getting students into university to help potential students choose subjects effectively. Make sure you ask questions about 'soft' subjects at options evenings and open events; never rely solely on the response of a single subject tutor who may be looking to recruit to their course. Get advice from a range of staff who can be impartial and have the necessary insight; you could try the UCAS co-ordinator, the head of sixth form or a careers adviser.

If you have some ideas about your degree choices, it is worth talking to admissions tutors to get an idea of their preferences; aim to do this before you choose your A levels (and after as well, as requirements may well change). It is also helpful to take advantage of university summer schools or visits, when you may be able to find out more, even if you don't yet know which subject you will end up studying.

Are some A levels easier than others?

That depends on who you talk to; some subjects will have more essay writing and coursework, while others will have concepts that you may find more difficult to grasp. Just take a look at a thread on The Student Room and see the many different answers to 'Which is the hardest/easiest A level?'; it is subjective, so everyone has a different view.

According to *The Hard Truth about 'Soft' Subjects*:

'[there was] "little evidence" that A-level subjects described as "soft" were any less demanding than their counterparts. Yet they have found inconsistencies.

'A recent analysis of the A-level results of 250,000 students by Durham University, commissioned by the Royal Society, found that a pupil would be likely to get a pass two grades higher in "softer" subjects such as General Studies or Business Studies, than in Mathematics or science.

'Critically though, our research suggested that many research-intensive universities do not regard the issue of whether certain subjects are easier to get high grades in as the crucial issue. Their subject preferences are generally based on a more nuanced understanding of the skills that a student will need to cope with – or excel in – a particular course. Factors include whether a subject encourages independent thought, whether its content is academic or practical, the level of internal and external examinations, and the amount of group work involved.'

Fazackerley, A. and Chant, J., *The Hard Truth about 'Soft' Subjects*, Policy Exchange

---

Degrees that don't require specific knowledge

Many of the subjects which you might expect would be essential to study a particular degree are not required after all. For example, you can get onto a computer science degree without ever having studied computing, but you are likely to need maths; the same goes for accounting.

Other degrees that don't require prior knowledge of a specific subject include:

- archaeology
- business
- history of art
- law
- media
- philosophy
- politics
- psychology
- sociology.

And there are many more.

Just as many degrees are open to students with any A level subjects, many careers are available to graduates of all disciplines. So your degree in politics, for example, might well lead to a completely unrelated area of work. For that reason, you might even be able to keep your options open for a few more years.

As there are few certainties around how you will use your education in the future, sometimes avoiding a very narrow focus can be beneficial. Breadth of subjects (or the inclusion of a contrasting subject) can bring scope and choice. Although specialising may be necessary, particularly for those choosing science options at the top universities, it does have its risks; the main problem is if you later change your mind.

'I didn't know what I wanted to study at university when I chose my subjects. I picked History A level, but when I decided that I wanted to study medicine, it turned out that I would need biology. I ended up picking up AS Biology in my A2 year.'

George Kennedy

I know what I want to study at university, so which subjects should I take?

If you know what you want to do at university or beyond, then your decisions should be slightly easier; start with where you want to end up and then take a few steps back. So if you see yourself entering a graduate training programme with a particular company, check out their requirements in terms of preferred degree and A levels, grades and so on. (Try to keep other options in mind, too, as things often don't turn out exactly as you plan them.)

Top Tip

Your grades are an important part of getting to university, but they continue to be important even after you have gained a degree. Graduate recruitment opportunities at some of the top firms in accounting, for example, often require a minimum of 300 UCAS points.

'My subjects gave me a flavour of what I do and don't enjoy. For example, I found that I was really bad at English literature, and this put me off applying for a course which emphasises the importance of English (law). The variety within my subjects allowed me to narrow down to the part of the subject that I enjoyed the most, so when I chose my degree I really knew what I wanted to study; I chose politics with international relations rather than just a straight politics course.'

Sarah Hembrough

Should I choose a subject that I struggle with just because it's needed for my chosen degree or career?

Plenty of students decide to press on with a subject against their better judgement because it is needed for their chosen degree or profession. This is the time to be honest with yourself and consider the real reasons behind your issues with the subject. Whether it is down to a personality clash with a teacher, not working hard enough or lack of interest in the GCSE syllabus, you need to be confident that these issues will have disappeared by the time you start your A level. If it comes to the crunch, don't rule out a rethink of your career choice: if you struggle with a subject, is a career which relies upon it the right choice?

Top Tip

On top of the subject and grade requirements, a number of degrees need practical experience relating to the discipline you intend to study. These degrees include teaching, social work, nursing, medicine and physiotherapy.

Which subjects for a degree in . . . ?

Essential and useful subjects for a number of degree courses are included below. Requirements vary depending on the institution, so don't forget to check your selected university's published entry requirements for the latest and most reliable information.

Accountancy
Accountancy doesn't always require specific subjects, although maths is sometimes needed (and is always useful).

Architecture
Some universities prefer maths and physics, while others find art and design useful. You will tend to need a portfolio of artwork, even if you haven't studied the subject.

Art and design
A level or equivalent art and design qualification, plus a Foundation Diploma in Art and Design. A portfolio from another creative course, such as graphics or textiles, could also help you gain a place on the Art Foundation Course.

Computer science
A number of universities require maths, while others prefer it.

Dentistry
Chemistry and biology are required, while maths or physics may be useful.

Dietetics
Biology and chemistry are generally required.

Drama
Specific subjects are not always needed. Drama and theatre studies or English literature might be required, plus an audition.

Economics
Economics is not required, although maths is needed for some degrees.

Engineering (aeronautical)
Physics and maths are both required.

Engineering (electrical)
Physics and maths are needed, while chemistry can be helpful.

Engineering (mechanical)
Physics and maths are essential.

English
Advanced level study of English is essential; subjects such as history and languages may enhance your application.

Environmental science
Required subjects vary between universities, but one or two from the sciences, geography and maths are often needed.

Geography
Geography is required, while geology, sciences and maths may be useful.

History
History is required, while languages or complementary subjects such as anthropology, sociology or philosophy might be useful.

Law

No specific subjects are needed, although essay-writing subjects may help (English literature or history, for example). Some universities prefer you not to have studied law beforehand.

Media

This subject can be studied from scratch at university, although English literature or media studies might be useful.

Medicine

At least chemistry and biology are required; some universities also look for one from maths and physics.

Modern languages

At least one language is required, although more than one can be useful. Some less common languages are taught at university without prior knowledge, but most universities like to see some proof of linguistic aptitude.

Music

Previous study of music is needed, both academically through A levels (or equivalent) and through grade exams at grades 6, 7 or 8. Some universities will consider candidates who haven't studied advanced level music provided they can demonstrate their abilities through graded practical and theory exams.

Nursing

Biology, or another science subject, is needed.

Occupational therapy

Biology may be required, while other social sciences can be useful.

Pharmacy

Chemistry and biology are essential, while physics or maths may be required.

Physiotherapy

Biology is nearly always required (although some universities will consider applicants with physical education or chemistry instead). Other universities look for a second science.

Psychology

Advanced level psychology is not needed to study the subject at degree level. Some universities favour a science background, although many accept a range of subjects. Maths can be useful, although a strong GCSE grade may suffice.

Sociology

Most universities do not specify subject requirements, although social sciences could be relevant. Some of the most competitive universities might consider more traditional subjects a better preparation.

Speech therapy
Biology is essential; languages are sometimes required, while English or psychology can be useful.

Surveying
No essential requirements.

Teaching
At least one National Curriculum subject is essential.

'I went to see a careers adviser when I was applying to college. I already knew I wanted to do English language and psychology. As I wanted to go into primary teaching, she suggested I do two core subjects, so I went with geography as I did it at IGCSE and enjoyed it.'

Becky Whitehead

Veterinary science
At least chemistry and biology are needed; some universities also look for one from maths and physics.

Top Tip

If you're planning a route to a regulated profession, make sure your degree is recognised by the relevant professional body; for example, the BPS (British Psychological Society) for psychology or RICS (Royal Institution of Chartered Surveyors) for building surveying.

'Luckily, all my A levels have contributed to helping me at university I eventually decided to do mental health nursing so maths helped me with calculating drug administrations, psychology helped with the theory and PE helped describe the importance of taking care of body and mind.'

Melissa Livingstone

What if I want to study abroad?
If you're intending to study abroad at university level, then it makes sense to choose a qualification that is well recognised and easily understood. Qualifications such as the International Baccalaureate and A levels are probably the most portable and many overseas universities include these qualifications within their entry requirements.

This doesn't mean that Scottish Highers, Cambridge Pre-U and others aren't accepted outside the UK; they may just be slightly less familiar. Universities will probably need to check your qualifications and compare them to the local school leaving certificates to determine the kind of offer you will receive.

Many other countries retain a broad curriculum up to the equivalent of sixth form, much like Scotland, followed by a first year at university that allows a continuation of general education. Qualifications offering breadth, such as the IB and Scottish Highers, should fit quite neatly into this style of education.

Top Tip

Lots of UK students choose the Republic of Ireland for university, as costs can work out lower than in England, Wales and Northern Ireland; for courses at the leading universities there you are likely to need four full A levels in academic subjects.

How can I avoid choosing the wrong subjects?

Most of the students who contributed to this book fell into two categories when reflecting that they had made the wrong subject choices.

- 'I should have chosen subjects that I would have enjoyed.'
- 'I wish I had chosen subjects that are well recognised by universities.'

Achieving both of these aims is not an easy task. The less traditional subjects at A level are very popular; some might seem more exciting, relevant and therefore more enjoyable, but top universities continue to favour the more traditional choices – often because they provide a better grounding for the academic study you will experience at university. There is less of an issue with the newer universities, which tend to be far more accepting of a variety of advanced level subjects.

Some subjects might seem easier (with the opportunity for better grades), but choose a softer option and you risk alienating some of the universities to which you aspire. Confusingly, some of the professional-sounding subjects (that appear to lead to high-flying careers) might just be another wrong turn; accounting, psychology and business are not always viewed in the same way as English literature, chemistry and history.

If you do manage to choose subjects that inspire you while also keeping your chosen universities interested, then you will hopefully spend a more enjoyable two years; you'll be more likely to achieve higher grades and will have a much better chance of success when trying to get into your chosen university.

How can I decide?

How do you make decisions? Do you gather all the information before making a logical and informed choice? Or do you go with your instinct? Do you talk it through with people you trust? Do you ignore it and hope it goes away? Many people use a combination of methods; if you're struggling to make a decision you could use some of the suggestions here.

You first need to get your head around what you are hoping to achieve with your studies: a route to university (if so, do you know what type of university or what course?), a chance to learn more about your subjects, an opportunity to confirm your interests or something else. Be honest and be as specific as you can. By the way, it's fine to choose A levels (or equivalent) if you don't know what to do and you want to keep your options open; many students do!

If it works for you, use a mind map to jot down all your thoughts about studying at this level and what you want to get out of it. Just note everything that comes to mind, no matter how random, without editing it. If you have already started your research, you might include some of the information you have discovered. Once you have finished, you can take a look through and start to organise your thoughts or filter out the parts that are less relevant. Narrow this down to a handful of key criteria that are essential (or desirable) to your choices and then rank these in order of importance. For example:

- prefer assessment by exams
- a subject that uses my mechanical skills
- subjects that complement one another
- at least two subjects that are well recognised by the top universities
- interested in studying at Durham or Edinburgh.

The next step is to develop a long list of perhaps six or eight subjects and see how closely each matches your key factors. If you like to work through things logically, you could use a pros and cons list or a decision matrix (see an example below) to narrow down your choices. Or you could talk things through with family, your teachers or a careers adviser.

Decision matrix

Key factors when deciding my A level subjects	Weighting	Accounting	Chemistry	Classical Civilisation	PE	Physics
Wanted by top universities	Most important (×5)	4 (4 × 5 = **20**)	10 (10 × 5 = **50**)	8 (8 × 5 = **40**)	2 (2 × 5 =**10**)	10 (10 × 5 = **50**)
Will I cope with a grade C in maths?	Fairly important (×4)	5 (5 × 4 = **20**)	2 (2 × 4 = **8**)	10 (10 × 4 = **40**)	9 (9 × 4 = **36**)	1 (1 × 4 = **4**)
Prefer assessment by written exam	Least important (×1)	10 (10 × 1 = **10**)	7 (7 × 1 = **7**)	10 (10 × 1 = **10**)	4 (4 × 1 = **4**)	7 (7 × 1 = **7**)
TOTAL		50	65	90	50	61

Once you know which factors matter most to you, you'll need to decide just how important each factor is in your decision making and then give it a weighting according to its importance. You can use a scale or a percentage. In this example, a scale of 1 to 5 has been used; as the main priority is a subject wanted by the top universities, it has been given a weighting of 5.

Mark each subject out of 10 according to how closely it matches each of your deciding factors. For example, physics scores 10 out of 10 as it is well recognised by the top universities. Classical civilisation scores 8, as it is accepted by the leading universities, but is not a subject they specifically require.

Next, you'll need to multiply the score by its weighting; this helps to place more importance on the aspects that matter most to you. Once you have done the same to each subject, you can add up the results to give an overall total. The subjects with the highest scores should be the ones that are most suitable based on your criteria. In this example, classical civilisation, chemistry and physics are the three most relevant subjects.

You could expand your decision matrix to include far more subjects and factors.

Remember that practical considerations, such as your GCSE grades and timetabling options, will also have a bearing on the decision. Think about the need to have a coherent programme rather than focusing on subjects in isolation. There probably isn't one single perfect combination of subjects and you may have to make some compromises in your choices.

Also, don't forget those important questions from Chapter One.

- Will I enjoy it?
- Will I do well in it?
- Where will it lead?

Now that we have covered the main considerations when choosing your qualifications and your subjects, the next step is to look in more depth at the subjects themselves.

PART TWO

SUBJECT DIRECTORY

The Subject Directory has lots of information about subjects you can study after GCSEs (or equivalent). Each section includes the following:

- a description of the subject
- examples of some of the qualifications available
- an outline of the course structure and assessment methods
- options for further study of the subject
- future career options.

As you browse the directory, you can start to look at how a subject might suit you, your strengths and any future plans. As you do so, remember to consider those essential questions.

- Will I enjoy it?
- Will I do well in it?
- Where will it lead?

ACCOUNTING

Good financial understanding is a key requirement for success in most areas of life. It is essential for businesses, governments, households and individuals. Accountants learn how to provide a record of trading activity and independently audit any activities. They also deal with tax liabilities, act as company directors or work with senior managers to help them plan their commercial activities.

Accounting is mainly divided into two areas: financial accounting and management accounting. The former deals with checking a company's accounts and preparing annual accounts; on the other hand, management accountants usually work for a particular company and assist managers with budgeting and financial planning.

Is it right for me?

Accounting students will need a keen interest in business, good attention to detail and a sound head for figures. If you've struggled with GCSE (or Standard Grade) Maths, this may not be the subject for you.

Subject options

You can study accounting as an AS or A level across much of the UK; it is offered as a Higher and Advanced Higher qualification in Scotland.

A/AS level in Accounting

Students will be introduced to the principles of accounting and will then start to apply them to real situations. The subject is a mixture of learning theories and applying principles to business case studies. Assessment is by examination.

At AS and A level, your studies might include some of the following units. Talk to your selected sixth form or college, or use the exam board website, to find out the exact syllabus (often called a specification).

Accounting principles (AS)
An introduction to accounting; accounting concepts; expenditure classifications; ledger entries and adjustments; final accounts.

Accounting applications (AS)
The journal; correction of errors; control accounts; adjustments; ICT in accounting; an introduction to budgeting.

Company accounts and interpretation (A2)
Preparation of final accounts for limited companies; financing; accounting standards; analysis and interpretation of accounts.

Management accounting (A2)
Budgets and budgetary control; standard costing and variance analysis; capital expenditure appraisal; stock; costing; social responsibility.

Top Tip

Accounting is not favoured by every university; the London School of Economics considers it a non-preferred subject, although the University of Sheffield includes it in its accepted list.

Higher and Advanced Higher in Accounting

Both the Higher and Advanced Higher are divided into units on financial and management accounting. Closed book assessment and examination are used.

Choosing other subjects to go with accounting

Popular choices include business studies, computing, law, economics, mathematics and some sciences. If you want to study accounting at degree level, some universities require A level Mathematics.

Top Tip

A level Accounting has some subject overlap with A level Business, so taking both subjects might impact on your application to university. Get advice from your school or college (or intended university) before you choose these subjects in combination.

Accounting at university

Most universities do not require A level Accounting as an entry requirement for their degree courses. In fact, some prefer more traditional A levels rather than an A level in Accounting or Business Studies. In most cases a good grade at A level Mathematics is more important.

Alternatives to straight accounting courses include accounting with economics, computing, business management, law or mathematics. If you choose a joint degree, check whether you will still gain exemption from professional accountancy examinations.

Accounting and your future career

Non-graduate jobs in accounting

It is possible to become a qualified accountant without going to university. You will need good grades at A level (or similar qualifications), as training schemes often require As and Bs. You will also need the aptitude and temperament to balance work with substantial further study successfully. You would have to complete a training contract with a firm of accountants and take professional studies and examinations. Opportunities are available with firms including KPMG (www.kpmgcareers.co.uk), Ernst & Young (www.ey.com), PricewaterhouseCoopers (www.pwc.co.uk) and Deloitte (www.deloitte.com/uk), as well as with smaller firms.

Alternatively, you could consider working as an accounts assistant or an accounts technician while studying for work-based qualifications at the same time.

You would also be able to apply for other non-graduate jobs; those requiring numerical skills, attention to detail and an interest in business would be relevant.

Graduate jobs directly related to accounting

After you have graduated, in order to obtain a professional accountancy qualification, you will need to study for further exams and have a period of approved work experience.

There will then be a range of different accountancy roles open to you. You could be employed by a firm of accountants, providing financial or business advice and other management services to fee-paying clients; these could range from private individuals to large commercial organisations and government bodies. Alternatively, you could be employed by a blue-chip organisation or public sector organisation and work with departmental managers to help them understand financial information.

Other graduate jobs where a degree in accounting could be useful

The knowledge and skills gained in this degree subject would be relevant to jobs across the financial and business sector.

- **Corporate, commercial and investment banking.** There is a wide range of jobs in this area. For example, corporate financiers' tasks include advising clients on the raising of capital while operations professionals ensure that transactions run smoothly.
- **Financial management.** There are opportunities in all areas of business, industry and commerce, and in both the public and private sectors.
- **Insurance, pensions and actuarial work.** Jobs include managing pension funds and the underwriting of insurance claims.
- **Investment management.** You might work as a trader or stockbroker, although this is not a career choice for the shy ones.

- **Management consultancy.** Management consultants are called in to help solve organisational problems experienced by a company, including finances, IT, human resources, and so on. It is a competitive area to get into.
- **Retail banking and personal financial services.** Bank managers may manage several branches and have responsibility for meeting sales targets and attracting new business. Credit analysts undertake risk assessments on loan requests.
- **Taxation.** You could work as a tax adviser, providing advisory and consultancy services in order to create the best tax strategies for your clients, or as an inspector, determining tax liability on behalf HM Revenue and Customs.

Find out more about accounting

- Accounting Web: www.accountingweb.co.uk
- Assessment and Qualifications Alliance (AQA): www.aqa.org.uk
- Association of Chartered Certified Accountants (ACCA): www.accaglobal.com
- Chartered Institute of Management Accountants (CIMA): www.cimaglobal.com
- Chartered Institute of Public Finance and Accountancy (CIPFA): www.cipfa.org.uk
- Financial Skills Partnership: www.financialskillspartnership.org.uk
- Institute of Chartered Accountants in England and Wales (ICAEW): www.icaew.com.
- Oxford, Cambridge and RSA Examinations (OCR): www.ocr.org.uk
- Scottish Qualifications Authority (SQA): www.sqa.org.uk

ARCHAEOLOGY

Archaeology literally means the study of things ancient; it's about understanding history from studying relics and antiquities that have been excavated from the land beneath our feet. This subject draws on other disciplines such as information technology, science and literature, but its closest ally is history.

In the absence of any written records, archaeology is often the only means of interpreting key historical events and identifying past civilisations. Students of A level Archaeology learn, among other things, how sites are identified for excavation, how to interpret and date the findings and how settlements are formed.

Is it right for me?

The study of archaeology is nothing to do with Indiana Jones. Much of the A level course is classroom-based, although you will have some visits or excavations. Any digs you get the chance to attend are likely to be slow and painstaking – nothing like the excitement of programmes such as *Time Team*.

You do not need prior knowledge of archaeology to study it at A level. The subject incorporates aspects of the arts and the sciences, including history, geography, religious studies, art and even physics. It is good for an all-rounder, as you need interest and strength in a number of subjects.

Top Tip

If you are more interested in people and cultures in the world today, rather than in the distant past, you may prefer the study of social anthropology, available as an AQA A level in Anthropology (www.aqa.org.uk/qual/gce/humanities/anthropology_overview.php) and as social and cultural anthropology through the International Baccalaureate Diploma (www.ibo.org/diploma/curriculum/group3/socialandculturalanthropology.cfm).

Subject options

Archaeology is available at GCE A level and AS level through the AQA exam board. For the latest syllabus information, contact your chosen school or college, or AQA (Assessment and Qualifications Alliance, www.aqa.org.uk). If the A level is not available locally, you may be able to study it via distance learning (see the Council for British Archaeology website for details, www.britarch.ac.uk/education/study/alevels).

A/AS level in Archaeology

Archaeology is largely classroom-based, but will also involve visits to sites of archaeological interest, so students can relate learned theory to practical situations. The AS level is assessed with an exam on each unit. For the A2, 60% of the marks will be made up of a world archaeology exam. The remaining 40% will be from coursework and a 3,500–4,000-word research investigation. Your archaeological studies will include the following units.

The archaeology of religion and ritual (AS)

This unit focuses on belief systems and activities related to those beliefs. It explores the terminology of ritual and religion. Students will explore the relevance of sites from prehistoric Europe, ancient Egypt and Roman Europe.

Archaeological skills and methods (AS)

You will learn how archaeologists make their discoveries and explore the stages of site investigation, from formation and discovery to excavation, dating and interpretation. Methods studied include lab investigation and dating techniques.

World archaeology (A2)

This unit covers society, economics and culture in the past, as well as the latest developments and debates in archaeology today.

Archaeological investigation (A2)

You will carry out your own archaeological investigation involving research activities and practical fieldwork; this could be site-based or involve the examination of discovered artefacts.

Choosing other subjects to go with archaeology

Subjects which go well with archaeology are history, geography, art, languages, classical civilisation, Latin and classical Greek.

There may be some subject crossover with courses such as classical civilisation and history but not enough to cause issues when applying to university.

Archaeology at university

As Archaeology A level is not available everywhere, it doesn't tend to be a requirement for degree level study. Archaeology is available as a Bachelor of Arts (BA) or a Bachelor of Science (BSc); sciences are important if you intend to apply for the BSc, whereas history, ancient history or classical civilisation may be needed for the BA.

Archaeology is a well-established subject at higher education (HE) level, even though it still remains a fairly specialised area. Students from this course gain both practical and analytical skills, so they have a lot to offer employers.

Top Tip

Two science subjects are required for BSc (Hons) Archaeology at Durham University, but they will accept mathematics and geography as sciences.

Archaeology degrees can vary quite a lot. Some are relatively modern in their application of the subject's practical skills, whereas others focus more on classical archaeology and its relationship with classical culture, such as the arts, religion and literature. You will have to decide what kind of archaeology you're most interested in and research your options carefully. All courses will have elements of fieldwork, which students usually carry out during the holidays.

Top Tip

Archaeology appears on University College London's list of preferred subjects at A level. It is of more limited suitability when applying to Trinity College, Cambridge (unless you are applying for archaeology and anthropology).

Combining archaeology with other degree subjects

There are a range of joint degrees where you can combine archaeology with other subject choices, including:

- archaeology and ethnography
- architectural history and archaeology
- archaeology and social anthropology
- classics and archaeology
- geography and archaeology.

Archaeology and your future career

The study of archaeology helps to develop a wide range of skills which are in demand with employers: analysis, evaluation, teamwork, record keeping and report writing, and independent, lateral and logical thought.

Non-graduate jobs in archaeology

There may be some assistant or clerical level positions in museums or galleries that could make use of your skills and knowledge. Furthermore, a range of administrative and support roles, for example in the Civil Service, demand the kinds of qualities mentioned above.

Graduate jobs directly related to archaeology

Archaeologists can be found in national heritage agencies, local authorities, national parks, museums, universities and colleges, archaeological societies, consultancies and independent museums, trusts and charities. The main vocational areas directly related to this subject are the ones listed below.

- **Archaeologist.** The job involves working with a team to plan and excavate, analyse and report findings.
- **HE lecturer.** Lecturers teach through writing and delivering lectures, tutorials and other activities. They carry out research and may write books or articles for publication.

Graduate jobs where a degree in archaeology could be useful

- **Heritage manager.** The job comprises the conservation, interpretation and promotion of historic buildings and sites, along with managing facilities and organising exhibitions and events.
- **Historic buildings inspector or conservation officer.** You would inspect and report on buildings of special historic or architectural interest for the purpose of preservation or conservation.
- **Museum education officer.** In this role, you would create a link between a museum collection and the interests or needs of visitors. This might involve developing informal or curriculum-based learning opportunities.
- **Museum or art gallery curator.** Responsible for the care and improvement of a collection, including exhibitions, catalogues and organisation.
- **Museum or gallery exhibitions officer.** Responsible for the planning and organising of permanent and travelling exhibitions. Further study, such as an MA/Postgraduate Diploma in Museum Studies, is highly desirable.
- **Tourism officer.** A tourism officer might promote heritage as an attraction to incoming tourists. The role includes marketing and promotion, information provision and development activities.

Careers open to all graduates

The vast majority (around 60–70%) of graduate jobs are open to students irrespective of their degree subject.

In addition to your qualification, employers are interested in skills, potential, personal qualities and experience. It's important to get involved in outside activities while you're a student to enhance your skills and knowledge.

Find out more about archaeology

- AQA: www.aqa.org.uk
- Council for British Archaeology: www.britarch.ac.uk
- Creative and Cultural Skills: www.ccskills.org.uk
- Current Archaeology: www.archaeology.co.uk
- English Heritage: www.english-heritage.org.uk
- Young Archaeologists' Club (for those aged up to 17): www.yac-uk.org.

ART AND DESIGN

Why study art and design? You will develop your creativity and unleash your imagination, learning to express yourself using a variety of practical methods. You will get the chance to learn about contemporary art and design, as well as works from other times and other cultures. In addition, your aesthetic appreciation will improve, along with your critical reflections on your own art and the work of others.

Courses at this level provide a practical and theoretical understanding of art and design in a variety of contexts, equipping you with the skills to study or work in the field. You'll learn a range of creative techniques, from painting or drawing methods to creating a practical design for a new living space.

One thing most art and design students have in common is a visual appreciation of their environment; you will learn different ways of conveying that vision through different media including decorative arts, sculpture, graphic design, ceramics, textiles and photography. From a theoretical point of view, students may also consider how art forms have developed over time and how they relate to their literary, social and political contexts.

Is it right for me?

Whether you are considering an art-based or creative career or just have a love of the subject, it is worth considering advanced level art. You will need to have some creative background; GCSE Art at grade B is often a requirement for A levels or Standard Grade at credit level for SQA Higher Art and Design. Sixth forms and colleges may ask to see some of your artwork before they accept you on the course.

The courses allow you to develop creatively, teaching you to use different media with different techniques. You may also start to specialise in the field of your choice. The amount of coursework to complete means that art and design is likely to take up a lot of your time.

There are many careers where art and design skills or creative awareness are important, for example architecture, graphics, interior design, advertising, film, fashion and photography.

Subject options

Options at this level include the GCE A/AS level in Art and Design, available through all the major exam boards; Applied A levels in Art and Design; SQA Higher and Advanced Higher; Cambridge Pre-U in Art and Design; International Baccalaureate in Visual Arts; and BTEC Foundation Diploma in Art and Design.

As an alternative to art and design, have you considered design and technology options in graphic products, textiles or three-dimensional design? Find out more on page 106.

Top Tip

What is the difference between A level Art and Design and Applied A level Art and Design? The latter encourages active experience, including links with employers and knowledge of professional practice. For example, you may be encouraged to work to a fixed brief, as you would with a client. It will introduce you to a range of artistic disciplines and can be studied as a broad course or offer the chance to specialise. You'll be able to develop a portfolio, with the possibility to progress straight to university if it is strong enough. If you're hoping to go straight onto a degree, you may have a better chance with the larger portfolio gained from the double award, rather than the single Applied A level.

A level Art and Design is suitable for students who may wish to study a selection of other subjects in addition to art. It is a broad course with a number of specialist options available. The GCE A level can prepare you for further study of art and design – normally, an Art Foundation Course, such as the BTEC Foundation Diploma in Art and Design, at a college or university. There are some exceptions, but most students wouldn't use A level Art and Design to go straight onto the first year of an art and design-related degree.

A/AS level in Art and Design

Lots of your teaching time will be spent in the art studio, but you'll also need to spend time on research, visiting galleries and so on.

The outline below is based on the AQA syllabus. Talk to your selected sixth form or college to find out exactly what you will be studying.

You can specialise in one area or broaden your choices by studying the art, craft and design option. You will extend your creative skills through practical work, producing a portfolio of coursework at AS level which makes up 50% of the marks. The remaining 50% of your AS marks is based on a five-hour supervised assignment comprising prep work and a finished piece (or development of a piece).

At A2, you carry out a personal investigation; this is a practical unit with supporting written work of up to 3,000 words. The other half of the A2 marks come from a 15-hour supervised assignment.

The AQA course offers six main areas of study for your practical, critical and contextual work; however, options may be restricted based on the facilities available at your college or sixth form.

Art, craft and design

This option allows you to produce work from two or more of the following areas of study.

Fine art
Choose from painting, drawing, mixed media, sculpture, installation, printmaking, film, TV or photography.

Graphic communication
You could include illustration, advertising, packaging, communication graphics, multimedia, animation, web design, film, TV or computer graphics.

Photography
Options include portraits, landscape, still life, documentary, photo-journalism, and experimental and photographic installation.

Textile design
Take your pick from fashion, printed or dyed materials, domestic textiles, wallpaper, interiors or constructed textiles.

Three-dimensional design
3D design could encompass sculpture, ceramics, jewellery, body ornament, theatre design, interior design, product design or architectural design.

A/AS level (Applied) in Art and Design

Although there may be some theoretical elements to the course, in essence this is very much a practical and vocationally based course. You will be doing a lot of independent work in the art studio under the guidance of your teacher. You will also get the chance to get out and about, sketching or visiting exhibitions to extend your awareness.

Assessment is based on a combination of portfolios of work and externally set assignments, some of which have a time limit for completion.

This information is based on the AQA course specification. The Applied qualification can be taken as a single or double award and the units are as follows:

- Investigation of 2D visual language (AS)
- Investigation of 3D visual language (AS)
- Working to a brief (AS)
- Historical and contemporary contexts (AS double)
- Professional practice, communication and meaning (AS double)
- Option unit (AS double)
- Application and development of 2D visual language (A2)
- Application and development of 3D visual language (A2)
- Working to self-identified briefs (A2)
- Cultural and critical studies (A2 double)
- Option unit (A2 double)

You can tailor your course according to your interests; AS double award students get to focus on at least one of the following options, while A level double award students will choose at least two different options:

- drawing and painting or printmaking
- photography, film and video
- graphic design
- public art
- textile art and fashion
- 3D design.

Higher and Advanced Higher in Art and Design

The SQA courses encourage creative thinking, independent thought, innovation and problem solving. You'll have the chance to explore artistic expression, design and critical reflection. The course covers the environment, communication and the mass media, along with cultural, social and historical influences.

Your studies at Higher level will incorporate 2D and 3D, technology and contemporary issues. There are three mandatory units: expressive activity, design activity, and art and design studies. Assessment is divided between a portfolio of expressive and design work, and a written question paper on visual arts and design.

At Advanced Higher level, all students take design enquiry (the process of providing a solution to a design problem) and either expressive activity or design study. The choice of unit determines whether you gain an Advanced Higher in Art and Design: Design or an Advanced Higher in Art and Design: Expressive. The qualification is entirely portfolio-based.

International Baccalaureate Diploma in Visual Arts

The IB Visual Arts course is available at Standard and Higher level. Higher level students have more time for their studies, which tends to lead to work of a greater depth and a larger portfolio.

Assessment is based on an investigation workbook, which includes visual and written critical evaluation, such as notes, photos, experiments, sketches and written reflection. You'll also be assessed on an exhibition or portfolio of your creative work.

Cambridge Pre-U in Art and Design

The Cambridge Pre-U qualification offers the study of fine art, graphic communication, 3D design, textile design or lens-based imagery. If you don't want to specialise, the unendorsed option allows work to come from at least two of these areas.

As the style of the programme is linear (i.e. the assessment comes at the end of the two-year course), you can really develop your creative and academic skills before you have to submit pieces of work.

Assessment is based on a portfolio of work (30%), an evaluative study of up to 3,500 words (30%) and a project (40%).

BTEC Foundation Diploma in Art and Design

In many cases, studying an advanced level art and design course at A level (or equivalent) will not adequately prepare you for further creative studies at university. The Foundation Diploma in Art and Design bridges that gap; you'll get the chance to experiment with various disciplines, before specialising in an area relating to your intended undergraduate studies. Many universities prefer applicants to have an Art Foundation Course, as they like the improved practical skills, maturity of work and strength of portfolio that it brings.

Through an intensive, one-year course, you will develop skills in independent thinking and improve the way you organise yourself and your work. You might get the chance to study specialist options that weren't available at sixth form and, along the way, learn which university choices will be most appropriate. You should also gain an understanding of how the different disciplines of art and design relate to one another and learn about art and design today.

Top Tip

As an alternative to the BTEC qualification, some universities offer their own Art Foundation Courses.

The course consists of three distinct stages: the exploratory stage, the pathway stage and the confirmatory stage.

- **Stage 1: exploratory.** This stage encourages students to explore their interests, skills and creativity in art and design. Units cover 'researching, recording and responding in art and design' and 'media experimentation in art and design'.
- **Stage 2: pathway.** This stage takes a closer look at specialisms within the subject (such as art, craft and design) and helps to develop students' portfolios, CV and presentation skills. The stage is made up of four units: 'preparation and progression in art and design'; 'information and interpretation in art and design'; 'personal experimental studies in art and design'; and 'extended media development in art and design'.

- **Stage 3: confirmatory.** This stage is dedicated to the externally assessed final major project.

By the end of the course, you will have produced a substantial body of work, prepared for an exhibition and developed a portfolio for university interviews.

Choosing other subjects to go with art and design

Your choice of supporting subjects really depends on what you intend to do afterwards. If you're interested in architecture, for instance, you may need qualifications in maths and physics; on the other hand, if you're interested in theatre design, choosing English literature and drama could help your cause.

Top Tip

Due to the subject's practical nature, art and design qualifications are not always recognised by the leading universities; University of Sheffield and London School of Economics will only accept it when offered with other, more suitable subjects. Of course, regardless of university, the subject is essential when applying for many creative degrees.

Art and design at university

Degree courses tend to specialise rather than offering the general courses available at A level standard; you will come across art and design courses such as:

- BA (Hons) Design
- BA (Hons) Fashion Studies
- BA (Hons) Fine Art
- BA (Hons) Textiles.

You might be able to combine more than one of these programmes to give breadth to your expertise. Popular subject combinations include: history of art, computing, business studies and literature.

Art and design and your future career

Non-graduate jobs in art and design

It's possible to get into some art and design-related jobs after A levels, such as working as a junior design assistant in a creative design agency. Other possibilities to get experience at this stage include working as a marketing assistant, helping with the creative side of publications and promotions. The role of assistant to a professional artist, photographer, designer or sculptor is also an option.

Graduate jobs directly related to art and design

Within art and design-related jobs, it is possible and quite common for a graduate to cross over to a different discipline from the one they studied (for example, fine art to graphic design). Related jobs include those listed below.

- **Arts administrator:** supports and generates artistic activity. The role may include marketing, promotion, bookkeeping, finance and general administration. It appeals to those who want to combine working with art and people; it requires business and administration skills rather than creativity.
- **Exhibition/display designer:** organises the design of exhibition and display stands, and liaises with clients to produce designs that communicate their desired messages.
- **Fashion clothing designer:** produces designs for clothing and accessories, and may specialise in an area such as sportswear.
- **Graphic designer:** produces visual solutions for the communications needs of clients. The role requires creativity and imagination, good IT skills and commercial awareness.
- **Illustrator:** produces illustrations for magazines, books, advertising, brochures, greetings cards, packaging, posters or newspapers. Specialisms include scientific, technical and medical illustration.
- **Museum/gallery conservator/restorer:** preserves and cares for collections of artistic or cultural objects. Many specialise in one type of object (furniture, for example). A good class of degree and some voluntary experience are often necessary for entry.
- **Textile designer:** creates designs in knit, weave or print to be used in the production of fabric or textile products.

Other graduate jobs where a degree in art and design could be useful

- **Advertising art director:** creates visual ideas to be used within advertising and works as part of a team alongside illustrators, photographers and those responsible for editorial. The role can involve any media.
- **Art therapist:** works with people who present a variety of problems ranging from mental/physical illness, emotional and learning difficulties to stress and trauma. He/she aims to enable the client to effect change and growth on a personal level, within a safe environment, through the use of art materials.
- **Museum/art gallery curator:** acquires, cares for, stores and presents a collection of artefacts or works of art in order to inform, educate and entertain the public. The role may include other elements, such as public relations, fundraising and customer care.

- **Picture researcher/editor:** finds suitable images for print and electronic publications, investigates copyright, negotiates fees and liaises with clients. Part-time and distance learning courses are available.
- **Secondary school teacher.** The role appeals to those who are interested in developing the skills and knowledge of others within the art and design curriculum. Secondary school teaching mostly involves teaching art or design, craft or technology as part of the National Curriculum.
- **Visual merchandiser:** creates window and interior displays in shops and department stores with the aim of increasing sales.

Find out more about art and design

- AQA: www.aqa.org.uk
- Artists Information Company: www.a-n.co.uk
- Cambridge Pre-U: www.cie.org.uk/qualifications
- CCEA: www.rewardinglearning.org.uk
- Creative and Cultural Skills: www.ccskills.org.uk
- Creative Skillset: www.creativeskillset.org
- Edexcel: www.edexcel.com
- International Baccalaureate Diploma: www.ibo.org/diploma/curriculum/group6/
- OCR: www.ocr.org.uk
- SQA: www.sqa.org.uk
- WJEC: www.wjec.co.uk
- Your Creative Future: www.yourcreativefuture.org.uk

BIOLOGY AND HUMAN BIOLOGY

Biology is all around us, so perhaps it is unsurprising that it is such a popular choice at advanced level. Many current issues have a biological aspect, from diet and ecological issues to cloning and the latest medical developments.

Biology students learn about all life on the planet – human, plant and animal. The subject is full of variety, ranging from how plants get their energy to how the human heart works and how biological systems relate to ecology and the environment. Some of the questions that advanced level biologists could be asked to consider include those listed below.

- What is the exact process of cell division in humans and animals?
- How does the human nervous system work in detail?
- How do viral and bacterial infections work and how does the immune system respond?
- What are ecosystems and how do they work?

Top Tip

You will develop skills in data collection and evaluation, investigation and deduction, and how to present your findings (and argue your case).

Is it right for me?

The subject is technical and builds on knowledge and understanding from GCSE or Standard Grade Biology, so you will need to have achieved well at this level. It is helpful to have a good grasp of chemistry and maths, as you will need to collect and manipulate data, and understand the chemical processes that take place in the world around us. It helps if you are naturally inquisitive about the world.

Biology combines practical skill, scientific methods and problem solving. It has links with subjects such as chemistry, maths and geography. Human biology may be of particular interest to those considering a career in the health or clinical professions.

Top Tip

Dissections are not compulsory.

Subject options

There will be some variation in topic depending on the qualification and syllabus (some may put a greater emphasis on the social and environmental context of biology, for example), but all options at this level will cover the core biological concepts. Human Biology AS and A levels are offered at some schools and colleges.

Biology and Human Biology A levels are offered by all the big exam boards (OCR, AQA, Edexcel, WJEC and CCEA). You can also study the subject as a Scottish Higher and Advanced Higher, or as part of the Cambridge Pre-U Diploma and the IB.

Whichever qualification you choose, you will learn about biology through a range of methods: classroom teaching, investigations, practical work, discussions and presentations. You will spend time carrying out experiments in the lab, doing microscope work and getting out on field trips.

A/AS level in Biology

The AQA AS level Biology syllabus gives you a solid grounding in the subject, covering biology and disease, and the variety of living organisms, plus a practical investigative assignment.

AS level is assessed by exams on each topic, with the practical assignment making up the remaining 10% of your marks.

At A2 level, you will build on your AS level studies by covering two topics: populations and environment, and control in cells and organisms. This is followed with a further practical assignment.

Assessment at A2 level is very similar, with two exams making up the majority of the marks and the assignment making up 10%.

Other exam boards will offer different course content or style of assessment – see their websites for details (details can be found on page 77).

A/AS level in Human Biology

There is some overlap with the biology syllabus, but the material is organised differently and is focused on the human species.

AQA AS level covers the body and its diseases, and human origins and adaptations, along with a practical assignment.

A2 level comprises bodies and cells in and out of control, and the air we breathe, the water we drink, the food we eat. You will be asked to investigate a topical subject for your practical assignment.

Assessment for both AS and A2 is by a mixture of coursework and examination, with two written exams and one practical assignment each year, which counts for 10% of the marks.

'Human Biology is only acceptable as a science subject if it is accompanied by other strongly science-based subjects. Our preferred science subjects are Biology, Chemistry, Physics or Maths.'

University of Bristol, School of Biological Sciences (www.bristol.ac.uk)

Top Tip

Human biology is accepted by a range of other universities, including University College London and the University of Edinburgh.

Higher and Advanced Higher in Biology

Biology is available at Higher and Advanced Higher level. The Advanced Higher explains how biological principles can be applied to the world around us. You will study cell biology, genetics and growth, and learn about the importance of biochemistry, molecular biology and environmental issues.

Teaching encourages the development of experimental skills and enhances problem-solving abilities.

International Baccalaureate Diploma in Biology

The IB Biology course is available at Standard level and Higher level. Four key concepts are explored, comprising 'structure and function', 'universality versus diversity', 'equilibrium within systems' and 'evolution'.

An experimental approach is key to this qualification. Assessment in based on written exams, internally assessed group work, and short-term and long-term investigations. The internal assessments make up 24% of the marks. Practical work is a higher proportion of the IB than of the other qualifications listed here.

Cambridge Pre-U in Biology

The Cambridge Pre-U Biology syllabus includes the familiar topics from molecular biology, cell biology, physiology, genetics, and so on; it also introduces emerging topics in molecular genetics, biotechnology and immunology.

The key areas of study are: cell biology, evolution and the fundamentals of life, whole organism biology and environmental biology.

Students will be expected to show knowledge through understanding, analysis and application, and experimental and investigative skills. Assessment takes place at the end of year two and includes two written papers; a practical exam provides 15% of the marks.

Choosing other subjects to go with biology

If you are particularly strong in the sciences, then a common combination is biology, physics (or maths) and chemistry, but a whole range of alternative subjects tie in nicely with biology; other options include psychology, sociology, PE, health and social care or environmental science. Essentially, biology is a well-recognised and well-understood subject that can be studied with most other A level subjects, whether you are heading for a career in the sciences, the arts or anywhere else.

Some degree courses require at least two sciences, so you should check with your chosen universities before deciding on your perfect combination of subjects.

Biology at university

Biology at a higher level is extremely popular and there are many different biology-related courses available, including biochemistry, biomedical science and genetics. If you have an interest in studying medicine, dentistry or veterinary medicine at university, advanced level biology is more or less essential.

Like most degrees these days, biology can be quite varied and flexible in its content, and most courses will have core subjects in the first year before students choose their specialist area. You may find that biological sciences degrees tend to offer a broader curriculum, but you should always check the precise nature of the course before you take the plunge.

Biology can be combined with a whole range of subjects, including chemistry, physics, geography, maths or psychology. A word of warning: if you need a biology degree for a particular job, you should check beforehand whether a joint or combined qualification is acceptable.

Top Tip

Biology is widely accepted by all the top universities; it is also classed as a facilitating subject (by 'Informed Choices', the Russell Group guide to post-16 decisions), which means that it is one of the subjects most likely to be needed for a range of degrees (not just degrees in biology).

Biology and your future career

Most biology students don't end up working as biologists. Biology is relevant to a vast range of job areas, from veterinary medicine to health professions such as radiography and nursing. You could choose from scientific options, for example marine biology, biochemistry or ecology; alternatively, you could opt for teaching, sport or psychology.

Non-graduate jobs in biology

Many employers requiring A levels do not really mind which subjects you have studied. In that sense, Biology A level is as good a choice as any. However, there are some non-graduate areas of work where Biology A level is particularly useful. These include:

- health-care jobs
- laboratory work
- work in a dental surgery as an assistant
- any job requiring attention to detail and practical skills.

Graduate jobs directly related to biology

There are several employment areas where a degree in biology is directly relevant. Some of the most popular jobs are listed below, but further study is often required.

- **Civil Service fast streamer:** is employed by the Civil Service on the Fast Stream development programme. Uses scientific knowledge to carry out research, develop policy, manage projects and provide general administration.
- **Clinical cytogeneticist:** provides an analytical interpretation and advice service to medical staff in hospitals.
- **Industrial science researcher.** An intellectually challenging role that involves teamwork with professionals from a range of disciplines. The role can involve developing new products, such as drugs, or new processes.
- **Life science researcher:** is employed in universities and health authorities and by employers in the pharmaceutical, health-care or biotechnology fields. The role involves investigating and analysing natural and living phenomena, gathering scientific information and generating knowledge.
- **Medical sales executive:** represents pharmaceutical companies to GPs, retail pharmacists and hospital doctors. The role involves promoting pharmaceutical products in an ethical manner.
- **Scientific lab assistants:** help scientists and others who are engaged in research, development, analysis or scientific investigations by carrying out a variety of technical and experimental tasks.
- **Secondary school teacher:** teaches the subject as a separate discipline and also with a multidisciplinary approach through integrated science teaching.

Find out more about biology

To find out more about biology at advanced level, along with the range of opportunities using the subject, visit the following websites:

- AQA: www.aqa.org.uk
- Cambridge Pre-U: www.cie.org.uk/qualifications/
- CCEA: www.rewardinglearning.org.uk
- Edexcel: www.edexcel.com
- International Baccalaureate Diploma: www.ibo.org/diploma/curriculum/group4/
- NHS Careers: www.nhscareers.nhs.uk
- OCR: www.ocr.org.uk
- Science Council: www.sciencecouncil.org
- SEMTA – Sector Skills Council for Science, Engineering and Manufacturing Technologies: www.semta.org.uk
- Society of Biology: www.societyofbiology.org/home
- SQA: www.sqa.org.uk
- WJEC: www.wjec.co.uk

BUSINESS STUDIES

Students of business learn about organisations and how they work, as well as the different markets businesses serve. Generally, students will look at case studies from particular businesses and apply what they have learned to those case studies. Students of this subject might consider some of the following questions.

- What factors make a business successful?
- What external influences affect organisations?
- What are the different ways of motivating staff?
- How do the different functions of finance, information and human resources work together?

In essence, students gain an understanding of how organisations operate and how to make effective business decisions.

Is it right for me?

If you want to learn about decision making in business, then you should consider this course. The subject is relevant whether you see yourself setting up your own business or taking up a key position in an established organisation. Even if you're planning to work in an unrelated area, such as creative arts, some business acumen can be a great help.

Top Tip

Want to develop your skills in teamwork, articulating your point, understanding data and investigating facts? Business studies will develop all of those – and more.

Alternative options include many of the Applied A levels, such as leisure studies or travel and tourism, or courses that cover some common ground, such as economics.

Subject options

This subject is available as a GCE A/AS level and a GCE Applied A/AS level offered by all the major exam boards. In addition, you can opt for the SQA Higher and Advanced Higher in Business Management, the Cambridge Pre-U Business Management and the International Baccalaureate Diploma in Business Management.

A/AS level in Business Studies

The outline below is based on the OCR specification. For an exact definition of the AS and A2 syllabus you will be studying, talk to your selected sixth form or college or have a look at the exam board website. In the OCR specification, assessment is by written exam. If you prefer coursework, you could take a look at the Applied A level. Units are as follows.

- **An introduction to business (AS).** The nature of business; classification of business; objectives; other influences.
- **Business functions (AS).** Marketing; accounting and finance; people in organisations; operations management.
- **Option Unit (A2).** The first A2 unit is chosen from 'marketing', 'accounting', 'people in organisations' and 'business production'.
- **Strategic management (A2).** Business objectives and strategy; business analysis; external influences; change.

A/AS level (Applied) in Business Studies

Although there is some similarity between this course of study and the general AS/A level, the emphasis here is more on how to work effectively in business rather than simply understanding it from an academic point of view. There is also a greater emphasis on careers within business. Here is a list of the units on the full OCR syllabus.

- AS Creating a marketing proposal (Portfolio)
- AS Financial providers and products (Portfolio)
- AS ICT provision in a business (Portfolio)
- AS Recruitment in the workplace (Portfolio)
- AS Running an enterprise activity (Portfolio)
- AS The impact of customer service (Exam)
- AS Understanding production in business (Portfolio)
- AS Understanding the business environment (Exam)
- A2 A business plan for the entrepreneur (Portfolio)
- A2 Constructing a financial strategy (Portfolio)
- A2 Launching a business online (Portfolio)
- A2 Launching a new product or service in Europe (Portfolio)
- A2 Managerial and supervisory roles (Portfolio)
- A2 Promotion in action (Portfolio)
- A2 Training and development (Portfolio)
- A2 Business law (Exam)
- A2 Managing risk in the workplace (Exam)
- A2 Strategic decision making (Exam)

The Applied A level can be taken as a single or double award; students on the A level double award will take 12 units, whereas AS level single award students need to take only three.

Higher and Advanced Higher in Business Management

At Higher level, you'll be focusing on units on 'business enterprise', 'marketing and operations' and 'finance and human resource management'.

The Advanced Higher looks at the external business environment and the internal environment, and it allows you to research a business of your choice.

At both levels, the units are assessed internally with coursework, while the overall course is assessed by written exam.

International Baccalaureate Diploma in Business Management

The IB option can be taken at Standard or Higher level and includes 'business organisation and environment', 'human resources', 'accounts and finance', 'marketing' and 'operations management'. Higher level students also cover 'business strategy'.

Assessment takes the form of written exams and a research project at Higher level, while the Standard level students sit written exams and produce a written commentary.

Cambridge Pre-U in Business and Management

The Cambridge Pre-U course allows its students to consider real businesses and discuss current topics. You will carry out a personal investigation resulting in a 3,500-word report. The units on 'business concepts' and 'strategic decisions' are assessed by exams taken at the end of the two years.

Choosing other subjects to go with business studies

In theory, you could combine business studies with any other subject, but popular choices include economics, maths, computing, accounting, law, geography, science and languages. However, watch out for the overlap with economics, as some universities won't accept both subjects together.

Top Tip

If you want to study business at one of the more traditional universities then bear in mind that they may prefer more traditionally academic subjects rather than more modern ones. Business Studies A level is accepted by some (but not all) of the top universities, while applied business might restrict your choices. Check entry requirements before choosing.

Business studies at university

Business is a popular subject at HE level and the courses vary widely, in both content and style. Some are very much academically focused, examining the theories of management, for example, whereas others are much more vocational, with an emphasis on the practice of management and links with the business world. You have to ask yourself which type you would prefer.

At a higher level, business-related courses can be called a variety of things: management, business management, business and finance, business operations, and so on. Each of these has a slightly different inflection, so it's important to check the precise content. Most courses, however, include some core modules about business and management, and then allow students to choose options over the last two years. Some courses might even specify learning a foreign language as part of the course.

How about combining business with another subject? Popular combinations at degree level include business and accounting, business and economics, business and maths, business and law, business and psychology or business and engineering. Most employers with a strong commercial focus aren't too worried about how you combine your degree.

Business studies and your future career

Non-graduate jobs in business studies

This subject will give you an insight into the business world, so employers may be more likely to take you on than those who have studied other things. Positions do exist in management and administration for those with A levels. Moreover, there is an increasing number of school leaver programmes offered by companies such as the Chartered Insurance Institute (CII), Accenture and Deloitte, which provide the opportunity to achieve a sponsored degree alongside employment.

A number of young entrepreneurs decide to set up their own businesses, in which case the skills gained from a course like this could provide a good foundation.

Graduate jobs directly related to business studies

A knowledge of business is useful if not essential in most careers. When recruiting for commercial or financial job opportunities, employers are prepared to consider graduates in any subject but some may give preference to a business studies background, whilst others include this as a definite requirement.

Other graduate jobs where a degree in business studies could be useful

Although the following occupations are open to graduates from any degree discipline, a business studies degree will provide useful background knowledge, evidence of some of the skills mentioned above and, possibly, some exemptions from papers in professional examinations.

- **Advertising account executive:** acts as a link between the client and the agency, taking responsibility for putting the proposal together and presenting it to the client. The executive co-ordinates the activities of the advertising team and administration.
- **Bank manager:** responsible for managing the daily business of a branch and for the development of new business, ensuring that sales targets are met and maintaining a customer-oriented retail team.
- **Chartered accountant:** provides financial information, maintains general accounting systems, performs audits and liaises with clients or management colleagues. Opportunities exist in industry, commerce, private practice and the public sector.
- **Distribution/logistics manager:** manages the supply, movement and storage of goods and materials. Plans, organises and co-ordinates material flow and storage through the process of manufacture from supplier to customer. This role also involves controlling the total distribution operation.
- **Investment banker, corporate finance:** advises private and corporate investors about their money and currency-related activities. He/she also seeks to promote related financial products appropriate to the clients' needs.
- **Management consultant:** provides a professional service to business, public and other undertakings by identifying and investigating problems concerned with strategy, policy, markets, organisation, procedures and methods.
- **Marketing executive:** promotes and sells products to the public. This role involves working on various projects to develop brands and promoting existing products.
- **Personnel officer:** develops and advises on all policies relating to human resources in an organisation.
- **Public relations officer:** uses all forms of media and communications to project and protect the appropriate image of an organisation or individual.
- **Retail buyer:** successfully purchases attractive merchandise whose price, quality and availability meet customers' needs. Buyers must provide commercially viable merchandise ranges at competitive prices, whilst maximising profitability.
- **Retail manager:** in charge of the day-to-day management of a department or store; he/she is responsible for staff, sales, customer service, effective cost control of stocks and resource management.
- **Sales executive:** promotes and maximises sales of a company's products or services in designated markets. This role also involves identifying new markets and new business, and acting as liaison between producer and the retailer or wholesaler.

Find out more about business studies

- AQA: www.aqa.org.uk
- Business in You: businessinyou.bis.gov.uk
- Cambridge Pre-U: www.cie.org.uk/qualifications
- CCEA: www.rewardinglearning.org.uk
- Edexcel: www.edexcel.com
- Financial Skills Partnership: www.financialskillspartnership.org.uk
- International Baccalaureate Diploma: www.ibo.org/diploma/curriculum/group3/
- OCR: www.ocr.org.uk
- SQA: www.sqa.org.uk
- WJEC: www.wjec.co.uk

CHEMISTRY

Chemistry is about understanding the fundamental nature of life from a chemical point of view. Students learn the skills to work in a laboratory; they also acquire knowledge related to the theories of chemistry and test some of those theories in practice.

How can you test for the presence of acid? Why and how do substances change when you heat them? What are the properties of that changed substance? How do we express that change on paper?

These are just some of the questions whose answers advanced level chemists need to contemplate and explore. You may have considered some of these issues at GCSE level, but now you will get the chance to investigate them in much more detail.

Is it right for me?

The subject builds on the basics studied at GCSE or Standard Grade Chemistry, so it is important that you grasped the key concepts at that level. You will develop an understanding of chemistry using mathematical concepts, so an understanding of maths is also helpful.

Top Tip

If you like to solve problems and explore logical challenges, and don't mind the need to memorise some essential information, then chemistry might be right for you.

Subject options

This subject is available at GCE A/AS level, Scottish Higher and Advanced Higher, International Baccalaureate Diploma and Cambridge Pre-U.

A/AS level in Chemistry

Chemistry students learn the theory and practice of the subject, so you will spend lots of time in a lab, observing practical demonstrations and carrying out supervised experiments. Most of the assessment will be based on written exams but there will also be an assessed practical examination.

The outline below is based on a typical chemistry specification. Speak to your sixth form or college (or check the exam board websites, see page 88) for the latest information.

Atomic structure, bonding and main chemical groups
Most courses thoroughly investigate atomic structure, chemical formulae, chemical bonding and groups of chemicals such as Group 7 (chlorine to iodine).

Organic and inorganic chemistry, energetics, kinetics and qualitative equilibria
This includes the introduction to alkanes, alkenes, alcohols and halogenoalkanes; industrial inorganic chemistry; chemical reactions (endothermic and exothermic); calculating the rates of chemical reactions; understanding the dynamic nature of chemical equilibria.

Laboratory chemistry
This focuses on carrying out chemistry in the lab; you will get the chance to develop your experimental skills.

Periodicity, quantitative equilibria and functional group chemistry
More advanced theories about chemical reactions; understanding chemical properties of certain parts of the periodic table; acids and bases; further organic chemistry (including acids, esters, carbonyl and nitrogen compounds).

Transition metals, quantitative kinetics and applied organic chemistry
Oxidisation; ionic bonding; reaction mechanisms and aromatic compounds; understanding rates of chemical reactions using quantitative techniques; learning tests to identify certain organic compounds; identifying certain chemical structures of organic compounds; using a spectrometer; understanding the importance of organic chemistry in relation to agriculture, the pharmaceutical business and other materials.

Higher and Advanced Higher in Chemistry
Chemistry is available at Higher level, and four units are also offered as part of the Advanced Higher: 'electronic structure and the periodic table', 'principles of chemical reaction', 'organic chemistry' and 'chemical investigation'.

Assessment at this level is based on a written exam and a practical assessment.

International Baccalaureate Diploma in Chemistry
The IB syllabus emphasises the experimental approach. Standard level chemistry can be taken by those with little or no background in the sciences, while the Higher level explores the subject in greater breadth and depth. Topics studied at both levels include: stoichiometry, bonding, atomic theory and kinetics.

Assessment involves three written papers. An interdisciplinary project, practicals and investigations provide 24% of the marks.

Cambridge Pre-U in Chemistry

You will study physical chemistry, inorganic chemistry, organic chemistry and analysis. Topics that you might not find elsewhere at this level include: Van Arkel diagrams, functional group level, carbon-13 NMR and anti-bonding molecular orbitals.

Assessment is based on three written exams and one practical assessment (making up 15% of the marks); all assessments take place at the end of year two.

'I feel that I came to university with a smoother transition than some other chemists, who were thrown a little by the difficulty of some problems. I would definitely say that Chemistry Pre-U gave me the advantage at the beginning of the course.'

Anthony Kane

Top Tip

Studying chemistry will help you to develop a range of transferable skills, including problem solving, critical thinking and conveying complex information.

Choosing other subjects to go with Chemistry

Some degree courses require at least two science subjects at A level, so many students choose to combine this subject with biology, physics and maths. Alternatively, chemistry can be combined with a range of other arts or humanities subjects.

Chemistry at university

Chemistry at HE level is extremely popular and there are many different available courses related to this subject, including biochemistry, medical biochemistry and chemical physics. Most of these related subjects would require an A level (or equivalent) in Chemistry. If you plan to pursue a career in medicine, pharmacy, dentistry or veterinary medicine, you will generally need advanced level chemistry.

Most chemistry degrees expand upon the areas studied at A level; teaching involves a combination of set lectures, small-group tutorials, assigned coursework and lab work. Studying chemistry at degree level will have some overlap with other sciences; however, students often choose to combine this subject with biology or physics.

Other joint degree programmes offered by universities include:

- chemistry with a European language
- chemistry with management

- chemistry with maths
- medicinal chemistry.

Top Tip

Chemistry is one of the handful of subjects most often needed by universities for a variety of different degrees. It is widely accepted by the leading universities in the UK.

'All of my subjects (chemistry, biology and physics) will help gain entry onto my preferred veterinary medicine course. Chemistry and biology are vital and universities also seem to prefer science and maths subjects for science-related degrees, so physics and maths (which I later dropped) were an obvious choice.

'I enjoy the subjects greatly, as I have a passion for science. I have always been naturally good at science, so it has been relatively straightforward to understand most of it.'

Michael Hall

Chemistry and your future career

Non-graduate jobs in chemistry

Most jobs using chemistry require higher qualifications. It may be possible to get some experience working as a lab assistant, dental assistant or veterinary assistant, but these often require further training, too. Nevertheless, the subject is highly regarded by employers in lots of different areas of work, so you can expand your job options beyond chemistry-related occupations.

Graduate jobs directly related to chemistry

- **Analytical chemist:** performs structural, quantitative, product and formulation analyses using state-of-the-art techniques, often in support of other scientists.
- **Biomedical scientist/medical laboratory scientific officer (MLSO):** carries out laboratory investigations on human samples necessary for the diagnosis, treatment and prevention of illness or disease.
- **Colour technologist:** produces dyes and pigments for the colouration of products such as textiles, paper, cosmetics and foodstuffs. They may also develop dyes for highly sensitive biomedical applications.
- **Industrial research scientist:** organises and carries out systematic investigations to develop new products or improve existing products to meet consumer demand for quality, safety and price.

- **Materials engineer:** conducts technical investigations related to the development and production of a wide range of materials, such as glass, metals, polymers and plastics.
- **Process development scientist:** scales up processes developed in the laboratory so that they may be used in manufacturing large quantities. The aim is to produce products for the market in an efficient, economical and safe way.
- **Product development scientist:** takes ideas or discoveries generated by research and then develops or formulates them to the point where new products can be manufactured. The work may involve developing new products or improving the performance of existing ones.
- **Quality assurance officer:** develops and applies tests to ensure that raw materials, intermediates and finished products meet specified standards of composition, texture, taste, appearance and performance.
- **Research scientist, physical sciences:** plans and conducts experimental research, evaluates ideas, and uses and develops theoretical knowledge in either theoretical or applied areas.
- **Secondary school teacher, further education lecturer or higher education lecturer:** teaches chemistry in schools or colleges of further education. Lecturers in higher education balance their teaching load with research and supervision of postgraduate researchers.

Other graduate jobs where a degree in chemistry could be useful

- **Clinical biochemist:** carries out tests on samples from patients to assist with the investigation, diagnosis and treatment of disease. This role involves liaising with clinicians on the interpretation of results.
- **Forensic scientist:** analyses samples in relation to crime and writes reports which are presented as evidence in courts.
- **Medical sales executive:** negotiates sales and generates new business between producers and their clients, either business to general public or business to business.
- **Patent agent:** acts as an agent for inventors or companies with new ideas or processes to protect the intellectual property for the client.
- **Scientific journalist:** researches and writes scientific news and articles for the general public or for more specialist audiences.
- **Toxicologist:** carries out and interprets laboratory and field studies to identify toxins and their effect on living systems and the environment.

Find out more about chemistry

- AQA: www.aqa.org.uk
- Cambridge Pre-U: www.cie.org.uk/qualifications/
- CCEA: www.rewardinglearning.org.uk

- Cogent – Skills for Science Based Industries: www.cogent-ssc.com
- Edexcel: www.edexcel.com
- International Baccalaureate Diploma: www.ibo.org/diploma/curriculum/group4/
- OCR: www.ocr.org.uk
- Royal Society of Chemistry: www.rsc.org
- Science Council: www.sciencecouncil.org
- SEMTA – Sector Skills Council for Science, Engineering and Manufacturing Technologies: www.semta.org.uk
- SQA: www.sqa.org.uk
- WJEC: www.wjec.co.uk

CLASSICS AND CLASSICAL CIVILISATION

Classical civilisation is the study of the politics, art, philosophy and literature of Ancient Rome and Greece. It allows students who don't have knowledge of the Greek and Latin languages to gain an appreciation of culture during the period between 1500 BC and AD 450. You will discover the origins of European languages and the basis for much of our culture.

Is it right for me?

Classical civilisation requires no prior academic knowledge or knowledge of classical languages, although essay-writing skills, an interest in reading and researching, and a questioning outlook are all beneficial. The course requires debate, discussion and the ability to develop an argument. If you enjoy history, drama, art, politics or philosophy, you should discover something of interest in classical civilisation.

Top Tip

Classics subjects at A level include Latin, classical Greek, classical civilisation and ancient history.

Subject options

This subject is available at GCE AS and A level (offered by the AQA and OCR exam boards) and as a Scottish Advanced Higher. The Cambridge Pre-U in Classical Heritage also covers a similar range of topics.

Other classics subjects are available at A level, Scottish Higher and Advanced Higher or IB.

A/AS level in Classical Civilisation

Regardless of the syllabus you follow, you will learn by examining a range of writing (in translation) from the period. There may be some opportunities to visit a Roman or Greek site of archaeological interest. Assessment is based on written exams.

Units for OCR A level Classical Civilisation have a predominantly literary focus, although they can be combined with units from ancient history, Latin and classical Greek. The AQA syllabus offers 20 topics from which you would choose four; this allows you to focus on subject areas that most interest you.

Archaeology: Mycenae and the classical world (AS)
You will learn different ways of discovering the past; you will understand different dating techniques and explore pottery, weapons and armour of the era.

Homer's Odyssey and society (AS)
Learn about the values of the society represented by Homer's *Odyssey*.

Roman society and thought (AS)
Through the study of literature, you will gain an appreciation of Roman history and society.

Greek tragedy in its context (AS)
You will be introduced to texts by Aeschylus, Sophocles and Euripides, learning about their importance from a literary and social perspective.

Greek historians (AS)
Through the study of historical texts by Thucydides, Herodotus and Plutarch, you will start to explore society, history and the politics of the era.

City life in Roman Italy (AS)
Examine the social, cultural and political context of Pompeii, Herculaneum and Ostia.

Roman Britain: life in the outpost of the Empire (A2)
The study of literary and archaeological records will develop your understanding of Romano-British society.

Art and architecture in the Greek world (A2)
You will learn about classical Greece through the study of sculpture and architecture of the time.

Comic drama in the ancient world (A2)
Study the works of Aristophanes, Menander and Plautus, and investigate their historical, cultural and literary relevance.

Virgil and the world of the hero (A2)
You will study the epic through Virgil's *The Aeneid* and the partial study of Homer's *Iliad*.

Top Tip

Interested in ancient languages? OCR offers an A level in Biblical Hebrew.

Higher and Advanced Higher in Classical Studies

You will learn about the politics, history, religion, morality and philosophy of Greece and Rome, with a focus on the social aspects of the classical world.

Assessment is based on a written exam and a 4,000-word dissertation.

Cambridge Pre-U in Classical Heritage

You can choose from a range of topics linked to 'foundations of history and culture (in Greece and Rome)', 'classical literature' and 'the classical heritage'. You will be assessed with written exams at the end of two years, along with a personal investigation to be written up under exam conditions.

Choosing other subjects to go with classical civilisation

This A level overlaps with many disciplines and would work well with arts and humanities, such as English literature, ancient history, philosophy, archaeology, history and many others. It can also be combined with a range of other subjects, including the sciences.

Top Tip

You may encounter the word 'classics' used in two different contexts with two slightly different meanings. It is sometimes used to describe the range of subjects which include classical civilisation, ancient history, Latin and classical Greek. But when it comes to choosing a degree course, classics is more likely to refer to the study of classical civilisation which incorporates Latin and Greek.

Classical civilisation at university

When you are searching for relevant courses at university, search under 'classical civilisation' but also 'classical studies' and 'classics'. The focus of most degree courses will be on ancient Roman and Greek history and civilisation. However, this will be a lot more wide-ranging and in much more depth than your advanced level study. There may also be a requirement for students to become familiar with written Greek and Latin so that they can analyse historical documents in the original language.

A level Classical Civilisation is not normally a requirement for these university courses, but it can give you a useful insight into the subject before you take it on at a higher level. Good grades in traditional arts or humanities subjects would also stand you in good stead. If you will be studying literature in the original language, then A level Latin or Classical Greek is sometimes required.

> # Top Tip
>
> Classical civilisation is widely accepted by the UK's leading universities.

Classics cuts across quite a few disciplines so it's quite common to see it combined with other subjects. Some joint programmes offered by universities include:

- classics and applied computing
- classical studies and French
- classical studies and philosophy
- war studies and classical studies
- classical studies with film studies.

There are many other possible combinations.

Other related degree courses include archaeology, classical languages, modern languages, European studies and comparative literary studies.

Classics and your future career

You will come across classicists in a broad range of careers, from politics, the Civil Service and banking to journalism, law and accountancy.

Non-graduate jobs in classics

This A level will give you lots of marketable, transferable skills for a variety of jobs. Even though you may not be using the knowledge you've learned, you will be able to use your ability to research, form judgements, analyse evidence and think logically.

Graduate jobs directly related to classics

There are very few jobs which are directly related to a classics degree and where a classical subject is essential.

- **Secondary school teacher.** There are a few Postgraduate Certificate in Education (PGCE) courses for graduates wanting to teach classics in state secondary schools. Opportunities also exist in primary schools, independent schools, sixth-form colleges and further or higher education.

Other graduate jobs where a degree in classics could be useful

There are many jobs where the transferable skills learned from a classics background are particularly useful, including the following ones listed below.

- **Administration.** Roles involve planning and organising services, providing information and collecting data to form the basis for future actions within the organisation, and informing the world outside the organisation. You could work in public service, industry, education, the health service, charities, voluntary or international organisations.
- **Archivist:** reserves, stores and safeguards records for permanent retention. This role also involves making records accessible for administrative or historical research purposes. Latin is necessary for work with older archives.
- **Civil Service fast streamer.** This role involves policy making or general management roles (staffing, finance, immigration, consular work) within embassies or high commissions abroad and in the Foreign and Commonwealth Office in London.
- **Editor.** This role involves copy-editing classical typescripts, and checking that the text reads fluently and aptly and is translated correctly. The editor also ensures internal consistency and that the text is free from errors of language, spelling or punctuation.
- **Museum/art gallery curator.** This role involves the collection, documentation, preservation, display and interpretation of materials for public benefit.
- **Solicitor:** prepares deeds and contracts of all types, manages legal cases, instructs counsel (barristers) in the higher courts and acts as an advocate for others in the lower courts. You could work in private practice as a generalist or specialist, in industry, public service, law centres, magistrates' courts or the armed services.
- **Technical author.** This role involves preparing technical information for publication in a way that is intelligible to a wide range of users. You need to produce clear, logical, unambiguous and accurate text. You must be able to communicate effectively with very different people, from engineers to schoolchildren.

Find out more about classical civilisation

- AQA: www.aqa.org.uk
- Cambridge Pre-U: www.cie.org.uk/qualifications
- Council for British Archaeology: www.britarch.ac.uk
- Creative and Cultural Skills: www.ccskills.org.uk
- Current Archaeology: www.archaeology.co.uk
- Institute of Conservation: www.icon.org.uk
- International Baccalaureate Diploma: www.ibo.org/diploma/curriculum/group3/
- OCR: www.ocr.org.uk
- SQA: www.sqa.org.uk
- *Times Literary Supplement* (classics): www.the-tls.co.uk/tls/reviews/classics_and_modern_languages/

COMMUNICATION AND CULTURE

What is culture and communication? How do we communicate effectively? How is culture communicated through the media? What is the difference between high culture and popular culture? How does culture relate to capitalism, globalisation and consumerism? These are some of the questions tackled by students of communication.

The formal study of this subject explores the theory and practice of communication and culture, and how they interconnect. The course involves the study of theories, practices and policies. You will investigate how culture and communication make us who we are and how they impact on our society.

Is it right for me?

If you like to analyse, criticise, debate and evaluate, then you might enjoy this subject. Communication and culture allows you to discover information for yourself and develop your own ideas, rather than memorising facts. You will get the chance to develop your own communication skills, consider how we interact, exchange information and persuade others.

Subject options

This subject is offered at GCE AS/A level by the AQA exam board.

A/AS level in Communication and Culture

Assessment is carried out by a combination of coursework, case studies, presentations and closed examinations. Half the marks at both levels are based on written exams and the other half on the coursework portfolio.

Understanding communication and culture (AS)
The nature of culture; definitions of culture; the meanings and practices of everyday life; high culture and popular culture; the relationship between culture and value; verbal and non-verbal communication; identity and self-presentation; group communication; reading images and products.

The individual and contemporary culture: portfolio (AS)
This is a piece of individual work based on one of the following topics: communication, culture and the individual, or cultural contexts and practices.

Communicating culture (A2)
A study of a cultural site; dominant and alternative approaches to the understanding of communication and culture; the relationship of capitalism, globalisation and consumerism to cultural products and practices; key concepts and cultural issues.

Further aspects of communication and culture (A2)
A major piece of independent work; personal and social identities; social and cultural rituals.

Choosing other subjects to go with communication and culture

Communication studies could work well with subjects such as English literature, drama, media studies, history, psychology, philosophy, sociology and politics.

Top Tip

If you are applying to one of the top universities, you will need to take care when choosing your additional A level subjects. In many cases, communication and culture is accepted only as a third or fourth choice, alongside two subjects from a university's accepted subject list. Please note that many of the newer universities do not have preferred subjects and are more interested in the grades you achieve and the quality of your application and reference.

Communication and culture at university

There are degree courses in communication, culture and the media, but there are others solely in communication studies or cultural studies. Look closely at the course detail – considering what you will study, and how you will be taught and assessed – and then choose the one you think you will find most interesting.

A degree in communication and culture focuses on the communicative and cultural activities that shape the world in which we live: everyday life, human interaction, global relations and technological developments. Courses focus on three main strands: communication in contemporary culture; communication in human interactions; and global contexts and communication media.

Complementary subjects include English, media studies, philosophy, history, sociology, linguistics and politics.

Communication and culture and your future career

Non-graduate jobs in communication and culture

An A level in Communication and Culture will give you an awareness of popular culture, skills in communicating effectively, and the ability to analyse issues and evaluate critically. These skills may enable you to get a junior position in advertising, marketing, public relations, the media and other areas of business.

Graduate jobs directly related to communication and culture

Many students on these courses are interested in gaining employment in all aspects of the media industry. Careers in the media, however, are highly sought after and competition is likely to be fierce.

- **Broadcast assistant (radio):** assists with production and presentation of programmes for local and national radio stations.
- **Broadcasting presenter:** fronts the programme; specific responsibilities vary depending on the programme.
- **Journalist:** reports on news and other areas of interest for newspapers, periodicals, radio and TV.
- **Multimedia programmer:** researches, develops and produces materials for new media-based company activities.
- **Programme researcher (broadcasting/film/video):** acts as an assistant producer with responsibility for conception and implementation of a programme.
- **Radio producer:** responsible for initiating ideas, selling these to commissioning editors and managing the technical and creative team to produce the final programme.
- **Television/film/video producer:** undertakes the artistic interpretation of materials and directs the production of shows or films.
- **Television production assistant:** provides organisational and administrative support for the programme director.

Other graduate jobs where a degree in communication and culture could be useful

- **Advertising account executive:** takes overall responsibility for co-ordination, planning and organisation of advertising campaigns.
- **Editorial assistant:** assists editorial staff in the commissioning, planning and production of books, journals and magazines.
- **Event organiser:** identifies potential business and researches, writes, plans and runs all types of conferences on behalf of a client or his/her own organisation.
- **Information officer/manager:** ensures effective communication of information relating to a particular field of interest.
- **Market research executive:** undertakes systematic research to determine the potential market for a product or service.
- **Public relations account executive.** PR agencies work for their clients in presenting their image to the public. They decide on strategies to be used and which media would be the most effective.

Find out more about communication and culture

- AQA: www.aqa.org.uk
- Creative Skillset: www.creativeskillset.org

COMPUTING

We have come to depend on computers to manage our work, home and social lives. Computing students gain a deep understanding of how computer systems work, from microprocessors to memory, information systems and networks.

How do you design and implement a computer system? What's the most appropriate IT application for a particular situation? What is a protocol? These are just some of the questions that students are asked to tackle at this level.

Is it right for me?

You need to have a mathematical mind and a logical approach. Can you work alone, pay attention to detail and keep focused? It's not all about individual work; you will also need to be able to work with others on group activities. You will be honing your skills in problem solving and analysis, and dealing with abstract concepts. Don't expect to spend the entire course using computers; a substantial part of it is classroom-based and theoretical.

Top Tip

There is no Cambridge Pre-U option in computing or ICT, but you may be able to take the A level alongside other Pre-U subjects. If not, and if you intend to study computer science at university, you'll probably need to choose maths as one of your options.

Subject options

This subject is available at AS and A level, and Scottish Higher and Advanced Higher. Computer science is offered as an elective subject in the International Baccalaureate Diploma.

Information and communication technology (ICT) is an alternative option, available at A level, Applied A level and Advanced Higher (Information Systems). Computing is more theoretical, focusing very much on computers and how they work, while ICT considers the broader context of how we use information technology, of which computers are a big part.

A/AS level in Computing

Case studies make up much of the teaching methods of this course; students work with them to generate IT-based solutions to various scenarios. Students usually have to do a substantial project, perhaps on systems design or software development. The rest of the assessment is usually by written exams.

The outline below gives a flavour of what the syllabus might include. Students taking the AS award only will have to study about 50% of the modules which are needed for the full A level award. For an exact definition of the AS and A2 syllabus you will be following, you should consult your school or college, or the exam board website (see page 102).

Computer systems
In this module students learn about the many different applications of computer systems; the social, legal and economic implications of IT; the different types of data files and data security; software and hardware; networking and maintenance.

Design and organisation of information systems
Students learn what constitutes an information system, and whether an information system is suitable for computerisation, and about organising data, designing and implementing software.

Computer systems design
Understanding databases; organising files; understanding hardware and software; networks and communications.

Systems development
Different ways of implementing an information system; project management; managing information; data structures; programming.

Top Tip

Although it isn't essential to have your own computer, it will help when it comes to independent work at home.

Higher and Advanced Higher in Computing

The mandatory units focus on computer systems, software development and software solutions. A further optional unit can be selected from 'artificial intelligence, computer networking, multimedia technology' (Higher only) and 'computer architecture' (Advanced Higher only). Assessment is based on a combination of coursework projects and exams.

International Baccalaureate Diploma in Computer Science

Computer science is available at Standard and Higher level. There are four course options on offer: databases, modelling and simulation, web science and object-oriented programming. At Higher level, students will be allowed to investigate current issues in depth. Practical programming skills are an essential part of the course, with the programming language determined by the staff at your chosen school or college.

Top Tip

Computer science became an International Baccalaureate Diploma Group 4 option (Experimental Sciences) in August 2012.

Choosing other subjects to go with computing

Subjects that combine neatly with computing include maths, physics (and other sciences), philosophy, electronics, business, law, accounting, and many others.

Top Tip

You may not need advanced level computing to study a computer science degree at a top UK university; however, you will need maths. Even if A level is not a requirement, a B or above in GCSE Maths may be needed by the leading universities.

Computing at university

There are a lot of IT-related courses available at HE level. Some are very theoretical, whereas others are very practical or applied in their emphasis. Computer science tends to be more academic and theoretical, but computer studies tends to be more practical. You should always check the specific nature of a course before applying, in order to determine what will suit you best.

Top Tip

Advanced level computing is accepted by some of the best universities in the country – but not all. Check lists of preferred or accepted A levels closely at the universities where you hope to study.

Trinity College, Cambridge, includes computing on its list of A levels that are suitable only as a fourth subject.

The University of Sheffield includes computing on its acceptable list of A levels, whereas ICT is acceptable only as a third or fourth choice subject.

Most computing courses, even if they are theoretical, will consider how IT is applied to business, industry and research. There are usually core components in the first year, with some flexibility in the final two years depending on your interests. Topics might include:

- bioinformatics
- communications and networks
- computational finance
- information security
- logic programming
- object-oriented modelling
- object-oriented software engineering
- web and internet technologies.

Assessment tends to be via a combination of final exams, coursework and project work.

The different combinations possible with the subject are numerous, but some joint programmes include:

- computer science with artificial intelligence
- computer science with French
- computer science with management
- computer science and maths
- computer science and physics.

Computing and your future career

Non-graduate jobs in computing

Given that nearly every organisation needs computers now, you will be an asset if you have an advanced understanding of them. In that sense, there is a range of junior positions for which you could apply. You may even be able to get work in IT support in some organisations without any further qualifications.

Graduate jobs directly related to computing

The vast majority of computing opportunities are at graduate level.

- **Applications developer:** writes and modifies programs to enable a computer to carry out specific tasks, such as stock control or payroll, typically for technical, commercial and business users.
- **Database administrator:** responsible for the usage, accuracy, efficiency, security, maintenance and development of an organisation's computerised databases.
- **Information technology consultant:** gives independent and objective advice on how best to use information technology to solve business problems. The work includes analysing problems, making recommendations and implementing new systems.
- **Software engineer:** specifies, develops, documents and maintains computer software programs in order to meet clients' or employers' need. He/she usually works as part of a team.
- **Systems designer:** takes the specification for the requirements of a computer system and designs the system, including hardware, software, communications, installation, testing and maintenance.
- **Systems developer:** sets up the computer operating systems and standard software services essential to the operation of any computer.

Other graduate jobs where a degree in computing could be useful

The following jobs will make some use of your IT background.

- **IT sales professional:** sells computer hardware, software and peripherals; he/she normally works in conjunction with sales representatives for a computer manufacturer.
- **Magazine journalist (computing):** researches and writes news and feature articles which are suited to the magazine's reader profile.
- **Recruitment consultant:** brings together jobseekers with vacancies on behalf of an employer (particularly for the IT sector).
- **Secondary school teacher:** teaches one or more specialist subjects to classes of secondary pupils aged 11–18. This role requires further training (for example, a PGCE). IT is currently a shortage subject.

Find out more about computing

- AQA: www.aqa.org.uk
- BCS – The Chartered Institute for IT: www.bcs.org
- e-Skills UK: www.e-skills.com
- International Baccalaureate Diploma: www.ibo.org/diploma/curriculum/group5/
- OCR: www.ocr.org.uk
- SQA: www.sqa.org.uk
- WJEC: www.wjec.co.uk

CRITICAL THINKING

Critical thinking is a bit different from most subjects, as it is not the study of a single discipline. On this course, you will learn to think about issues in a variety of different ways and to develop critical reasoning skills. Among other things, you will learn how to construct an argument (and how to see the flaws in other people's reasoning), test hypotheses and consider different ways of making decisions.

Unlike most other advanced level courses, critical thinking is based on the enhancement of skills rather than knowledge; the skills you will develop on this course will prepare you for HE, employment and the general demands of daily living.

This is a challenging course, which should complement and enhance your other studies in the arts, sciences or humanities. Although it will not be considered as part of your university offer, the skills you develop will be in great demand.

Is it right for me?

Are you interested in problem solving? Do you want to expand your skills in clear and logical thinking? Do you want to improve the ways in which you communicate? The ability to think critically is a key part of higher education and working life today. Many advanced level subjects require logical reasoning and the consideration of abstract concepts, but most students will not have had the chance to develop these skills to any great extent at GCSE or Standard Grade.

Subject options

This subject is available as GCE A/AS level.

A/AS level in Critical Thinking

The outline below is based on the AQA specification. Teaching is mainly classroom-based but there may be some case study work, which also forms part of the exam. Assessment is by written papers. The OCR exam board also offers this qualification.

Foundation unit (AS)

How to recognise reasoned argument and its contexts; interpreting and evaluating reasoning; identifying evidence, ambiguity and persuasive language within reasoning; recognising bad reasoning and countering it with cogent responses; the basic vocabulary of reasoning.

Information, inference and explanation (AS)

Presenting evidence and information; numerical and statistical reasoning; patterns and correlations; plausible explanations; making inferences from evidence; using data and information to construct arguments.

Beliefs, claims and arguments (A2)

Knowledge, belief and their relevance to critical thinking; evidence, beliefs and claims to knowledge; testing hypotheses; patterns of reasoning, logic, ethics, principles and rhetoric.

Reasoning and decision making (A2)

Reasoned decision making; using information to assess and identify consequences; value-based decision making; assessing, judging and evaluating arguments.

Top Tip

Many schools and colleges now offer the level 3 Extended Project (EP). The EP provides a context for developing the critical thinking and project management skills essential to success at university and at work. The EP assesses your ability to plan, research, complete and evaluate the success of a report.

International Baccalaureate Diploma: Theory of Knowledge

The International Baccalaureate Diploma has Theory of Knowledge (ToK) at its core: another opportunity to consider critical thinking, but this time the focus is on knowledge itself. It is a means to help you discover and express your views, to share ideas and to learn from others. The International Baccalaureate Diploma is an interdisciplinary programme; ToK can help you to make the links between the knowledge gained from the different elements of the programme: subject knowledge, experience or extended essay research.

Cambridge Pre-U: Global Perspectives and Research

The Global Perspectives and Research (GPR) element of the Cambridge Pre-U also helps you to develop the skills to recognise, analyse and evaluate different arguments. The course covers five themed elements: ethics, economics, environment, technology, and politics and culture.

Choosing other subjects to go with critical thinking

Critical thinking complements almost any subject at this level but works particularly well with philosophy, religious studies or government and politics; it can provide a nice counterbalance to the sciences. It should be taken in addition to your other A level choices – perhaps as a fourth A level – as it is unlikely to be included in your university offer.

Critical thinking at university

Given that critical thinking is an important skill needed for most HE courses, there are no specific degree programmes in the subject; however, if you are keen on critical thinking, you might be particularly attracted to subjects such as philosophy and law.

Critical thinking and your future career

Employers appreciate people who have a broad base of knowledge and who can think for themselves; critical thinking aims to equip students with both of these things.

Find out more about critical thinking

- AQA: www.aqa.org.uk
- AQA Extended Project: www.aqa.org.uk/qualifications/projects/extended-project-epq.php
- Cambridge Pre-U: www.cie.org.uk/qualifications
- International Baccalaureate Diploma: www.ibo.org/diploma/curriculum/core/
- OCR: www.ocr.org.uk

DESIGN AND TECHNOLOGY

Design and technology students learn all about the ways in which products in society are designed, created and implemented. At one end of the spectrum this may focus on the creative and artistic design process, while at the other it may be all about design and technology in an industrial context.

You will also gain a critical understanding of the influences of design and technology processes from a historical perspective and in current practice, studying effective and inspiring design and designers. The use of information technology is also emphasised as a way of enhancing design and technology processes. As a student of design and technology, you will be encouraged to use your own creativity and innovative skills to produce your own high-quality products.

Is it right for me?

There are some key differences between the various design and technology subjects at advanced level but, essentially, students are creative with the potential for great ideas. Depending on the option you choose, some ability to draw, design or create will be useful. It is important that you like making things and solving problems for practical (and sometimes aesthetic) reasons.

If you are interested in brilliant design, you'll need to understand the relationship between design, materials, manufacture and marketing. You will get the chance to develop your creativity and practical and enterprise skills. Strength in subjects such as maths and physics, art, ICT, and design and technology at GCSE level is relevant.

Top Tip

To do well in this subject you will need a practical mind, good business sense and creative flair.

Subject options

This subject is available at GCE A/AS level, with options in food technology, systems and control technology, and product design (resistant materials technology, graphic products, 3D design or textiles). It also appears as a subject on the International Baccalaureate Diploma programme and as a Scottish Higher and Advanced Higher, albeit with a different title (see page 108).

A/AS level in Design and Technology

You would specialise in one of the following options.

- **Food technology.** Working with a variety of ingredients and equipment, you will develop original products through testing, preparation and evaluation.
- **Systems and control technology.** You will design and make products using electronics, basic programming, mechanics, materials science, and so on; along the way, you will develop your technological know-how and understanding of engineering.
- **Resistant materials.** Using materials such as wood, metals or plastics you will design and make products with a range of machinery and equipment.
- **Graphic products.** Learn how to convey a message using visual media on paper, using computers or in 3D – from promotional materials and packaging to online or print media.
- **3D design.** You will learn to make structures and products – and even design buildings (initially, by drawing and later by 3D modelling on a computer). Develop a design from an idea on paper to a 3D product, using computers and technology.
- **Textiles technology.** By studying the creative use of techniques and materials, you will develop your own products. You might study traditional and contemporary processes.

The outline below provides an idea of some of the topics you might study, whichever option you choose. The subject is taught by a mixture of teacher-led activities and hands-on practical work. Students have to work to design briefs and produce portfolios and projects throughout the two years. Around half of your marks will be based on practical coursework, with the rest coming from written exams. For the latest and most accurate information, speak to your sixth form or college, or check out the exam board website (see page 110).

Materials, components and application (AS)
An understanding of components or ingredients; preparing and testing materials; the use of technology in the manufacturing process.

Learning through designing and making (AS)
Students have to complete independent project work in relation to developing a product.

Design and manufacture (A2)
Learning how to create design specifications; understanding the different characteristics of a range of materials; large-scale manufacturing processes; design processes; quality control; estimating the potential appeal of a product; health and safety issues.

Design and making practice (A2)

This is a synoptic unit where students have to make connections from all they have learned so far. The particular emphasis is on the step-by-step process of creating a workable and marketable design and product.

Higher and Advanced Higher in Design Technology

The Scottish Qualifications Authority offers separate subject options in 'home economics: health and food technology', 'product design' and 'technological studies'. Assessment is based on written exams and a design project.

International Baccalaureate Diploma in Design Technology

At both Standard and Higher level on the International Baccalaureate Diploma, you will select an option in which to specialise:

- CAD/CAM
- electronic product design
- food science and technology
- human factors design
- textiles.

You will learn how to gather information, process it and plan to solve the design problem. Relevant considerations when developing a design include social, technological, economic, environmental, political, legislative and ethical aspects.

The final grade is made up of projects and investigations for 36%, with the remainder derived from written exams.

Choosing other subjects to go with design and technology

Design and technology works in combination with many other subjects. Those with an artistic aptitude could choose A levels in the creative field and those who are more interested in the technical side could consider subjects such as maths, physics, computing or electronics. Business studies or economics might also be relevant.

Top Tip

For some of the top universities, including University College London and University of Sheffield, design and technology has limited suitability and might only be considered alongside two accepted subjects, such as maths and physics.

Design and technology at university

Degree courses in the design and technology field have different emphases but most have strong links with industry; some offer a sandwich placement as part of the course, which is a great way to gain experience alongside your qualification. Art- or technology-related subjects are usually preferred but not always essential.

Degrees related to design and technology may include some of the following modules:

- computer-aided modelling
- computing for designers
- design for sustainable development
- design practice
- electronic systems
- internet and interface for designers
- management and marketing
- materials science and processing
- universal design.

The skills and knowledge gained from design and technology relate to a whole range of HE courses, such as architecture, product design, engineering and IT.

Design and technology and your future career

Non-graduate jobs in design and technology

It may be possible to get junior positions (technician level) in construction, manufacturing, computer-aided design or engineering.

Graduate jobs directly related to design and technology

- **Exhibition/display designer:** organises the design of exhibition and display stands; he/she liaises with clients to produce designs that communicate their desired messages.
- **Fashion clothing designer:** produces designs for clothing and accessories; he/she may specialise in an area such as sportswear.
- **Production engineer.** The role involves planning, managing and maintaining production methods and processes to make the most efficient use of resources.
- **Production manager.** The role involves organising and scheduling production, selecting and controlling process variables, setting and meeting targets and people management.
- **Quality assurance officer.** The role involves establishing and operating systems that ensure quality standards in products, packing, delivery or labelling. It also requires troubleshooting and technical investigations.

- **Technical sales engineer.** The role involves technical advisory work, sales and after-sales service.
- **Textile designer:** creates designs in knit, weave or print to be used in the production of fabric or textile products.

Other graduate jobs where a degree in design and technology could be useful

- **Advertising art director:** creates visual ideas to be used within advertising. He/she works as part of a team alongside illustrators, photographers and those responsible for editorial. The role can involve any media.
- **Information scientist.** The role involves finding, storing, evaluating and disseminating scientific, technical and commercial information.
- **Information technology and management services (industrial engineering, work study, IT, systems, etc.).** Roles involve investigating business, commercial and industrial problems and data-processing requirements.

Find out more about design and technology

- AQA: www.aqa.org.uk
- Creative and Cultural Skills: www.ccskills.org.uk
- Creative Skillset: www.creativeskillset.org
- Design Council: www.designcouncil.org.uk
- Edexcel: www.edexcel.com
- Improve – Food and Drink Skills Council: www.improveltd.co.uk
- International Baccalaureate Diploma: www.ibo.org/diploma/curriculum/group4/
- OCR: www.ocr.org.uk
- Proskills UK – Sector Skills Council for the Process and Manufacturing Sector: www.proskills.co.uk
- SEMTA – Sector Skills Council for Science, Engineering and Manufacturing Technologies: www.semta.org.uk
- SQA: www.sqa.org.uk
- WJEC: www.wjec.co.uk

DRAMA AND THEATRE STUDIES

As a student of advanced level drama and theatre studies, you will learn to understand, analyse and then create imaginative theatre. You will have the opportunity to develop your skills of performance and theatre design. You will gain an understanding of the techniques playwrights use to bring their plays to life. The skills gained while studying this course will give you a good start for a career in the theatre, but it is also a good all-round subject for those who simply want to deepen their interest and enjoyment of the area.

Is it right for me?

This subject is an academic discipline taught through practical methods. You will need to be an active participant with a love of theatre, but it is not just about acting or performance. The course requires you to study, reflect and evaluate before performing (or theatre designing). You will need to be creative, share ideas, work with others and accept direction.

Initial written theoretical study of the theatre is later applied to a practical assessment of a performance. At A2 level, this extends to the preparation of an original piece of theatre. You will develop academic, physical and artistic skills.

Subject options

A range of qualifications are available, although each takes a slightly different approach to the content, the teaching or the assessment of the subject.

The GCE A/AS level is offered by Edexcel, AQA and WJEC. OCR runs an alternative course in Performance Studies, as well as an Applied A/AS level in Performing Arts (see page 215). Drama and Theatre is on offer as a Cambridge Pre-U subject, or you can choose SQA Higher or Advanced Higher Drama. Theatre can be studied as part of the International Baccalaureate Diploma programme.

A/AS level in Drama and Theatre Studies

There is some classroom learning as part of the course, but you will also be spending a lot of time doing practical performance work, possibly in a drama studio. A good grade at GCSE English Literature would help you with this course, but it's not always a prerequisite. Assessment is by a combination of written exams, coursework and assessed performances.

The following outline is based largely on the Edexcel A/AS level syllabus. Your chosen sixth form will be able to give you details of the syllabus you will follow.

Exploration of drama and theatre (AS)
You will learn how to analyse plays and understand the ways in which they are interpreted for performance through language, structure or dramatic elements.

Theatre text in performance (AS)
You will demonstrate your skills as an actor or theatre designer in a performance environment.

Exploration of dramatic performance (A2)
You will work with others to create an original piece of theatre, building on the theory and practical skills learned at AS level.

Theatre text in context (A2)
You will make a detailed study of both a play and a period of historical theatrical importance.

Higher and Advanced Higher in Drama

The Higher qualification gives you the opportunity to cover investigative theatre, to study text in a theatrical context and to learn about contemporary Scottish theatre. You will investigate a topic before adapting your findings into a dramatic performance. In addition to classroom-based study, you will learn and develop practical skills through workshops, from the perspective of both actor and director. Your skills and learning will be stretched further at Advanced Higher level, expanding to include world theatre and its practitioners. Assessment at both levels is based on exams and practical exams.

International Baccalaureate Diploma in Theatre

At both Standard and Higher level, the course includes 'theatre in the making', 'theatre in performance' and 'theatre in the world'. You will have to complete an independent project. The practical requirements of the course can be fulfilled as a performer or as part of the production team.

Cambridge Pre-U in Drama and Theatre

The course has four components: world drama and theatre, repertoire, devised drama and a performance investigation. Assessment takes place at the end of the second year and involves exams, live performance, the production of original drama and an independent investigation resulting in a 3,500-word essay.

Choosing other subjects to go with drama and theatre studies

Good companions for this subject include English literature, media studies, art and design, music, languages or history.

Check the university admissions criteria where you intend to apply. As a general rule, drama and theatre studies tends not to be accepted by the most competitive universities, unless in combination with two other preferred subjects.

For example, the London School of Economics views drama and theatre studies as follows:

'The Departments of Anthropology, International History, International Relations, Social Policy and Sociology consider drama and theatre studies equally with other generally preferred subjects. They will therefore consider drama and theatre studies alongside one other subject from the non-preferred list.

'However, the majority of departments continue to feel that drama and theatre studies is not appropriate or relevant in content to their degree programmes and still consider it to be "non-preferred".'

For full details and the latest information, see www.lse.ac.uk.

Top Tip

Drama and theatre studies is widely accepted as an entry requirement for drama courses at university, but you should choose your other subjects carefully if you're planning to apply to a top institution. English literature at advanced level may be accepted as an alternative.

Drama and theatre studies at university

There are many different types of courses related to theatre studies out there. Some specialise in particular aspects of drama and theatre, such as performance, directing, stage design, lighting, and so on, while others go for a broad overview of drama and the theatre. You have to ask yourself, which one will suit me best? Some courses include a year studying abroad at another university.

Modules from a typical degree programme in this area might include:

- critical theories
- elements of performance
- explorations in space
- practical skills
- staging histories
- writing and performance.

This subject may be offered in combination with English literature, a modern language, history, and many more.

Drama and theatre studies and your future career

Non-graduate jobs in drama and theatre studies

If you want a career in performance or in the technical side of the theatre, you will probably have to go and do further study. However, it's possible to get your foot in the door straight after A levels by working in an administrative role within a theatre box office, for instance.

Graduate jobs directly related to drama and theatre studies

The availability of some of the following jobs may depend on the type of degree and relevant work experience you have obtained. Some jobs will require relevant postgraduate study and, if you want to become a performer, you may need further professional training.

- **Actor.** Using speech, body language and movement, an actor communicates a character and situations to an audience.
- **Drama therapist.** The role involves using drama to treat or educate people with health or emotional difficulties through therapeutic techniques.
- **Secondary school teacher.** The role involves teaching drama, music or other curriculum subjects in schools and colleges.
- **Theatre director:** co-ordinates all the artistic aspects of a dramatic presentation from inception, through production stages and rehearsals, to the final performance.
- **Theatre stage manager:** organises and co-ordinates rehearsals and performances, and liaises between the director and the technical staff.
- **Wardrobe manager:** supervises the making, buying, hiring and maintenance of costumes, accessories and wigs, and controls the budget for all these items.

Other graduate jobs where a degree in drama and theatre studies could be useful

- **Arts administrator:** facilitates the planning and promotion of visual and performing arts activities, sometimes specialising in areas such as finance and marketing.
- **Community arts worker.** This role focuses on the promotion of the arts in the community, often through working with young people in schools and youth centres.
- **Journalist.** There are many specialist publications covering the arts but entry is very competitive. Graduates could start in mainstream broadcast or print journalism and specialise or go freelance later.
- **Programme researcher:** supports the TV/film/radio producer by helping to organise and to plan the programme.

- **Television production assistant:** organises and co-ordinates programme activities, booking performers and facilities, and providing administrative support.

Find out more about drama and theatre studies

- AQA: www.aqa.org.uk
- Cambridge Pre-U: www.cie.org.uk/qualifications
- Creative and Cultural Skills: www.ccskills.org.uk
- Edexcel: www.edexcel.com
- Equity (UK trade union for professional performers and creative practitioners): www.equity.org.uk
- International Baccalaureate Diploma: www.ibo.org/diploma/curriculum/group6/
- National Association of Youth Theatres: www.nayt.org.uk
- National Council for Drama Training: www.ncdt.co.uk
- OCR: www.ocr.org.uk
- SQA: www.sqa.org.uk
- WJEC: www.wjec.co.uk

ECONOMICS

Economics is big news these days and studying this subject will help to provide some context to the financial news that affects everyday life. As a student of economics, you will learn how the markets work and the factors that make them crash or fail. You will also consider how economies develop, how countries manage their economies and the place of the UK in the global market.

Economics is a social science which uses scientific methods, covering both the quantitative and qualitative. The subject considers how we deal with the finite resources we have, how they are allocated and the methods we use to make these choices, whether from the perspective of an individual consumer or an entire country.

On a more specific level, students may consider how economic forces affect things such as house prices, petrol prices and the price of a range of consumable goods. You will become familiar with concepts such as inflation, balance of payments and the pros and cons of the single European currency.

Is it right for me?

Economics is an important subject if you want to know how the world works. You don't need to be a maths whizz-kid to study A level Economics (although you will tend to need strong maths skills if you choose to take economics at university level). It is not a purely theoretical subject; you will need to be able to argue your case and compare theory to economics in the real world.

You will develop skills in communication, research, independent thinking, evaluation and working with others.

Top Tip

Microeconomics focuses on the factors affecting individuals, businesses and markets; macroeconomics concentrates on the aspects that affect societies, governments and countries.

Subject options

Economics is available at GCE A/AS level through all the major exam boards. Edexcel also offers GCE A/AS level in Economics and Business Studies. In addition, economics can be studied as part of the International Baccalaureate Diploma, Cambridge Pre-U and the Scottish Qualifications Authority's Higher and Advanced Highers.

A/AS level in Economics

Much of the subject is teacher-led in the classroom but students may also consider case studies and TV programmes, along with the analysis of newspaper reports and charts, graphs and tables. Students should have a good head for figures and possess good analytical skills; a good grade in GCSE Maths will help you in this area. Assessment is mainly by written exam, although there may be some coursework, too.

The outline below provides an idea of the topics you might encounter at A level. For an exact definition of the syllabus you will be studying, you should consult your chosen sixth form or college, or consult the exam board website (see page 121).

Your course will cover most or all of the following:

- economic development
- industrial economics
- labour markets
- managing the economy
- markets – how they work
- markets – why they fail
- the UK in the global economy.

A/AS level in Economics and Business Studies

This subject looks at the relationship between the two subjects. More specifically, it applies economics concepts to business issues. Assessment is carried out by a mixture of closed examinations and coursework.

Topics covered include:

- competition, markets, supply and price
- elasticity of demand
- how exchange rates affect businesses
- profit margins
- purchasing patterns
- what do customers want?

Top Tip

Economics helps you to develop strong analytical skills and provides a valuable basis for a wide range of degrees.

Higher and Advanced Higher in Economics

Once again, with this qualification you will learn how to apply theory and analyse economic change, and you will become familiar with the factors and decisions that affect life in Scotland, the UK and the rest of the world. At Advanced Higher, you will extend your Higher level learning by studying national and international economic issues, along with the way companies behave.

The Higher course is assessed by means of an exam, while the Advanced Higher requires a written exam and a dissertation.

International Baccalaureate Diploma in Economics

Economics is available at both Standard and Higher level, where students tackle the following topics: microeconomics, macroeconomics, international economics and development economics. You will learn through applying economic theories to real issues.

Students are assessed by coursework, a portfolio based on three issues from the news, and exams.

Cambridge Pre-U in Economics

The course teaches the theory that supports the workings of today's economy through a syllabus focused on three topics: microeconomics, the national economy and international economics. Students get the chance to learn about current issues such as China and the global economy, and the global credit crunch.

Assessment is by three final exams taken at the end of year two; one is multiple choice, the other is essay-based and the third is an investigation essay written under exam conditions.

Choosing other subjects to go with economics

Popular choices to combine with economics include mathematics, history, politics, philosophy, sociology, computing or business; however, like most subjects it can be combined with any A level discipline.

Top Tip

Economics tends to appear on the preferred subject lists of the top universities, including University College London, London School of Economics and University of Sheffield.

Economics at university

Some degree courses are very mathematical, so A level Maths will be just as useful as A level Economics if you want to do a degree in the subject. The most prestigious courses, such as the one offered by the London School of Economics (LSE), will demand the very highest A level grades to get a place. Having said that, economics is a subject offered by many institutions, so it should still be possible to get a place somewhere else, even with slightly lower grades.

There is some variation in economics degrees around the country but most of them include the following core subjects:

- economics
- elementary statistical theory
- macroeconomic principles
- mathematical methods
- microeconomic principles
- principles of econometrics.

There may also be the option to study more specialist topics:

- Africa and the world economy
- Europe and the global economy
- further mathematical methods (calculus)
- game theory
- locational change and business activity
- managerial accounting
- operational research methods
- philosophy of economics
- the politics of international economic relations.

'I really enjoyed the breadth and stretch of Cambridge Pre-U Economics. I also felt I could express myself better in exams and it definitely reinforced my decision to study economics at university.'

Sam Miller

Combining economics with other degree subjects

Very well-known combinations include philosophy, politics and economics (PPE), economics with history, maths and economics, business management with economics, and economics with law. Economics with a foreign language is also becoming more common. If you intend to work as an economist, it's probably safer to study pure economics.

Economics and your future career

Non-graduate jobs in economics

A level Economics is highly regarded by employers and should stand you in good stead if you decide to start your career without going on to further study. Banks, retail organisations, insurance companies and some areas of the City and financial services take people on with good A levels, either onto training schemes or straight into work. It is worth noting, however, that some jobs are only accessible with a degree.

Graduate jobs directly related to economics

The role of economist is probably the most obvious work area directly related to your course. Most economists are concerned with practical applications of economic policy. They use their understanding of economic relationships to advise businesses and other organisations, including insurance companies, banks, securities firms, industry and trade associations, unions and government agencies. Entry to the profession is very competitive. Successful candidates tend to have a strong academic record and, often, a higher degree as well.

Other graduate jobs where a degree in economics could be useful

- **Accountant.** This role involves providing financial information and maintaining general accounting systems, performing audits and liaising with clients or management colleagues. Opportunities exist in industry, commerce, private practice and the public sector.
- **Actuary.** This role involves assessing probabilities and risk, traditionally in the insurance and pensions sectors although increasingly in other areas. It requires strong mathematical and statistical skills.
- **Corporate, commercial and investment banker.** This role involves providing a broad range of financial services and advice to companies, institutions and governments. This includes dealing with mergers and acquisitions, arranging or underwriting equity or debt issues, and identifying and securing new deals with clients.
- **Insurance underwriter:** assesses risks and premiums to be charged, and liaises with clients and brokers. Other insurance industry roles, such as broking, claims and sales, are likely to involve more client contact.
- **Investment analyst:** undertakes research to provide ideas and information to fund managers, who use it to make decisions relating to the investment portfolios that they manage.
- **Management consultant.** This role involves advising private and public sector organisations on business issues. Management consultants are primarily concerned with initiating and implementing technological, organisational and behavioural change.

- **Market research executive:** conducts or commissions market research by planning and controlling projects, usually for independent research agencies.
- **Political party research officer:** responsible for making sure that the party for which they work is able to develop realistic new policies in response to (or in anticipation of) changing social, political and economic conditions.
- **Statistician:** concerned with the collection, analysis, interpretation and presentation of quantitative information. Statisticians design samples, collect data using a variety of methods, process data and advise on the strengths and limitations of results.
- **Trader.** This role involves undertaking transactions in stocks and shares, bonds, foreign exchange currencies, options or futures with traders at commercial banks, investment banks and large institutional investors.

Find out more about economics

- AQA: www.aqa.org.uk
- Cambridge Pre-U: www.cie.org.uk/qualifications
- CCEA: www.rewardinglearning.org.uk
- The *Economist*: www.economist.com
- Edexcel: www.edexcel.com
- Financial Skills Partnership: www.financialskillspartnership.org.uk
- Government Economic Service: www.civilservice.gov.uk/networks/ges/
- Institute of Economic Affairs: www.iea.org.uk
- International Baccalaureate Diploma: www.ibo.org/diploma/curriculum/group3/
- OCR: www.ocr.org.uk
- SQA: www.sqa.org.uk
- WJEC: www.wjec.co.uk

ENGLISH

Students of English can focus on just language or literature – or choose both. If you are considering picking English language, you should think about some of the following questions.

- What are the origins of the English language?
- How has it changed over time?
- How is it used differently according to different situations, contexts and purposes?
- What makes the journalism in one newspaper different to another?
- What are jargon, idiom and cliché?

Through a close examination of literary texts, English literature students are asked to consider questions about life. Literature encourages us to think about a range of issues and intersects with many other subjects, such as history, psychology, philosophy, religion, art and sociology. The kinds of issues English literature students could consider include those listed below.

- What is the author's view of contemporary society?
- What literary methods does the poet use to create a particular effect in the poem?
- How does Shakespeare's language differ from our own?
- What are the main recurring themes in this novel?

English language and literature allows students the opportunity to study English from both a linguistic and a literary perspective. You will have the chance to study a far more varied range of texts than if you opted for a pure literature course and the focus is less on structure, semantics and linguistics than it is on a pure language course. Some of the questions that students of this course will consider include the following.

- How do language and literature link together?
- How is language used in literary genres such as poetry, prose and drama?
- How do I critically compare two or more pieces of literature and/or language?
- How is language adapted according to different audiences?

Is it right for me?

It might be the right subject choice if you are interested in ideas, have an enquiring mind and love to read. You'll need to have strong written skills, so a good grade in English at GCSE is important.

You will use creative writing skills for advanced level English language, or language and literature combined. English literature will help you to develop your understanding of the written word, expand your vocabulary and give you the skills to express yourself eloquently. In order to interpret what you read, you will need to have good attention to detail and be aware of hidden meanings.

You will be expected to share your ideas and may have to challenge your own assumptions, through discussion and debate with others.

Subject options

English is available as an AS and A level, the SQA Higher and Advanced Higher, the International Baccalaureate Diploma and the Cambridge Pre-U.

A/AS level in English Language

The information below should give you an idea of what an English syllabus might cover. For the latest and most accurate information on what you will be studying, you should consult your school, college or the exam board website (see page 128).

Introduction to language study
You will explore a variety of texts to learn some of the characteristics of the English language, including structure, stylistics, semantics and linguistics.

Using language
This element of the course allows you to develop your own writing skills and compare what you have written to a series of texts.

Interacting through language
You will investigate how language is used in face-to-face encounters and identify the speaking and listening skills required to be an effective communicator. The course includes theorists' views of face-to-face communication and linguistic analysis.

Language variation and change
You will examine how language is used in different times and settings, and how the language has developed from early modern times to the present day. Students are also taught how contemporary English is used differently in different geographical locations.

A/AS level in English Literature

Students read a range of literary texts in different genres, but syllabuses will include the following elements.

Prose/fiction
Most syllabuses include a stipulation that students will gain a knowledge of modern and older fiction; some exam boards also make the distinction between pre- and post-war writing. Popular texts include Charlotte Brontë's *Jane Eyre*, F. Scott Fitzgerald's *The Great Gatsby*, Arthur Miller's *Death of a Salesman* and at least one play by Shakespeare (*King Lear*, *Othello* or *Measure for Measure*, for example).

Poetry

English has a rich history of poetry and therefore exam boards have a lot to choose from. Again, choices try to reflect both modern and older poets, and set texts can include some of Chaucer's *Canterbury Tales* and Shakespeare's sonnets, along with selected poems from the following writers:

- Anne Stevenson
- Emily Dickinson
- John Keats
- Seamus Heaney
- Sylvia Plath
- T. S. Eliot
- Tony Harrison
- W. B. Yeats
- William Blake.

Top Tip

English literature is one of the subjects most often required for entry to a range of university courses – not only English degrees – so it might help to keep your options open if you aren't sure of your future plans.

A/AS level in English Language and Literature

The following outline is based on the OCR specification. Teaching on the A level is a combination of close textual analysis and group discussions around particular themes. Students are expected to do lots of reading outside the classroom to support their learning. Essay writing is a key component of the course. Assessment is via a combination of coursework, closed examinations and open book examinations. The qualification is also offered by other exam boards, including AQA and WJEC.

Speaking voices (AS)

This unit requires you to study the narrative voice in prose or fiction. Students focus on the individual voices that create meaning.

Changing texts (AS)

Students write original pieces covering both literary and non-literary styles, and provide a commentary on their own writing based on the insights gained from both literary and linguistic techniques.

Dramatic voices (A2)

You will study two plays from different eras, linked by a theme. Set texts include *Dr Faustus* (Christopher Marlowe) and *Rosencrantz and Guildenstern Are Dead* (Tom Stoppard), or *The Duchess of Malfi* (John Webster) and *Top Girls* (Caryl Churchill).

Connections across texts (A2)

This module focuses on how language and literature can be used and interpreted in relation to value, status and classification.

Higher and Advanced Higher in English

At Higher level, studies include compulsory units on literature and language. The Advanced Higher has a mandatory unit in literature and a specialist study dissertation; you can select your final unit by choosing from 'language study', 'textual analysis', 'reading the media' or 'creative writing'. Final grades are based on exams and coursework.

International Baccalaureate Diploma in English

Options are available in literature, language and literature, and literature and performance. All students must choose one of these three options. You should develop skills in the appreciation of language and literature, literary criticism, written and oral expression, and cultural differences. Assessment is based on written and oral exams or coursework.

Cambridge Pre-U in Literature in English

With a focus on literature, you will study poetry, prose and drama. The syllabus encourages varied reading and the development of a critical understanding and response. Students are assessed by written exams at the end of the two-year course, with a further 25% of the marks coming from a personal investigation.

Choosing other subjects to go with English

It's common for students to combine English with other arts, humanities or social sciences, such as history, psychology, sociology, religious studies, art, archaeology, classical civilisation or a foreign language. Certainly, the kind of skills used in these subjects would reinforce and complement the ones developed in the study of English language and literature. However, this subject would also provide a good contrast for students who are studying the sciences.

Top Tip

Although English literature is widely accepted by the top universities, you may be surprised to find that English language is less valued by some.

In response to a question on UCL's website (www.ucl.ac.uk/english/prospective/ug/faqs.htm) clarifying whether A level English Language is suitable for BA (Hons) English at UCL, the answer is: 'No. Candidates taking the combined A level in English Language and Literature are sometimes accepted. However, we regard the English Literature A level, which exposes students to a wider range of literary works, as a better preparation for our very challenging course.'

On the other hand, all English options (literature, language and combined) appear on the University of Sheffield's list of acceptable A level subjects.

English at university

At degree level, there are many courses that include language and literature and many where it's possible to study literature and language as single subjects. To get a place on one of these degree courses you would need a good A level grade in at least one of the following: English language and literature, English literature or English language.

Degrees in English may have core components, such as 'Anglo-Saxon literature' or 'the English language', but students are also given the flexibility to add modules of their choice to complete the degree. Specialist options might include 'the literature of James Joyce' or 'semantics', for instance.

Some degree courses have a foreign language and literature element, so knowledge of a foreign language could be a help. It's common to see English language or literature combined with subjects such as history, philosophy, sociology or music. Since English language and literature courses are already offered as a joint option, they tend not to be combined with anything else.

Advanced level English is a useful and relevant subject for any essay-based degree course.

'English lit was a vital subject choice for getting onto my journalism course, as you really need to show that you can write and have a good knowledge of writing. I think theology helped with forming opinions and putting them into a written format. I think I learned a lot at A level about myself and the way I write.'

Charlotte Randall

English and your future career

Non-graduate jobs related to English

Many employers requiring A levels or equivalent do not really mind which subjects applicants have. In that sense, English is as good a choice as any, as it gives students all-round critical thinking, empathy and analytical skills. Furthermore, there may be some non-graduate areas of work where English is still more useful than some other subjects because you will have developed strong skills in both written and oral communication. Jobs where these skills are especially useful include:

- marketing or sales assistants
- jobs requiring a lot of communication or telephone work
- trainee news reporter
- library assistant
- tour guide.

Graduate jobs directly related to English

If you wish to use your degree directly there are several employment areas where a degree in English is particularly relevant. Some of the most popular jobs are listed below. Further training is needed in some cases.

- **English as a foreign language teacher/English as a second language teacher.** This role involves teaching English to foreign students in either the UK or overseas.
- **HE lecturer in English language and literature.** This role involves teaching university students about language and literature. After your degree, you would generally need an MA and a PhD to get a lectureship.
- **Primary school teacher and secondary school teacher.** Opportunities exist in secondary and primary schools as well as in independent schools, sixth-form colleges and in further or higher education.

Other graduate jobs where a degree in English could be useful

There are careers which traditionally attract English graduates more than others and which can make use of many of the skills that are acquired through studying the subject.

- **Advertising account executive:** co-ordinates, plans and organises advertising campaigns in consultation with clients.
- **Advertising copywriter:** writes original advertising copy to promote and sell products or services in the press, on television and radio, or online.
- **Charity officer.** This role involves a wide range of responsibilities, including aspects of marketing, finance, fundraising and public relations. It may also include organising events, managing volunteers and meeting targets.
- **Commissioning editor:** monitors the progress of print and digital publications from conception through to publication, liaising with all those involved in the production process. He/she develops ideas for new publications and responds to market forces.
- **Marketing executive:** formulates a marketing plan for a product or service and brings it to fruition.

- **Newspaper journalist:** reports on news and other items of current interest for newspapers.
- **Programme researcher (broadcasting/film/video):** generates programme ideas, researches background material, and briefs production teams and presenters.
- **Public relations officer:** projects and maintains a desirable image of an organisation and keeps the public informed of developments of general interest.
- **Television/film/video producer:** responsible for turning ideas into programmes within the allocated budget.

Find out more about English

- AQA: www.aqa.org.uk
- Cambridge Pre-U: www.cie.org.uk/qualifications
- CCEA: www.rewardinglearning.org.uk
- Creative and Cultural Skills: www.ccskills.org.uk
- Creative Skillset: www.creativeskillset.org
- Edexcel: www.edexcel.com
- International Baccalaureate Diploma: www.ibo.org/diploma/curriculum/group1/
- National Council for the Training of Journalists: www.nctj.com
- OCR: www.ocr.org.uk
- Society of Authors: www.societyofauthors.net
- SQA: www.sqa.org.uk
- WJEC: www.wjec.co.uk

ENVIRONMENTAL STUDIES

Environmental studies is all about how humans interact with their environment. Given the growing public and political concern about environmental issues, it is hardly a surprise that this subject is becoming increasingly popular. Students investigate the scientific concepts in relation to environmentalism but also the social, political and economic aspects of managing the environment, such as sustainability and conservation.

Is it right for me?

If you've got an interest in green issues, then you might be interested in environmental studies, but the subject is much broader than that. You will gain an extensive scientific knowledge of the issues affecting our planet; this incorporates aspects of geography, economics, geology, politics and sociology. You will develop skills in the collection, analysis and evaluation of information, as well as teamwork, communication of ideas, processing of numerical data and problem solving.

In order to do well on this course, you will need a good grasp of sciences and maths at GCSE or Standard level.

Top Tip

Environmental studies is a science subject, involving scientific investigations, practicals and fieldwork.

Subject options

Environmental studies is available at GCE A/AS level, as part of the International Baccalaureate Diploma (Environmental Systems and Societies) and as a Scottish Higher.

A/AS level in Environmental Studies

The outline below is based on the AQA specification. There is no coursework in the AS or A level. Assessment is by written exam.

The living environment (AS)

Why conservation is important; methods of effective conservation; national and international conservation efforts; ecology, organisms and the environment.

The physical environment (AS)
Atmospheric gases, water and mineral nutrients; human exploitation and the effective management of physical resources; unsustainable natural resources.

Energy resources and environmental pollution (A2)
Energy supply shortage and possible solutions; pollutants; minimising the release of toxic materials.

Biological resources and sustainability (A2)
Human population growth and its demands on the environment; food production and forestry systems; human lifestyles and sustainability.

Higher in Managing Environmental Resources

This option is available at Higher level only. Its aim is to develop your knowledge and experience of environmental studies through scientific methodology. You will study 'resources in existence', 'natural resource use', 'investigating ecosystems' and 'land use in Scotland'. Assessment is based entirely on written exams.

The SQA is currently developing a Higher qualification in environmental science.

International Baccalaureate Diploma in Environmental Systems and Societies

This subject is classed as an interdisciplinary subject and is available at Standard level only. It can be selected as an option under 'experimental sciences' or 'individuals and societies'. The course will encourage you to consider the scientific, ethical and socio-political aspects of your subject.

You can benefit from this course without prior studies in science or geography, but it helps to be aware of scientific methods and environmental issues. The course is hands-on, incorporating lab and fieldwork. The final assessment is based for 20% on practical activities, with the remainder based on written exams.

Choosing other subjects to go with environmental studies

Environmental studies obviously goes very well with geography and biology, but other subjects that are compatible include geology, chemistry, politics, economics and law.

Top Tip

Trinity College, Cambridge, will accept environmental studies only as a fourth A level; however, University College London and University of Sheffield consider it an accepted or preferred subject.

As it is not available everywhere, most degree courses won't specify that an A level in Environmental Studies is needed, but most prefer at least one science (some universities require two) or a qualification in geography.

Environmental studies at university

At HE level, courses in this area are usually called either environmental science or environmental studies. The former, not surprisingly, tends to have more of a scientific emphasis, whereas the latter looks in more detail at the social and political aspects. Many courses emphasise the importance of integrating biology, chemistry and geography, thus leading students to understand the science of human impact on the environment and therefore (when considered in the context of a social, legal and political framework) helping to develop solutions to some of the major environmental issues facing the world.

Instruction takes the form of lectures, tutorials, seminars, practicals, fieldwork and research projects, all of which vary between departments and universities. Fieldwork may include specific field project modules, as well as projects on air and water quality. Most students are required to undertake final year research projects and these, too, may include a substantial element of fieldwork.

It is quite common to see this subject combined with physics, biology, chemistry, maths, geography, development studies, politics or computer science.

Environmental studies and your future career

Non-graduate jobs in environmental studies

Most jobs working in the environmental field involve further training, but you may be able to get some experience in environmental charities, especially if you have good administrative or secretarial skills. Your A level in this subject will have developed your skills in analysis, logical thinking and problem solving, and you should always try to demonstrate these to potential employers, whatever the sector.

Graduate jobs directly related to environmental studies

There has been an increase in the range of careers where an environmental science or environmental studies degree is one of the requirements. In some cases, postgraduate qualifications may be required (or may be beneficial to enhance your skills). Some of the related jobs include the following.

- **Countryside manager:** works for a local authority to manage countryside and visitor services within that area.
- **Environmental education officer:** supports, sustains and develops environmental issues within the community. The role may involve school visits,

giving talks, leading walks, producing educational resources and developing innovative ways of promoting sustainable development.

- **Environmental manager:** implements initiatives through local authorities in the UK (e.g. sustainable development programmes, programmes for the reduction of pollution and other environmentally linked policies in their area).
- **Nature conservation officer:** responsible for the protection, management and development of wildlife habitats in a national or country park, private estate or other conservation site.
- **Recycling officer:** responsible for local authorities' environmental policies for waste reduction, re-use and recovery. He/she develops plans, implements and monitors a variety of recycling schemes.
- **Waste disposal officer:** works with local authorities, which are responsible for waste regulation, or with waste disposal companies in the fields of site operations, control and monitoring of the environmental effects of waste disposal, and development of new methods of managing all types of waste disposal (recycling, high temperature incineration, and so on).
- **Water quality scientist.** This role involves scientific analysis of water samples for the purpose of maintaining quality to set targets and standards.

Other graduate jobs where a degree in environmental studies could be useful

- **Environmental consultant:** works on client contracts in areas such as water pollution, air and land contamination, waste management, environmental impact assessment, environmental audit, ecological management, and environmental policy.
- **Environmental health officer:** monitors and ensures the maintenance of standards of environmental and public health – including food and food hygiene, safety at work, housing, and noise and pollution control – in accordance with the law.
- **Property and construction:** landscape architecture, town planning, cartography and geographical information systems.
- **Public health and consumer protection:** occupational and public health, health and safety inspectorates, and environmental health.
- **Secondary school teacher:** geography or science, depending on the core subjects taken within the first degree.
- **Toxicologist:** carries out scientific identification and studies the effects of harmful chemicals, biological materials and radiation on living systems and the environment to see how they can be avoided or minimised.
- **Transportation planner:** identifies the need for transport infrastructure, manages travel demand and changes people's travel behaviour in line with government guidelines (reducing car use and promoting walking, cycling and public transport, for example).

Find out more about environmental studies

- AQA: www.aqa.org.uk
- Department for Environment, Food and Rural Affairs (Defra): www.defra.gov.uk
- Environment Agency: www.environment-agency.gov.uk
- International Baccalaureate Diploma: www.ibo.org/diploma/curriculum/group3/
- LANTRA – Sector Skills Council for Land-based and Environmental Industries: www.lantra.co.uk
- SEMTA – Sector Skills Council for Science, Engineering and Manufacturing Technologies: www.semta.org.uk.
- SQA: www.sqa.org.uk

FILM STUDIES

As a student of film studies, you will broaden and deepen your knowledge and enjoyment of film. The emphasis of the course is on how films convey meanings in different ways and how they are subject to the social, cultural, political and economic forces of the day. As well as analysing different genres of film, you will compare Hollywood and British films, and analyse specific cinematic techniques. Understanding how the film and cinema industries operate, and the relationship between film production and consumption, is also part of this course.

Is it right for me?

Do you love film? Are you interested in gaining an academic understanding of film-making? Film studies introduces you to technical, historical, business, literary and creative aspects of film; it's not about relaxing and eating popcorn!

Film studies is an essay-writing subject and therefore strong written skills are important. You will learn through watching films, discussion and textual analysis.

Subject options

Film studies is available at GCE A/AS level through the WJEC exam board; it is also offered at Standard and Higher level as part of the International Baccalaureate Diploma.

Top Tip

If you're looking for a more technical and practical alternative to film studies, how about A/AS level in Moving Image Arts (CCEA) or Cambridge Pre-U in Art and Design (Lens-based Imagery), which includes photography, film and video?

A/AS level in Film Studies

An A level in Film Studies will encourage students to explore films in a variety of ways: such as a form of art, a method of communication and as an industry. The A level will cover topics such as those listed below. Assessment is usually a mixture of written examinations and research and creative projects.

Exploring film form (AS)

This unit focuses on analysing the form and style of certain types of film. You will learn about *mise en scène*, cinematography and editing; the relationship between form and how an audience interprets a film is also an important part of this.

British and American film (AS)
In this unit, students focus on topics in UK and US film and complete a comparative study. You will study the relationship between producers and their audiences, and the use of narrative and genre in the creation of meaning.

Film research and creative projects (A2)
Students complete a film-related research project and a creative project.

Varieties of film experience: issues and debates (A2)
Students learn about world cinema and spectatorship and have the opportunity to complete an in-depth critical study of a single film.

International Baccalaureate Diploma in Film

Students on the International Baccalaureate Diploma will develop their analytical response to films along with their creative abilities. The aim of the course is to deepen theoretical understanding and encourage a critical approach to the analysis of film.

At both Standard and Higher level, students will cover 'textual analysis', 'film theory and history' and 'creative process – techniques and organisation of production'. A broader and deeper understanding of the subject is obtained at Higher level. Assessment includes an independent study, oral presentation and a completed film project.

Choosing other subjects to go with film studies

Subjects that complement this one include media studies, English literature, communication and culture, languages, sociology and history. Make sure there isn't too much overlap between your subjects because exam boards may not permit the combination and universities may not accept the grades for both. Your chosen sixth form or college will be able to advise you further.

Top Tip

Film studies may need to be supplemented by more traditional A level subjects if you want to be considered by one of the leading universities. It would need to be combined with two more accepted subjects at the University of Sheffield; however, University College London includes film studies on its accepted subject list. It is suitable for some arts options at Trinity College, Cambridge.

Film studies at university

There are many film courses at university level. Some are very academic and theoretical, whereas others are more practical or vocational in their approach. You have to decide which type of course appeals to you more. There are also many related courses in media studies or media arts which include the study of film.

The breadth of your studies will be much greater at degree level than at A level. Typical modules of a degree in film studies might include:

- art and film
- the avant-garde
- border crossings in American cinema
- British cinema from the 1950s
- cinema in 1920s Berlin, Paris and Moscow
- European cinema
- film style, interpretation and evaluation
- introduction to narrative cinema
- sound and cinema
- the documentary film
- topics in American cinema.

Subjects that are often combined with film studies include English literature, a modern language, drama, history and politics.

Film studies and your future career

Non-graduate jobs in film studies

Your advanced level studies should develop your essay-writing skills, critical thinking and ability to communicate ideas. An A level in Film Studies will give you good skills and an insight into the film industry, as well as the academic aspects of film. Getting into the film business is notoriously difficult and you have to be prepared to make contacts and to work often on an unpaid basis to build experience until you get your first break. Non-media careers are still open to you, of course.

Graduate jobs directly related to film studies

Many students on film studies courses are interested in gaining employment in all aspects of the media industry. Careers in the media, however, are highly sought after and competition is likely to be fierce.

- **Broadcast assistant (radio):** assists with the production and presentation of programmes for local and national radio stations.
- **Broadcasting presenter:** fronts the programme; specific responsibilities vary depending on the programme.
- **Journalist:** reports on news and other areas of interests for newspapers, periodicals, radio and TV.
- **Multimedia programmer:** researches, develops and produces materials for new media-based company activities.
- **Programme researcher (broadcasting/film/video):** acts as an assistant producer with responsibility for conception and implementation of a programme.

- **Radio producer:** responsible for initiating ideas, selling these to commissioning editors and managing the technical and creative team to produce the final programme.
- **Television/film/video producer:** undertakes the artistic interpretation of materials and directs the production of shows or films.
- **Television production assistant:** provides organisational and secretarial services for the programme director.

Other graduate jobs where a degree in film studies could be useful

- **Advertising account executive:** takes overall responsibility for co-ordination, planning and organisation of advertising campaigns.
- **Editorial assistant:** assists editorial staff in the commissioning, planning and production of books, journals and magazines.
- **Event organiser:** identifies potential business and researches, writes, plans and runs all types of conferences on behalf of a client or his/her own organisation.
- **Information officer/manager:** ensures effective communication of information relating to a particular field of interest.
- **Market research executive:** undertakes systematic research to determine the potential market for a product or service.
- **Public relations account executive.** PR agencies work for their clients in presenting their image to the public. They decide on strategies to be used and which media would be the most effective.

Find out more about film studies

- International Baccalaureate Diploma: www.ibo.org/diploma/curriculum/group6/
- British Film Institute: www.bfi.org.uk/education-research
- Creative Skillset: www.creativeskillset.org
- WJEC: www.wjec.co.uk

GENERAL STUDIES

General studies is a bit different from most subjects in that it is not the study of a single discipline; its purpose is to broaden students' minds by teaching aspects from various different disciplines and areas of life. As well as acquiring knowledge of contemporary and historic matters, one of the aims of the course is to develop skills of critical and logical thinking, so that you can form your own opinions about issues in the world.

Is it right for me?

General studies will help you to think across a range of subjects; you will develop your critical thinking and the ability to make an argument and draw conclusions. This subject will improve your communication and presentation skills and give you experience in working independently or as part of a team. The skills it enhances are highly relevant to advanced level study, university study and the world of work. The qualification should broaden your studies and encourage a critical understanding of current issues.

Although general studies isn't consistently accepted as part of a university offer, it can be a good way to demonstrate breadth of understanding, beyond your academic subjects.

Subject options

This subject is available as GCE A/AS level and is offered by Edexcel, OCR and AQA exam boards.

Top Tip

Other ways to enhance your breadth of knowledge include the level 3 Extended Project (EP), level 3 Core Certificate of the Welsh Baccalaureate, Global Perspectives and Research (Cambridge Pre-U) and Theory of Knowledge (International Baccalaureate Diploma).

A/AS level in General Studies

For an exact definition of the syllabus you will be studying, you should check with your sixth form or college or take a look at the exam board website (see page 140 for details). Some of the themes studied include:

- culture, morality, arts and humanities
- critical thinking and analytical skills

- science, mathematics and technology
- society, politics and the economy.

Assessment is usually by written exams.

Choosing other subjects to go with general studies

General studies should be taken in addition to your regular subjects, as it will generally be accepted only as a fourth A level for entry to university – if at all. For this reason, and because of the breadth of the syllabus and the skills you develop, any other subjects may be studied alongside the general studies course.

General studies at university

The vast majority of universities do not recognise general studies as a qualifying subject; however, some will accept it for specific courses, while others recognise its value when deciding whether or not to make an offer or whether to consider a student who has just missed the grade requirements.

Some university views on general studies are listed below. Admissions policies change from time to time, so for the latest and most accurate information, see the relevant university website.

'General Studies A level is welcomed but not normally included as part of the standard offer unless otherwise stated in the course details.'

University of Manchester, www.manchester.ac.uk

'The University recognises all A level subjects, including general studies and critical thinking, for the purposes of general entry requirements but individual degree programmes may require specific previous subject knowledge to A level (or equivalent standard).'

University of Hull, www.hull.ac.uk

'A level General Studies is not normally accepted as an approved subject.'

University of Edinburgh, www.ed.ac.uk

'We accept general studies as an A level for all of our programmes except BA Economics and Politics.'

Politics and International Studies, University of Leeds,
www.polis.leeds.ac.uk

'All A-level subjects are accepted, including general studies. You should check with individual admissions offices for specific exclusions.'

University of Glasgow, www.gla.ac.uk

There are no degree programmes in general studies, but the skills and general knowledge you develop should be useful for all areas of study at university level.

General studies and your future career

There are no specific jobs related to this subject, but employers appreciate people who have a broad base of knowledge and who can think for themselves; general studies aims to equip students with both of these things. However, like many universities, many employers don't recognise this subject as a legitimate A level subject.

Find out more about general studies

- AQA: www.aqa.org.uk
- Edexcel: www.edexcel.com
- OCR: www.ocr.org.uk

GEOGRAPHY

Geography is a truly interdisciplinary subject, calling on and developing skills in research, numeracy and spatial awareness, as well as critical and analytical thinking.

Students of geography learn about the environment in which we live and the way humans interact in that environment. You will study physical geography (the physical aspects of the Earth) alongside human or urban geography (how humans use and adapt to their surroundings) and the interaction between the two. Some of today's most political issues – including decisions to build new motorways or runways, immigration, food shortage and famine – relate to human geography. Physical geography is based on the scientific aspects of the world around us.

Top Tip

You do not always need to have studied geography at GCSE or Standard level to study it at advanced level.

Is it right for me?

If you're interested in the world and enjoy problem solving, then you might want to read on. Geography has relevance to a range of humanities and science subjects, including biology, physics, maths, history, politics, economics and sociology.

To do well at this subject, it helps to be a good all-rounder with the ability to think and analyse different types of data. You will learn through an interesting variety of methods, including fieldwork, visits and surveys or the interpretation of data, maps and weather reports. You will probably be spending some time outdoors, whatever the weather.

You will develop a range of skills: from research and investigation or communicating complex ideas to the understanding and interpretation of natural phenomena.

Subject options

Geography is available at GCE A/AS level, Scottish Higher and Advanced Higher, International Baccalaureate Diploma and Cambridge Pre-U.

Top Tip

Alternative subject options include WJEC's A/AS level in World Development and Edexcel's Global Development AS level.

A/AS level in Geography

Most of the exam boards offer courses with some of the following elements. For an exact definition of the AS and A2 syllabus you will be studying, you should consult your chosen sixth form, college or the exam board itself (see page 146 for websites).

As is the case for most subjects, there is an element of learning from textbooks and taking notes in class; however, geography students also get the opportunity to learn through a variety of additional methods which include fieldwork, visits and surveys. Assessments are increasingly based on exams. For example, the AQA specification includes two written exams – one on classroom work and one based on fieldwork – each year. Some of the typical topics covered are listed below.

Physical geography

- Water on land
- Climatic hazards and change
- Energy and life

Human geography

- Population dynamics
- Settlement processes and patterns
- Economic activity

Challenge and change in the natural environment

- Coasts: processes and problems
- Geomorphological processes and hazards (the shaping of the Earth's surface by environmental forces)
- Cold environments and human activity
- Sustainability

Higher and Advanced Higher in Geography

At Higher level, you will study 'physical environments', 'human environments' and 'environmental interactions'; assessment is based entirely on written exams.

At Advanced Higher, you will cover 'geographical methods and techniques', 'geographical study' and 'geographical issues'. Assessment is made up of coursework, including a research report and evaluative essay, which make up 70% of the marks for the year. A written exam accounts for the remaining 30% of the marks.

International Baccalaureate Diploma in Geography

The qualification includes human and physical geography, and the study of scientific and socio-economic methods. You will get the chance to investigate issues such as sustainability and poverty from a local, national or global perspective. The core themes at Standard and Higher level are 'population in transition', 'disparities in wealth and development', 'patterns in environmental quality and sustainability' and 'patterns in resource consumption'. Optional themes include 'hazards and disasters', 'urban environment' and 'geography of food and health'. Higher level students also study an extension topic on global interactions.

Assessment is based mainly on exams, although 20% of the mark at Higher level (25% at Standard level) comes from an investigative fieldwork report.

Top Tip

The study of geography can help you to get a place on a range of different degrees. It is a facilitating subject, often needed by the leading universities for a number of their courses, so studying it might help to keep your degree options open.

Cambridge Pre-U in Geography

The Cambridge Pre-U Geography course includes four components: 'geographical issues', 'global environments', 'global themes' and a research topic. Each component is assessed by a written examination taken at the end of the two-year programme.

Choosing other subjects to go with geography

Geography can be very scientific at one end of the spectrum and very social at the other, so it works very well with a wide range of subjects. Common combinations include environmental science, biology, history, mathematics, physics and chemistry.

If you want to study geography at university level, you should think carefully about your subject selection; some degree courses are very science-based while others are much more focused on humanities. Most university courses require the study of A level (or equivalent) Geography, although some courses (for example, those with a more geological focus) may ask for two sciences at A level.

Geography at university

Geography at degree level can be offered as a science subject (BSc) or an arts subject (BA), or both. This largely depends on the outlook of the department and the emphasis of a particular course. A BSc in Geography tends to concentrate more on physical geography, while the BA in Geography tends to focus more on human geography. Some universities offer flexibility, thus enabling students to choose options from both degree programmes.

'My subject choices (geography, maths and physics) were based on the assumption that I would be accepted to study meteorology. Although I am now studying a different discipline (natural hazard management and geography), it is a subject that I thoroughly enjoy and I cannot wait to have a job in the field I have been studying.'

Melissa Handley

Fieldwork is an important part of a degree in geography and many institutions run fieldwork trips in Britain and abroad.

Modules that could form part of a typical degree programme in geography include:

- geography, society and development
- global environmental change
- global environmental issues
- global environmental problems and policies
- historical geographies of urbanism
- hydrology
- methods in geographical analysis
- natural hazards
- readings in geography
- the natural environment
- tropical forests in a changing environment.

If allowed by the institution, geography can be combined with many other degree subjects, such as a modern foreign language, environmental science, history, computer science, development studies, English or biology.

Top Tip

For certain courses, at some universities, geography is considered as a science subject. Websites and prospectuses will normally make this clear, so don't assume that this is always the case.

Geography and your future career

Non-graduate jobs in geography

You will gain a wide variety of skills from studying advanced level geography, which you could apply to several different areas of work; however, if you want to work in a geography-related area, you will normally need to study the subject to degree level first.

Relevant transferable skills include teamwork, skills in the use of IT, analytical skills, the ability to interpret and communicate different forms of data and to draw conclusions, numerical skills and awareness of current affairs.

Graduate jobs directly related to geography

Some of the following jobs require further training or study and relevant practical experience.

- **Cartographer:** evaluates sets of geographical data and presents them in the form of diagrams, charts and spreadsheets as well as conventional maps.
- **Distribution/logistics manager:** manages the supply, movement and storage of goods and materials. The role involves planning, organising and co-ordinating the flow and storage of materials through the whole supply chain process from manufacturer to customer.
- **Environmental consultant:** works in areas such as air and land contamination, water pollution, noise and vibration measurement, waste management, environmental policy and ecological/land management.
- **Geographical information systems manager:** manages a team of IT professionals who use computer-based systems to handle geographical information.
- **Remote sensing scientist:** processes aerial photographs and satellite images by computer in order to fit them to maps or to enhance specific features of interest and to assess their significance.
- **Secondary school teacher:** develops schemes of work and plans lessons in line with national objectives. As a secondary school teacher, you must also keep up to date with developments in your subject area and with new resources and methods.
- **Town planner:** directs or undertakes the planning of land use. This involves taking into account the views of interested parties in order to find a balance between the conflicting demands of housing, industrial development, agriculture, recreation, the transport network and the environment.
- **Transportation planner:** identifies the need for a transport infrastructure and devises transport strategies in line with government guidelines, such as reducing car use by promoting walking, cycling and public transport. Statistical analysis is used to forecast developments.

Other graduate jobs where a degree in geography could be useful

The following represent some common areas of employment chosen by geographers.

- **Local government administrator:** responds to the needs of individual departments, sometimes as a specialist in administration, finance or personnel. The role involves assisting in the formulation of policies and procedures, and co-ordinating their implementation.
- **Nature conservation officer:** protects, manages and enhances wildlife habitats. This role may include promoting and implementing local biodiversity action plans through negotiation with planners and developers, conservation tasks, visitor liaison or educational and interpretative work.
- **Tourism officer:** develops and promotes tourism in order to attract visitors and to produce significant economic benefits for a particular region or site.
- **Urban general practice surveyor:** values, manages and markets residential and commercial property, acting as an agent for clients in the purchase, leasing or sale of property.

Find out more about geography

- AQA: www.aqa.org.uk
- Association for Geographic Information: www.agi.org.uk
- Cambridge Pre-U: www.cie.org.uk/qualifications
- CCEA: www.rewardinglearning.org.uk
- Department for Environment, Food and Rural Affairs (Defra): www.defra.gov.uk
- Edexcel: www.edexcel.com
- Environment Agency: www.environment-agency.gov.uk
- International Baccalaureate Diploma: www.ibo.org/diploma/curriculum/group3/
- LANTRA – Sector Skills Council for Land-based and Environmental Industries: www.lantra.co.uk
- OCR: www.ocr.org.uk
- Royal Geographical Society: www.rgs.org
- SQA: www.sqa.org.uk
- WJEC: www.wjec.co.uk

GEOLOGY

Geology is a multidisciplinary science that provides an insight into the origins of the planet and how it has changed over time. Geologists use science to understand the history of the Earth and to forecast its future.

Through the study of advanced level geology, you will explore the physical properties of the Earth but also the causes of natural disasters such as volcanoes, earthquakes and tsunami. You will learn all about the characteristics of the Earth's surface, as well as the rocks and minerals that make up the planet's crust, mantle and core.

Is it right for me?

No previous knowledge of geology is required to study it at advanced level. If you enjoyed science and maths at GCSE level and you are interested in the scientific study of the Earth, then geology might be a good choice.

The course introduces you to the history of the planet, what the Earth is made of and its processes. You will learn through fieldwork and lab investigations on rocks, fossils or minerals, which will require you to use scientific methods to solve problems. It helps if you enjoy being outdoors and have a keen interest in science and a curiosity about how the world works.

Top Tip

Geology includes aspects of physical geography, biology, chemistry and physics.

Subject options

A/AS level Geology is offered by the exam boards OCR and WJEC. The Scottish Qualifications Authority offers geology as a Higher qualification, although it is not currently available at Advanced Higher level.

A/AS level in Geology

Geology is a science subject, so practical and lab work are important elements. Assessment is via written exams, fieldwork and coursework. On the OCR A level syllabus 10% of the final marks come from coursework, with the remainder from written exams. The outline below is based on the OCR exam board specification.

Global tectonics (AS)

The structure of the Earth; earthquakes; continental drift and plate tectonics; geological structures.

The rock cycle – processes and products (AS)

The rock cycle (the study of igneous, sedimentary and metamorphic rocks); sedimentary processes and products; igneous processes and products; metamorphic processes and products.

Geology practical 1 (AS)

Students complete a practical task, possibly as fieldwork.

Environmental geology (A2)

Water supply; energy resources; metallic mineral deposits; engineering geology.

Evolution of life, Earth and climate (A2)

Formation of fossils; morphology and organisms; fossil evidence; climate change; dating methods and interpreting geological maps.

Geology practical 2 (A2)

Students complete a further practical task, possibly as fieldwork.

Top Tip

Geology is a subject that is respected and favoured by the top universities, but it tends not to be an entry requirement so would not be classed as a facilitating subject.

Higher in Geology

At Higher level, you will study topics such as of plate tectonics, the Earth's magnetic field, the structure of the Earth, and fossilisation. Assessment is based on written exams and a fieldwork report.

Choosing other subjects to go with geology

Advanced level geology works well with science and humanities subjects including biology, chemistry, physics, geography, archaeology and environmental studies. Candidates concentrating on arts, humanities or languages may choose to broaden their subject knowledge by taking a science such as geology.

Geology at university

If you want to study geology at a higher level you will probably need advanced level qualifications from the following subjects: physics, chemistry, biology, maths, geology and geography. Some universities will accept subjects from a broad range of science disciplines including environmental science, computing, design and technology, PE, psychology and electronics.

Top Tip

You will need one or two sciences at advanced level to be considered for a geology degree; A level (or equivalent) Geology tends not to be a requirement.

Some of the geology-related degree programmes on offer include:

- computational geoscience
- environmental geoscience
- geology
- geology and geophysics
- geophysics.

Subjects that go well with geology at degree level include physics, biology, computer science, geography, archaeology and environmental science. There will be variations in the combinations universities are prepared to offer.

Geology and your future career

Non-graduate jobs in geology

You will gain lots of varied skills from geology, which you could apply to various types of work. These skills include numeracy, analytical ability, good judgement and IT skills. If you want to work in a geology-related area, you will probably have to study the subject at a degree level first.

Graduate jobs directly related to geology

Geologists are needed in a range of settings to report on natural resources, environmental issues or geological risks.

- **Engineering geologist:** assesses the impact of ground conditions on development schemes such as tunnels, buildings, pipelines, docks, bridges and other structures.
- **Geoscientist:** locates and proves the existence of oil, gas, minerals and water reserves, estimating the extent and quality of the find.
- **Hydrogeologist:** identifies the type, distribution and structure of rock strata and their impact on the movement and accumulation of groundwater.

- **Minerals surveyor:** assists in the planning of mineral workings, ensuring the stability of mine sites and advising on the future restoration or redevelopment of exhausted sites.
- **Mudlogger.** Based on an oil drilling rig, the role involves collecting and monitoring information and samples from drilling operations to report back to drilling teams and oil companies.
- **Seismic interpreter:** interprets geophysical and geological data to produce maps of structures and to evaluate the prospect of recovering hydrocarbons.
- **Wellsite geologist:** supervises the recording of an oil or gas well, co-ordinates the collection and interpretation of well data, and communicates the results to management and other colleagues.

Other graduate jobs where a degree in geology could be useful

The following examples illustrate some areas of work that can give you the opportunity to use the skills and knowledge gained from a geology degree.

- **Geographical information systems manager:** digitises geographical information, such as the location of bridges, flood defences or plant species, using GPS tools in the field or converting paper maps to GIS datasets. It also involves managing the storage, analysis and presentation of the data held.
- **Hydrologist:** analyses water flow through pipes and channels for the engineering and control of water. The focus of the work is on surface water and can include estimating yields of water and investigating its quality.
- **Waste disposal officer.** Tasks could include managing a landfill site and organising household waste collection systems, including tendering for contracts and researching and implementing methods of toxic waste disposal.

Find out more about geology

- British Geological Survey: www.bgs.ac.uk
- Earthworks: www.earthworks-jobs.com
- Geological Society: www.geolsoc.org.uk
- Natural Environment Research Council (NERC): www.nerc.ac.uk
- OCR: www.ocr.org.uk
- SQA: www.sqa.org.uk
- WJEC: www.wjec.co.uk

GOVERNMENT AND POLITICS

Whatever your political views, you cannot escape the effects of politics. A course in government and politics will help you to understand the process of how the UK and other elected governments function. In addition, you may also cover issues such as human rights, justice, war and peace.

Some of the questions that you may be asked on this course include the following.

- How have political systems changed over time?
- How do political structures and voting systems work?
- What is democracy and how does that concept vary according to different contexts and periods of history?
- What are the responsibilities of governments and how do they exert their power?
- What are some of the differences between the US and UK political systems?

Is it right for me?

Government and politics is a contemporary subject; you will study changes as they happen but also with an eye on the past. The subject is theoretical and essay-based (not just about debate and discussion), but you will enhance your understanding of theories by applying them to current affairs. The subject has wide appeal, as politics touches on all aspects of society and our lives.

You do not need prior knowledge of politics (although a healthy interest in the news is helpful) but good written skills are important. You will develop skills in research and analysis, communication and the development of an argument.

Subject options

This subject is offered at GCE A/AS level by a range of exam boards. It is available as a Cambridge Pre-U subject and a Scottish Higher qualification.

A/AS level in Government and Politics

Teaching is mainly classroom- and textbook-based but you may also look at news reports, political party manifestos and many other texts related to politics. Sometimes schools and colleges invite speakers to come and talk to students or organise visits to political organisations. Assessment is mainly by written exams (for example, the AQA syllabus is assessed by two written exams each year).

An A level course in Government and Politics will normally include the following topics, although the titles of the units may vary between the different exam boards:

- people and politics
- governing in the UK
- participation and voting behaviour
- introducing political ideologies
- introducing international politics
- the EU and European issues
- governing in the USA
- international politics in the UK.

Higher in Politics

This option is currently only available at Higher level and covers 'political theory', 'political structures' and 'political representation'. Assessment is carried out by written exams.

Top Tip

Government and politics appears on the preferred subject listings for University College London and University of Sheffield; on the other hand, Trinity College, Cambridge, considers it to have 'more limited suitability' as a third or fourth choice providing a route to arts subjects only.

Cambridge Pre-U in Comparative Government and Politics

This course encourages students to communicate effectively, to articulate informed opinion and to consider the traditions and philosophy of politics. You study four units: 'concepts and institutions', 'parties and ideas', 'ideologies and philosophies' and 'contemporary international debates: contexts and comparisons'. Assessment is made up of four written exams at the end of the second year.

Top Tip

The International Baccalaureate Diploma is currently running a pilot programme in global politics which should become widely available in September 2015.

Choosing other subjects to go with government and politics

This subject goes well with many others, including English, history, law, business, economics, sociology and media studies.

Government and politics at university

You won't normally need to have studied government and politics at advanced level to apply for a BA Politics degree. Institutions usually ask for three good grades; in some cases no subjects are specified, while others favour subjects from the arts, social sciences or humanities. For example, Newcastle University prefers one subject from history, government and politics, geography, English and philosophy.

Most university degrees tend to be based on a combination of core and optional modules. Optional courses may include:

- advanced policy analysis
- comparative politics of Western Europe
- environmental policy
- European Union
- fascism
- history of political thought
- Islam and the Middle East
- Karl Marx
- politics of development
- political leadership in the twentieth century.

Some courses may also involve some fieldwork, where students spend some time with political organisations (such as a political party or a pressure group) or may go abroad to organisations such as the European Parliament, NATO or the European Commission.

Degree level politics works well with subjects such as law, economics, history, philosophy, sociology and modern languages.

Government and politics and your future career

Non-graduate jobs in government and politics
Students can gain access to a few related jobs after an advanced qualification; these include junior positions in the Civil Service or in local government. Additionally, the skills that you will gain from the course are transferable to many different areas of work.

Graduate jobs directly related to government and politics
There are very few careers where a first degree in politics is essential. The following jobs are some of the most closely related to a politics degree, but they may also require relevant experience or further training.

- **Charity fundraiser and charity officer:** entry for both types of work may initially have to be on a voluntary basis.

- **Political party agent:** responsible for press coverage, publicity and liaison between the local party and the Member of Parliament.
- **Political party research officer:** employed in a variety of settings, including higher education, political parties and independent agencies. This role includes working for Members of Parliament and Members of the European Parliament.
- **Public affairs consultant (lobbyist):** represents the client's case to those in government who make decisions that affect them. The client may be a large company, a trade association, a pressure group or a local authority.

Other graduate jobs where a degree in government and politics could be useful

- **Civil Service fast streamer:** responds to the needs of individual departments, sometimes as a specialist in administration, finance or personnel. The role involves assisting in the formulation of policies and procedures and co-ordinating their implementation.
- **Journalist:** responsible for gathering news and reporting in both written and broadcast media. This involves developing contacts, interviewing people, attending press conferences and producing copy to a deadline.
- **Personnel officer:** responsible for advising on all policies relating to the use of human resources, and for the organisation and implementation of policies for workforce planning, recruitment, training, terms and conditions of employment and benefits.
- **Police officer.** First and foremost, graduates should be committed to the role of a police officer. However, those with potential and continued high performance may be fast-tracked for promotion.
- **Public relations account executive:** responsible for the transmission of positive information to particular audiences in order to influence their attitudes by using press and media liaison, company newspapers and journals.
- **Social researcher:** designs, formulates and carries out social research in a variety of settings, including central and local government, independent research institutions and trades unions. This will only be appropriate if your degree scheme contains a component of research methodology.
- **Solicitor:** advises individuals and organisations on legal problems, prepares wills, contracts and other legal documents, and researches and advises on points of law.

Find out more about government and politics

- AQA: www.aqa.org.uk
- Cambridge Pre-U: www.cie.org.uk/qualifications
- CCEA: www.rewardinglearning.org.uk
- Civil Service Fast Stream: www.civilservice.gov.uk/recruitment/fast-stream

- Edexcel: www.edexcel.com
- OCR: www.ocr.org.uk
- SQA: www.sqa.org.uk
- UK Parliament: www.parliament.uk
- WJEC: www.wjec.co.uk
- Read daily newspapers, particularly the broadsheets, e.g. *The Times, Guardian, Daily Mail*

HEALTH AND SOCIAL CARE (APPLIED)

The emphasis of this course is very much on the vocational contexts of health and social care. It offers a pathway for candidates wishing to progress to higher education courses in this area, as well as providing a useful introduction to employment in the sector.

You will learn about values, rights and responsibilities, how to communicate effectively, health and well-being, and understanding human behaviour.

Some of the questions that health and social care students should consider include the following.

- What are the most effective ways of caring for particular age groups?
- What is the role of exercise in the maintenance of good health?
- What are the career paths available in the health and social care field?

Is it right for me?

This subject might be relevant if you see yourself working in a health or social care role in the future but would like to learn more about the issues affecting the sector and the range of opportunities open to you.

You will gain some understanding of sociology and psychology in the context of health and social care. The course teaches you about the professional relationship between carer and patient (or client) and the relevant legislation and principles that apply to work in this field. You will also develop some of the skills that are required within this sector.

It is not necessary to have any prior knowledge of health and social care before studying it at advanced level (skills in English are more important). The skills learned through this course will be helpful to a range of helping and supporting roles, from childcare and counselling to nursing and social work.

Top Tip

You don't have to study health and social care to work in the field, but it will give you an invaluable insight into what matters in the sector.

Subject options

This course is available as a GCE Applied A/AS level (single and double award) and at Scottish Higher level.

A/AS level in Health and Social Care

AS level study focuses on the needs of clients, while A2 will develop your learning by covering the issues that relate to service delivery.

This subject is taught by a mixture of tutor-led activities, independent research and reading, and practical work. The context for this subject is very much work-related; you might visit health and social care settings or speakers might be invited to talk about their work or current issues. Assessment is by a mixture of internal examination of prepared portfolios of work and written exam.

The outline below is based on the syllabus from OCR. AQA, CCEA and WJEC also offer the qualification. For an exact definition of the GCE syllabus you will be studying, you should consult your school or college, or the exam board (see page 160).

Courses generally include a mixture of compulsory and optional units. Here are the main areas covered across the A2 double award.

- Promoting quality care (AS)
- Communication in care settings (AS)
- Promoting good health (AS)
- Health and safety in care settings (AS)
- Caring for people with additional needs (AS)
- Working in early years care and education (AS)
- Health as a lifestyle choice (AS)
- Complementary therapies (AS)
- Caring for older people (AS)
- Care practice and provision (A2)
- Understanding human behaviour and development (A2)
- Anatomy and physiology in practice (A2)
- Child development (A2)
- Mental health issues (A2)
- Social trends (A2)
- Research methods in health and social care (A2)

Top Tip

At GCE AS level, single (three units) and double (six units) awards are available; an AS level double award is equivalent to two AS levels.

At GCE A level, single (six units) and double (12 units) awards are available; an A level double award is equivalent to two A levels.

Higher in Care

This one-year course focuses on three units: 'psychology for care', 'sociology for care' and 'values and principles in care'. Assessment takes place at the end of the year and is based on two closed book exam papers.

Top Tip

You're not recommended to choose health and social care as a main A level subject if you're applying to medical school. Medical schools tend to favour the more academic A levels rather than the applied options. Queen's University Belfast will accept a maximum of either one Applied A level or one Applied AS level, so it is always worth checking the exact requirements with your preferred universities.

Choosing other subjects to go with health and social care

This course could be combined with many subjects but the most compatible include biology, sociology, psychology, government and politics, PE and business studies.

Health and social care at university

There are many different health and social care options available at university level. Some students may opt for subjects such as sociology or social policy, whereas others may be interested in courses such as health studies or health economics. Each course is different and may require specific subjects at advanced level for you to be able to gain a place; health economics, for instance, would probably require an economics background rather than one in health and social care.

Courses are available in the following areas:

- community and youth studies
- community health
- health studies
- midwifery
- nursing
- primary care
- social work.

Often these courses aim to give you a professional qualification in a particular area (social work, for example). If you wanted a more academic course, you could consider a degree such as social policy, health-care policy or sociology.

Top Tip

Most of the courses that lead to a professional qualification, such as nursing or social work, tend to ask for plenty of relevant experience alongside your academic qualifications.

Some students choose to combine their subject with other disciplines, including sociology, social policy, politics, public sector administration, biology or management.

Health and social care and your future career

Non-graduate jobs in health and social care

It is possible to get trainee posts in some areas of work in health and social care without first getting a degree. These include jobs as care assistants and in some areas of nursing and social care. It's also possible to get administrative positions in these environments (in the NHS or social services, for example).

Graduate jobs directly related to health and social care

For many professional roles allied to medicine, such as nurse, dietitian, podiatrist or occupational therapist, it would be necessary to complete a full vocational course at undergraduate or postgraduate level. Other options closely related to health and social care often require some further postgraduate training.

- **Health promotion specialist:** promotes awareness of health issues to individuals and the community.
- **Health service manager:** responsible for the provision of local health care through the management of hospital, GP or community health services.
- **Nutritional therapist:** advises clients on how to improve overall health and well-being by assessing needs, problems, diet and lifestyle, and recommending changes.
- **Personal trainer:** provides physical fitness instruction and prescription of exercise and fitness programmes for individuals.
- **Physiotherapist:** treats a range of health problems through massage, movement, exercise and technology. Although qualified status requires a degree in physiotherapy, posts as physiotherapy assistants are also available, providing valuable experience.
- **Social worker:** aims to provide a service to individuals and families facing problems which they are unable to manage alone. Entry involves gaining work experience and completing a degree course.

Other graduate jobs where a degree in health and social care could be useful

- **Charity officer.** The size of the organisation determines the responsibilities of this role. Besides administrative tasks, the position may include fundraising, policy, public relations and education. Relevant experience may be necessary – either voluntary or paid.
- **Civil Service administrator (mainstream entry).** Civil Service departments employ administrators in a variety of roles, but tasks may include organising services and resources, strategic planning, implementing policies, research and report writing.
- **Counsellor:** helps people who are struggling to cope with problems, decisions, transitions and crises. The role usually requires voluntary and life experience, along with an accredited counselling qualification.
- **Further education lecturer.** This role involves delivering specific modules or courses in post-compulsory education. A professional health qualification could enhance your chances.
- **Local government administrator:** responds to the administrative needs of individual departments. The role involves assisting in the formulation of policies and procedures.
- **Sales executive (medical):** represents pharmaceutical companies to GPs, retail pharmacists and hospital doctors.
- **Sports administrator.** The role varies depending on the organisation but may include organising events, training sessions or conferences; marketing and public relations; producing literature; liaising with other agencies; and financial and business administration.

Find out more about health and social care

- AQA: www.aqa.org.uk
- CCEA: www.rewardinglearning.org.uk
- Civil Service Careers: www.civilservice.gov.uk/recruitment
- Community Care: www.communitycare.co.uk
- NHS Careers: www.nhscareers.nhs.uk
- OCR: www.ocr.org.uk
- Skills for Care and Development: www.skillsforcareanddevelopment.org.uk
- Skills for Health: www.skillsforhealth.org.uk
- SQA: www.sqa.org.uk
- WJEC: www.wjec.co.uk

HISTORY

History continues to be seen as an academically sound subject, not least because it develops lots of useful skills. Empathy and the ability to evaluate written information critically and to weigh up evidence are just some of the qualities history students learn to demonstrate. The study of history does not simply focus on learning about the past; it's also about understanding how we view the past from today's perspective.

History students may be asked to consider the following kinds of questions.

- What has been the global effect of 9/11?
- What are the ramifications of the reigns of prominent politicians and monarchs?
- What were the circumstances that led to the outbreak of World Wars I and II?
- How reliable are certain types of historical evidence?
- Why did Henry VIII split from the Catholic Church in Rome?

Is it right for me?

If you like to read, discuss, analyse and write, then you might enjoy history. As well as having an interest in past events, it helps if you are curious about society and current affairs.

Top Tip

Don't worry if you haven't studied history before; you may still be able to study it at advanced level, as long as you have strong English skills.

You will need to remember plenty of facts and figures, but memorising alone is not sufficient; you will also need to be able to reflect critically, analyse and clearly explain your reasoning. You will develop some useful skills in the use of data, investigation and deduction, and the communication of ideas.

'A level is a lot more in depth. For GCSE History, marks will be awarded for knowing certain facts and dates but for A level History, you need all of these and a clear argument. Essay-writing skills are a big part of the A level exams.'

Sian Burke

Subject options

All the major exam boards offer GCE AS/A level in History. It is also available as a subject choice in the Cambridge Pre-U and International Baccalaureate Diploma and as an SQA Higher and Advanced Higher course.

A/AS level in History

For an exact definition of the AS and A2 syllabus you will be studying, you should consult your school, college or the exam board itself. Class lessons may include group discussions, watching relevant historical programmes and analysing historical documents. As with subjects such as English literature, the volume of reading and writing is high, so you need to be prepared for this before you choose history.

Assessment varies between exam boards; some may have exams only, while others have elements of assessed coursework, independent projects and open book examinations.

The main variations in the subject depend on the particular period chosen by your school or college, along with the type of history studied (social, political or religious history, for example).

Most courses will ensure that candidates get experience of the following:

- significant historical events, issues or people
- a range of historical perspectives
- the diversity of society
- the history of more than one country or state
- a substantial element of English history
- continuity and change over a particular period.

This is achieved in a variety of ways by different exam boards but is likely to include at least some of the following options.

Periods of English history
Most A level specifications include the study of a particular period of English history. This could be any period from 1000 to 1970, with a tendency to focus on up to 150 years at a time.

Periods of European and world history
Students may also have the opportunity to study a period of non-British history from about 1000 to 1900.

The study of historically significant people
Some courses offer the option of an in-depth study of great historical figures, such as:

- Charlemagne
- Chamberlain

- Elizabeth I
- King John
- Lenin
- Napoleon I
- Oliver Cromwell
- Peter the Great
- Philip II
- Stalin.

The study of historical themes

As well as studying individuals, some exam boards offer the opportunity to study historical themes, such as:

- rebellion and disorder in England 1485–1603
- the Catholic Reformation in the sixteenth century
- the decline of Spain 1598–1700
- war and society in Britain 1793–1918
- civil rights in the USA 1865–1980.

Independent study

In some cases, students can do some independent study on a particular period, theme or historical figure as part of assessed coursework.

Top Tip

History is considered to be a facilitating subject, according to 'Informed Choices' (the Russell group guide to making decisions about post-16 education). As it is one of the subjects most often required by the leading universities, studying it might help to keep your degree options open.

Higher and Advanced Higher in History

At Higher level, you will cover Scottish, British and European history, and will be assessed by exam and extended essay.

On the Advanced Higher course, you will choose a field of historical study from a range which includes 'Scottish independence 1286–1329', 'Japan: from medieval to modern state 1850s–1920' and 'Soviet Union 1917–1953'. You will answer a question paper and also research and write a dissertation.

Top Tip

The skills gained in the study of history relate to many career paths; these include journalism, law and politics.

International Baccalaureate Diploma in History

History is available at Standard and Higher level on the International Baccalaureate Diploma. Your school or college will decide whether you will concentrate your study on 'twentieth-century world history' or 'the key developments in Europe and the Islamic world, 500–1570'. Assessment is based on written exam papers and a historical investigation.

Cambridge Pre-U in History

The Pre-U offers a range of historical periods in British or European history, along with 'US history 1750–2000' and 'African and Asian history 1750–2000'. You are expected to study more than one region and will be assessed at the end of the two years with written exams and externally marked question papers.

Choosing other subjects to go with history

History is often combined with arts, languages, social sciences and humanities, such as English literature, sociology, geography, philosophy, archaeology, classical civilisation, economics and government or politics. It can also prove an interesting counterbalance to sciences.

History at university

Pure history remains a very popular choice at university level. It is seen as an academically rigorous discipline and employers appreciate the skills that historians develop. Related courses include economic history, international history, political history and ancient history. In most cases, you would need A level History to get on to these courses.

Like many degrees these days, history can be quite varied and flexible in its content. Most courses will have some core subjects (usually studied in the first year) and then will give students the possibility to specialise by choosing particular modules. The options are likely to include most areas of British, European and world history; students will often consider theories of history as well as historical periods.

History can be combined with many other disciplines to form a joint degree. As many arts, humanities and social science degrees include an historical context, history is an ideal accompaniment for any of them (for example, geography and history, politics and history or German and history).

'I want to become a museum curator so history will provide me with the necessary knowledge needed for the career.'

Rachel Etherington

History and your future career

Non-graduate jobs in history

Many employers requiring A levels do not really mind which subjects applicants have studied. In that sense, history is as good a choice as any. However, there may be some non-graduate areas of work where history is more useful than other subjects because of the particular skills and knowledge acquired. These include:

- administrative work
- management
- sales
- marketing
- working as an assistant in a museum or gallery.

Graduate jobs directly related to history

History-related occupations include the following, although many require further study.

- **Academic librarian/information manager/records manager:** responsible for the acquisition, organisation and dissemination of information and materials within the library system or information unit.
- **Archaeologist:** studies the past through material remains.
- **Archivist:** acquires, selects, arranges, stores, preserves and retrieves records not in current use but deemed to be of historical value.
- **Genealogist:** traces and charts lines of descent or family trees. This role offers the possibility of freelance work.
- **Museum/art gallery curator:** responsible for the care and improvement of a collection including exhibitions, catalogues and acquisitions.
- **Secondary school teacher:** teaches history to 11–18-year-olds in schools.

Other graduate jobs where a degree in history could be useful

The following represent some other potential areas of employment.

- **Arts administrator:** brings together artists and audiences to support and generate artistic activity.
- **Civil Service fast streamer:** Fast Stream entry graduates are involved in helping senior staff, and through them ministers, to formulate and implement policy. Graduates also enter as junior managers with administrative and management responsibilities.
- **Journalist:** gathers and presents news and features to the public.

- **Marketing executive:** manages the marketing of a product or service from research and development through to the launch. This can include promotion and advertising to the public or businesses.
- **Primary school teacher:** develops and fosters the appropriate skills and social abilities to enable the optimum development of children, within the framework of the National Curriculum.
- **Sales executive:** promotes and maximises sales of a company's products or services in designated markets. The role also involves identifying new markets and new business, and acting as liaison between producer and the retailer or wholesaler.

Find out more about history

- AQA: www.aqa.org.uk
- Cambridge Pre-U: www.cie.org.uk/qualifications
- CCEA: www.rewardinglearning.org.uk
- Council for British Archaeology: www.britarch.ac.uk
- Creative and Cultural Skills: www.ccskills.org.uk
- Edexcel: www.edexcel.com
- Historical Association: www.history.org.uk
- International Baccalaureate Diploma: www.ibo.org/diploma/curriculum/group3/
- Museums Association: www.museumsassociation.org
- OCR: www.ocr.org.uk
- SQA: www.sqa.org.uk
- WJEC: www.wjec.co.uk

HISTORY OF ART

History of art is a fairly specialised subject that introduces students to a wealth of art, architecture and decorative arts from some of the world's most famous artists. As well as learning about the techniques used by artists, students learn about:

- the historical, social, religious and political context in which the pieces of art were produced
- which themes are repeated in art throughout the centuries
- which artists have been the most influential
- how the political hierarchy patronised artists to further their political ends.

Is it right for me?

You will need a strong interest in art, sculpture and architecture, along with a curiosity about the historical and social settings that resulted in such works. It's important you have an appreciation for art and visual culture, but you don't need to have creative skills yourself. You do, however, need strong written skills; this is an essay-based subject. You will need to be able to remember facts and figures but also to analyse and reflect on your understanding of the subject.

You will strengthen your observational skills, develop the knowledge and the vocabulary to analyse art and architecture, and learn how to articulate your ideas.

Subject options

Both AQA and CCEA offer an A/AS level in History of Art. Cambridge International Examinations offers the Pre-U certificate in Art History at Principal level. There seems to be a focus on Western art in the A level syllabus, while the Pre-U also includes some non-Western pieces.

A/AS level in History of Art

The first year provides you with a grounding in art appreciation, while the second year allows you to study the subject in greater depth, along with the option to focus on your areas of interest.

As you might expect, this subject involves looking at images in books, on slides, on stained glass windows, and in museums and galleries. There may be visits to places of art historical interest. Of course, there is the usual classroom and textbook work. Students are also encouraged to do independent reading to support their learning in the classroom. Assessment is by written examination.

An outline based on the AQA syllabus is listed below. You should talk to your chosen school or college to check the exact specification you will be following, as this can vary.

Visual analysis and interpretation (AS)

An introduction to the methodology and terminology of the history of art.

Themes in history of art (AS)

Students learn some significant art historical themes from classical Greece to the art of the twentieth century.

Investigation and interpretation (1) (A2)

Schools have the option of teaching any of the following:

- art and architecture in fifteenth-century Europe
- art and architecture in seventeenth-century Europe
- art and architecture in nineteenth-century Europe
- art and architecture in Europe and the United States of America 1946–2000.

Investigation and interpretation (2) (A2)

Schools have the option of teaching any of the following:

- art and architecture in thirteenth- and fourteenth-century Europe
- art and architecture in sixteenth-century Europe
- art and architecture in eighteenth-century Europe
- art and architecture in Europe and the United States of America 1900–1945.

Top Tip

Most universities will not insist on A level History of Art as an entry requirement for a history of art degree. If the latter is what you want to study, universities may ask for subjects including English, history or perhaps a foreign language.

Cambridge Pre-U in Art History

In the first year, you will study 48 works of art, encompassing visual analysis and contextual knowledge. You will also get the opportunity to study two historical topics, from Gothic art and architecture or the Renaissance right up to art and architecture in the twenty-first century.

In year two, you will carry out an investigation into a theme – perhaps landscape, still life or art and architecture in the city – and you will sit an exam on this subject. You will also complete a 3,000-word dissertation on your choice of topic.

Assessment takes place at the end of the second year and is based on exams and your personal investigation in conjunction with a viva. The viva involves a short presentation and discussion with an examiner about your personal investigation.

Choosing other subjects to go with history of art

History of art obviously goes well with subjects such as art and design, history, English literature and classical civilisation. However, you can study this subject alongside almost any other, including maths and the sciences.

Top Tip

History of art is widely recognised; it appears on the accepted lists at the University of Edinburgh and the University of Sheffield.

History of art at university

A degree in this subject will really develop some of the themes explored at advanced level. Many courses include some fieldwork or visits to places of artistic or architectural influence. Modules might include some of the following.

Core modules

- introduction to the history of art
- the classical tradition
- theory and historiography.

Optional modules

- impacts of the late antique c.350–850
- the art of Anglo-Saxon England, c.600–1066
- the age of the cathedrals: architecture in England c.1050–1250
- East and West: art of the Crusading era
- European art of the High Middle Ages
- art and patronage in fifteenth-century Florence
- art in Venice: from Bellini to Tintoretto
- the art of Holy Russia: painting, piety and power in the principality of Moscow c.1500–1680.

At degree level, art history is most commonly combined with English or history and occasionally with classics, archaeology or a foreign language.

History of art and your future career

Non-graduate jobs in history of art

It may be possible to get a starter position in an auction house, gallery, museum, design company or the antiques business straight after A levels, but increasingly these professions are being seen as graduate entry. Other areas are open to you, too, and you shouldn't have to restrict yourself to jobs related only to history of art.

Graduate jobs directly related to history of art

Most jobs directly related to the history of art require some form of further study, training or experience. Some of the jobs you could consider are listed below.

- **Auctioneer/valuer (fine arts):** identifies and values pieces of art, secures them for auctions and compiles catalogues. This role also involves organising, attending and supervising auctions.
- **Historic buildings inspector/conservation officer:** inspects and reports on buildings of special architectural or historic interest to ensure their preservation and conservation.
- **Museum education officer:** creates a link between a museum and audiences and develops learning opportunities and materials for children or adults in or outside formal education.
- **Museum or gallery conservator/restorer:** assesses and analyses the condition of a particular type of object or types of art. The role also involves carrying out treatments to arrest decay while maintaining the object's integrity.
- **Museum or gallery curator:** responsible for the development and management of a collection, including acquisitions, cataloguing and storage, as well as marketing and presentation to the public through exhibitions, documentation and talks.
- **Museum or gallery exhibitions officer:** researches, organises, mounts and selects objects for exhibitions in museums or art galleries.

Other graduate jobs where a degree in history of art could be useful

- **Archivist:** manages a public or private collection of records (or images) which have historic value by selecting, acquiring, cataloguing and preserving them.
- **Arts administrator:** supports, generates and is responsible for the organisation of artistic activities and groups. Duties include budgeting and marketing.
- **Event organiser:** researches, organises and publicises events which allow businesses and customers to meet. He/she is responsible for choosing venues and liaising with exhibitors, contractors, caterers and the press.

- **Heritage manager:** responsible for the conservation and all aspects of public access to heritage sites. This role also involves developing and marketing a site to visitors, while preserving its character.
- **Heritage officer/interpreter:** communicates the significance of a place or object to visitors through exhibitions, displays, re-enactments and publications.
- **Tourism officer:** develops and promotes tourist attractions to visitors and the tourism industry through events, marketing campaigns and information.

Find out more about history of art

- AQA: www.aqa.org.uk
- Association of Art Historians: www.aah.org.uk
- Cambridge Pre-U: www.cie.org.uk/qualifications
- CCEA: www.rewardinglearning.org.uk
- Creative and Cultural Skills: www.ccskills.org.uk
- Historical Association: www.history.org.uk
- Institute of Conservation: www.icon.org.uk
- Museums Association: www.museumsassociation.org

HOME ECONOMICS

Home economics is a subject that is often misunderstood; this is probably because it used to be all about how to cook and how to work with textiles. Today, home economics at advanced level is a topical subject focused on food, nutrition and health, and how these relate to the society in which we live.

- What are the nutritional properties of proteins and fat?
- How does diet affect life expectancy and quality of life?
- How dangerous are bacteria, additives and agricultural chemicals?

As a student of home economics, these are just some of the questions you may debate and answer during the course.

Is it right for me?

Home economics includes nutrition, science and finances; you will study diet, health and the impact of the choices people make.

Home economics students build up their knowledge of health and well-being, management of resources, nutrition and consumer issues. You will get the chance to learn about technological developments and scientific advances.

Although the subject builds upon GCSE Home Economics, this is not a requirement, so you may still be able to study this subject at advanced level without the corresponding GCSE.

If you have an interest in nutrition, food science, product development or environmental health then home economics could be the right choice for you.

Top Tip

Advanced level home economics is not really a route to becoming a chef; it is a theoretical course, alongside which you will carry out practical investigations and food testing.

Subject options

This subject is available at GCE A/AS level and is offered by AQA, OCR and CCEA. Note that each home economics course can have a slightly different focus. It is also available as a Scottish Higher and Advanced Higher course, known as Home Economics: Health and Food Technology.

A/AS level in Home Economics

The following is based on the CCEA specification. Assessment is carried out by a mixture of final written exams and the research assignment, which makes up 25% of the marks.

Nutrition for optimal health (AS)

Macro- and micro-nutrients and other dietary constituents; nutritional requirements and dietary recommendations.

Priority health issues (AS)

Current research in relation to diet and health, mental health, sexual health; targets, strategies, initiatives and campaigns for optimising health are also studied.

Consumer issues (A2)

Food safety issues; ethical issues for consumers; financial management issues for consumers; consumer information; consumer protection and redress.

Research-based assignment (A2)

Students research an area covered in the specification above and produce a 4,000-word report about it.

Higher and Advanced Higher in Home Economics

The Scottish Qualifications Authority offers Home Economics: Health and Food Technology, which combines practical work with theory and food testing. At Higher level, the syllabus focuses on the properties of food: physical, chemical, nutritional, biological and sensory. At Advanced Higher level, this extends to include the psychology of food, alongside the food chain, food politics and nutrition. Assessment is based on written exams along with a dissertation at Advanced Higher level.

Top Tip

The Scottish Qualifications Authority also offers Home Economics: Lifestyle and Consumer Technology, which covers healthy eating, food preparation skills, and some aspects relating to parenting and child development.

Choosing other subjects to go with home economics

This subject goes well with many others, including the sciences, sociology, health and social care or PE, depending on your interests.

Home economics at university

Home economics courses at university might be called home economics, food and consumer management or food design and technology. You don't necessarily need to have studied home economics beforehand to get a place. If you're interested in related subjects, such as nutrition or dietetics, then most universities prefer you to have studied science subjects.

Degree courses might include:

- consumer law
- food, nutrition and health
- food tourism and gastronomy
- food science
- media and food
- principles of human nutrition.

Top Tip

Home economics appears on the University of Sheffield's and LSE's non-preferred list of subjects, so you would need to supplement it with two preferred A levels if you wanted to be considered by one of these institutions. Check the requirements for your chosen universities.

Home economics and your future career

Non-graduate jobs in home economics

Students could apply to a few jobs that are related to home economics straight after an advanced level qualification. These include working in hospitality and catering, perhaps for a chain of hotels. If you're interested in the consumer side of the subject then it would be possible to start off in a junior administrative role in a consumer agency (such as the Food Standards Agency).

Graduate jobs directly related to home economics

There are very few careers where a first degree in home economics is essential. Some jobs are closely related to a home economics degree but they may also require particular A level subjects (often sciences), experience or further training.

- **Dietitian.** This work will appeal if you're attracted to the nutritional aspects of food science. It involves both a therapeutic and preventative role. Qualification as a dietitian is acquired via a BSc or MSc in Dietetics or a two-year postgraduate course. Candidates need to have a good knowledge of biochemistry and physiology, as well as an ability to relate well to people.

- **Food technologist or scientist in product/process development.**
  This role involves working in three main areas: product development, quality assurance and retailing, with a potential overlap between all three. The aim is to produce food which is safe and nutritious with a consistent flavour, colour and texture. He/she develops new products and processes, and modifies existing ones. He/she works in industry, but also in government and local authority food inspection departments.

Other graduate jobs where a degree in home economics could be useful

- **Industrial buyer or retail buyer:** procures or purchases the highest quality and appropriate quantity of goods and services at the most competitive rate to meet user need according to specified criteria. The work requires continuous development of market knowledge and contacts for new products and services.
- **Production manager:** takes responsibility for all stages of the manufacture of a product, including the planning, co-ordination and control of industrial processes. This can present a range of challenges, both technically and in terms of managing production workers.
- **Quality assurance (QA) manager:** acts to ensure that each product contains the correct materials, correctly made, properly packed, transported, labelled and up to standard when released to the customer. This role involves responsibility for maintaining the quality system and giving advice on any required changes and their implementation. The QA manager also provides training, tools and techniques to enable others to achieve quality.

Find out more about home economics

- AQA: www.aqa.org.uk
- CCEA: www.rewardinglearning.org.uk
- Improve – Food and Drink Skills Council: improveltd.co.uk
- Institute of Food Science and Technology: www.ifst.org
- OCR: www.ocr.org.uk
- SQA: www.sqa.org.uk

INFORMATION AND COMMUNICATION TECHNOLOGY (ICT)

The study of information and communication technology (ICT) will introduce you to a whole range of practical and academic issues relating to computing and information systems. The subject should equip you with some excellent skills and also help to prepare you for university, whether or not you want to work in the ICT field.

Some of the questions that will be answered by studying ICT include the following.

- What is an information system?
- How are ICT projects managed effectively?
- How do I create a website?
- How do I design a spreadsheet?
- What is the most appropriate use of software for different purposes?

Is it right for me?

If you are interested in understanding how organisations and individuals use computers and technology, then ICT might be right for you.

Top Tip

If you are more interested in the theory of computing and how computers work, rather than the use of computers and technology, you might consider computing instead.

You don't need to have any prior knowledge of IT to study this subject but a practical mind, an interest in the subject and good spatial awareness will be a help.

You will get the opportunity to learn about computer systems, networking, hardware and software, along with the use of ICT in business and in life. Handy skills that you will develop include investigation, deduction and problem solving along with project management, teamwork and the ability to communicate your point of view. You will develop a range of technical and creative skills that should be relevant to a variety of different jobs or settings.

Subject options

This subject can be studied as a GCE A/AS level and as an Applied GCE A/AS level. A SQA Higher and Advanced Higher in Information Systems are also available.

A/AS level in ICT

The overall aim of this course is to encourage students to develop an understanding of the fundamentals of ICT and to provide the knowledge and skills suitable for participation in an evolving information-based society.

For an exact definition of the AS and A2 syllabus you will be studying, you should consult your school, college or the exam board itself. ICT is taught through a mixture of classroom input and practical work in the IT lab. Assessment is through written exams and a practical coursework project. ICT courses will include some (or all) of the following elements.

Information, systems and communications
The building blocks of information systems.

Structured practical ICT tasks
Students learn practical skills in design, software development, testing and implementation.

Practical applications of ICT using standard/generic applications software
Students learn about standard applications software as well as online relational and non-relational databases.

Communications technology and its application
This aspect focuses on how IT technology is used as a communication tool between individuals and businesses. Issues such as networking and further uses of ICT are explored.

ICT project
Students work on their own project throughout the course. This is usually an IT solution to a problem encountered by a user.

ICT systems and systems management
This element of the course focuses in more detail on IT and communication systems for business as well as ICT solutions to many business problems.

A/AS level (Applied) in ICT

So what is the difference between the A level in ICT and the Applied A level in ICT? The Applied option is more vocational, and often features more coursework, but should be equally challenging.

Teaching is similar to the traditional A level but there is a much more practice-based emphasis. Real-life case studies, visits to organisations using IT in interesting ways and talks from IT professionals are often part of the teaching methods used. Assessment is mainly by internally assessed portfolios of evidence with the occasional written exam. There are four possible routes for gaining an award in this subject: AS single award (three units), AS double award (six units), A level single award (six units) and A level double award (12 units).

The applied course goes into more detail about some of the ICT functions and how they can be applied in real life; students can choose from a larger range of options with a more specialised vocational focus. As you can see from the example modules below, the applied course is much more about how to do things rather than theoretical or historical considerations:

- advanced spreadsheet design
- creating a website
- data handling
- ICT solutions
- interactive multimedia
- programming
- publishing
- systems analysis
- web management.

Top Tip

Some of the leading universities will not accept Applied A levels (including ICT) for entry to some of their courses. For example, Keele University will not accept Applied A levels for entry to medicine.

Higher and Advanced Higher in Information Systems

At Higher level, you will study 'using information' and 'relational database systems'; you will choose your third unit from 'applied multimedia', 'expert systems' and 'the internet'. Students are assessed by a written exam and a practical coursework task.

The Advanced Higher course extends your knowledge to cover 'database analysis and design' and 'database implementation and testing'. You will have the opportunity to investigate an organisation of your choosing, which will give you some insight into business behaviour. This forms part of your assessment, alongside a written exam.

Choosing other subjects to go with ICT

Good supporting subjects for this one would include business, maths, sciences, art and design, geography, accounting or design and technology. Some students choose ICT and computing together, although this is a narrow combination of subjects that may restrict your university choices.

ICT at university

Students don't necessarily need to have studied advanced level ICT to take it at degree level, but some universities will specify at least one scientific or technical A level.

There is a wide variety of ICT and computer science courses, alongside a selection of more specific degrees, such as software engineering, forensic computing or information systems. Some courses are very theoretical, whereas others are very practical or applied in their emphasis. You should always check the specific nature of a course before applying.

Computing courses, even if they are theoretical, will often consider how IT is applied to business, industry and research. The range of modules covered might include some of the following:

- bioinformatics
- communications and networks
- computational finance
- information security
- logic programming
- managing information systems
- object-oriented software engineering
- object-oriented modelling
- web and internet technologies.

Assessment is carried out via a combination of final exams, coursework and project work.

The different combinations possible with the subject are numerous, but you could combine a degree in ICT or computer science with artificial intelligence, French, management, maths or physics.

Top Tip

ICT is an accepted subject which meets the general entry requirements for the University of Edinburgh and University College London. However, it is accepted only as a fourth subject at Trinity College, Cambridge.

ICT and your future career

Non-graduate jobs in ICT

Given that nearly every organisation needs computers now, you will be an asset if you have an advanced understanding of them, so there should be quite a few junior positions for which you could apply. You may even be able to get IT support work in some organisations without any further qualifications.

Graduate jobs directly related to ICT

Some of the more common jobs include the following.

- **Applications developer:** writes and modifies programs to enable a computer to carry out specific tasks, such as stock control or payroll, typically for technical, commercial and business users.
- **Database administrator:** responsible for the usage, accuracy, efficiency, security, maintenance and development of an organisation's computerised databases.
- **Information technology consultant:** gives independent and objective advice on how best to use information technology to solve business problems.
- **Software engineer:** specifies, develops, documents and maintains computer software programs in order to meet clients' or employers' needs. He/she usually works as part of a team.
- **Systems developer:** sets up the computer operating systems and standard software services essential to the operation of any computer.
- **Systems designer:** takes the specification for the requirements of a computer system and designs it, including hardware, software, communications, installation, testing and maintenance.
- **Web designer:** responsible for the design, layout and coding of a web page. This is known as the 'front end' of websites, as it is what the user sees. The work may also involve multimedia activities, such as video clips, music and other media. Web designers are also known as web producers, internet engineers and multimedia architects.

Other graduate jobs where a degree in ICT could be useful

Information technology is used in every single sector of the economy. The following jobs will make some use of your IT background.

- **IT sales professional:** gives technical advice and guidance to customers pre- or post-installation of their computer systems; he/she may work in conjunction with sales representatives for a computer manufacturer.
- **Magazine journalist:** researches and writes news and feature articles which are suited to the magazine's reader profile.
- **Recruitment consultant, particularly for the IT sector:** obtains the brief for job vacancies from clients and then matches candidates with the relevant qualities to these vacancies and arranges interviews with the clients.
- **Secondary school teacher:** teaches one, or more, specialist subjects to classes of secondary pupils aged 11–18. ICT is currently a shortage subject.

Find out more about ICT

- AQA: www.aqa.org.uk
- Blitz Academy (advice on working in the computer games industry): www.blitzgamesstudios.com/blitz_academy
- CCEA: www.rewardinglearning.org.uk
- Chartered Institute for IT: www.bcs.org
- Creative Skillset: www.creativeskillset.org
- e-Skills UK: www.e-skills.com
- OCR: www.ocr.org.uk
- SQA: www.sqa.org.uk
- WJEC: www.wjec.co.uk

LAW

This subject gives you a good insight into how the English legal system operates. It examines how laws come into being and how they are upheld. As well as the systems of law and justice, students are introduced to the many different types of law that are practised in the UK and their implications for everyday life. In the study of law, students may also engage with some important and interesting issues such as human rights, euthanasia, the impact of EU legislation on our lives and much more.

Is it right for me?

You will develop skills in logical and analytical thinking which, along with a basic understanding of the law, can be useful in many areas of work. The course will help you to understand the process and the reasoning behind the making of laws. You will also develop your knowledge of your own rights and responsibilities.

You don't need any prior knowledge of law to study it at this level. You will be learning a lot of facts about the legal system, which you will then analyse. There is a lot of reading and writing for this subject (as there is when working as a lawyer), so strong written skills are important. For the exams, you will need to memorise case details while also showing your understanding. You may find some common ground with advanced level study in government and politics, and some aspects of history.

Should I study A level Law if I intend to study law at university?

There has long been a debate about whether law is accepted as an A level subject by the top law schools. Certainly, it was not well recognised 10 years ago, but some law departments that didn't consider the subject in the past are now coming round to the idea.

In 2009, the exam board AQA surveyed all UK universities offering law degrees, asking whether they would view A level Law in the same way as other A levels, such as English and History. More than 140 responded positively, including a number of the colleges at Oxford and Cambridge, Durham University, Newcastle University and King's College London. The University of Manchester and London School of Economics indicated that law would need to be supplemented by preferred subjects (see Top Tip on page 183), whereas some universities did not respond. For full details, see store.aqa.org.uk/qual/gce/pdf/AQA-2160-W-UNI-LAW.PDF.

A slightly different outcome was unearthed by the Policy Exchange report *The Hard Truth about 'Soft' Subjects*, as part of their investigation into 'soft' subjects. They discovered that many of the leading research-based universities actually take fairly low numbers of students with A level Law. This was particularly the case at Imperial College, Queen's University Belfast,

University of St Andrews, University College London, University of Oxford and University of Bristol.

If you want to study law at a top university, you may be safer choosing traditional academic subjects. Some leading universities clearly include A/AS level Law on the list of subjects that they don't consider academically rigorous enough (see Top Tip below). This information may change from time to time, so if you have any preferred universities at this stage, you should refer to them for the latest information.

Top Tip

Lancaster University Law School indicates the following: 'We accept A level Law on a par with other A levels.' (See www.lancs.ac.uk/fass/law/prospective/undergrad/admissions.php.)

Warwick University School of Law states: 'We treat Law in the same way as any other subject. We have no preference either way. It is neither an advantage nor a disadvantage.' (See www2.warwick.ac.uk/fac/soc/law/ug/admissions/faq/.)

Other universities are not so positive. For example, the London School of Economics features A level Law on its non-preferred list, which means you would need to choose two other preferred subjects to be considered. Please note that offering three preferred subjects is the favoured combination. (See www2.lse.ac.uk/study/undergraduate/howtoapply/lseentryrequirements.aspx.)

Subject options

This subject is available at GCE A/AS level.

A/AS level in Law

For an exact definition of the AS and A2 syllabus you will be studying, you should consult your school, college or the exam board itself. This subject is offered by AQA, WJEC and OCR. The specifications cover more or less the same ground; differences are mainly in how the material is organised and what the modules are called.

The following outline is based on the AQA syllabus. You will be taught through classroom activities, discussions and applying your theoretical learning to scenarios. You may get a chance to visit a law court. This subject is entirely exam-based and contains no coursework.

Law making and the legal system (AS)

Parliamentary law making; delegated legislation; statutory interpretation; judicial precedent; the civil courts and other forms of dispute resolution; the criminal courts and lay people; the legal profession and other sources of advice and funding; the judiciary.

The concept of liability (AS)

Underlying principles of criminal liability; the courts: procedure and sentencing; liability in negligence; the courts: procedure and damages; formation of contract; breach of contract.

Criminal law (offences against the person) or contract (A2)

Murder; voluntary manslaughter; involuntary manslaughter; non-fatal offences against the person; defences; formation of contracts; contract terms; discharge of contract.

Criminal law (offences against property) or tort, and concepts of law (A2)

- Criminal law (offences against property): theft and robbery; burglary; blackmail; fraud; making off without payment; criminal damage; defences.
- Law of tort: negligence; occupier's liability; nuisance and escape of dangerous things; vicarious liability; defences; remedies.
- Concepts of law: law and morals; law and justice; judicial creativity; fault; balancing conflicting interests.

Choosing other subjects to go with law

Law goes well with a broad range of subjects including English, languages, history and government and politics. It can also complement finance-related subjects such as accounting, business or economics. Some students will combine law with science or maths.

Law at university

A law degree is usually called LLB Laws (Bachelor of Laws) and it will cover the basics in the first year, expanding what is taught at A/AS level:

- criminal law
- elements of contract law
- European law
- public law.

In the second and third years, students have the chance to take some more specialised units, which are aligned to their personal or career interests, perhaps choosing from:

- banking law
- copyright and designs
- human rights law
- international trade law
- medical law
- Russian legal institutions.

Combining law with other degree subjects

Law can be combined with other subjects at degree level. The combinations vary from university to university, but might include:

- law and accounting
- law and business
- law and a modern foreign language
- law and sociology
- law and philosophy.

Top Tip

If you intend to practise law in the future, check that any combined or joint course is a qualifying degree that meets the requirements of the JASB (Joint Academic Stage Board).

Law and your future career

Non-graduate jobs in law

Law is seen by employers as an academically sound and rigorous subject and therefore students with this subject under their belt will be in demand. However, it's also important to emphasise the other transferable skills gained from this qualification, such as problem solving, analytical skills and writing skills. Jobs working in law are mainly reserved for graduates but you may be able to work in junior positions in legal contexts, such as administration in a law firm.

Graduate jobs directly related to law

- **Solicitor and barrister:** both of which require postgraduate qualifications and training.

Other graduate jobs where a degree in law could be useful

There are a number of careers where legal knowledge and skills can be put to use.

- **Advice worker:** employed by local and central government and the voluntary sector. Advice and information are provided to the public or to special client groups in person, in writing and over the telephone.
- **Ancillary legal professions.** If you are attracted to work in the legal field, you could consider an ancillary role. A law degree is not required and postgraduate qualifications are not necessary for all of them. Occupations include barrister's clerk, legal executive (England and Wales), licensed conveyancer and legal secretary.
- **Chartered accountant:** works to ensure effective use of financial resources of individuals or organisations. This role can include auditing, financial management and planning, and giving financial advice.

- **Civil Service fast streamer:** employed in all government departments. Some have legal responsibilities (for example, in the Department for Constitutional Affairs or CPS).
- **Excise and inland customs officer.** This role involves regulating the entry of certain goods through ports and airports, controlling the movement of dutiable materials within the UK and the assessment and collection of VAT.
- **Immigration officer at passport control:** meets passengers and assesses their eligibility for admission.
- **Inspector of health and safety:** inspects factories, quarries, offices, farms and other places of work. He/she ensures that working conditions and machinery are safe and comply with regulations.
- **Local government administrator:** employed in all departments in local authorities.
- **Police officer:** maintains law and order, protects persons and property, prevents crime and deals with emergencies.
- **Prison officer:** keeps people committed by the courts in custody and looks after them with humanity, helping them to lead law-abiding and useful lives in custody and after release.
- **Probation officer:** supervises people placed under probation orders and other forms of suspension and those released from custody.
- **Tax inspector:** determines the tax liabilities of individuals and businesses on behalf of HM Revenue and Customs, including assessment and examination of accounts.
- **Trading standards officer:** promotes, maintains and develops fair trading by inspecting premises, advising traders and consumers, and investigating complaints.

Find out more about law

- AQA: www.aqa.org.uk
- Bar Council: www.barcouncil.org.uk
- Bar Standards Board: www.barstandardsboard.org.uk
- Law Society of England and Wales: www.lawsociety.org.uk
- Law Society of Northern Ireland: www.lawsoc-ni.org
- Law Society of Scotland: www.lawscot.org.uk
- OCR: www.ocr.org.uk
- Skills for Justice: www.skillsforjustice.com
- Solicitors Regulation Authority: www.sra.org.uk
- WJEC: www.wjec.co.uk

LEISURE STUDIES (APPLIED)

This is an Applied A/AS level and has a number of main aims: to give students an insight into the leisure industry within the UK and EU, to equip students with some of the skills and techniques that will enable them to develop a career in the leisure industry, and to encourage an understanding of the benefits of a healthy and active lifestyle. It is ideal for those who want a broad background in the leisure and recreation industry, and the course will allow them to progress to further study, university or employment. This sector keeps growing: people continue to spend money on leisure activities and the industry needs well-qualified people.

Is it right for me?

If you're interested in working in the leisure industry, and if you like project work and investigations, then this subject might interest you. The leisure industry includes sport, fitness and recreation but also extends to cover a range of pursuits including museums, attractions, festivals and shopping. Think of the things people do away from the workplace to have fun, get fit or relax – that's leisure.

No prior knowledge of the industry is required. You will study the theory of the leisure industry and learn some of the knowledge and skills required to be successful in it.

Top Tip

You will develop skills in problem solving, research, evaluation, analysis, critical understanding and working alone or as part of a team.

Subject options

This subject is available at Applied A/AS level (single award) offered by OCR and Edexcel. The AQA Applied A level in Leisure Studies, which includes the double award, is being withdrawn.

A/AS level (Applied) in Leisure Studies

The different exam boards cover very similar ground; the main differences are the titles of the modules and the way in which the material is organised and structured. The following outline is based on the OCR specification. As well as classroom work and independent research into the sector, you might get the chance to visit different types of leisure and recreation organisations. The majority of your assessment will be based on a portfolio of coursework, but there will also be some written exams. Your chosen sixth form or college will be able to advise you on the content of your particular course.

Exploring leisure (AS)
Definitions within the leisure industry; range, scale and importance of the leisure industry in the UK and Europe; sectors within the leisure industry; key factors which influence access, participation and barriers in leisure; role of the media in leisure.

Customer service in the leisure industry (AS)
Principles of customer service; needs of internal and external customers; customer service skills and personal presentation; assessing the quality of customer service in leisure.

Leisure industry practice (AS)
Safe working practices in the leisure industry; key aspects of marketing used in the leisure industry; budgeting in leisure organisations; measurement of quality in leisure organisations; key business systems used in leisure organisations.

Event management (A2)
Event feasibility; teamwork; marketing the event; financing the event; occasion management; carrying out the event; evaluation of the event.

Human resources in the leisure industry (A2)
Employment opportunities in the leisure industry; human resource planning; recruitment and selection; induction, training and development; staff motivation; performance management and termination of employment; influence of technology on HR and on training needs within the leisure industry.

Leisure in the outdoors (A2)
Development of leisure in the outdoors; types of leisure in the outdoors; organisations involved in leisure in the outdoors; choosing, planning and participating in a project in the outdoors; managing the impacts of leisure in the outdoors.

Choosing other subjects to go with leisure studies
This subject goes well with PE and with other applied subjects, such as business studies, ICT, and travel and tourism. However, the content of the Applied A level in Leisure Studies may overlap with travel and tourism, PE and business studies, so you should check with your sixth form or college whether this will cause any issues for you.

The scientific content of A level PE might make it a more appropriate choice than leisure studies for some degrees, including certain sports science or physiotherapy courses. See *How do universities view PE?* on page 226.

Leisure studies at university

There are a number of different leisure- and recreation-related degrees, such as leisure and recreation management, sports science or recreation and leisure studies. Check the entry requirements and the content for each course as there may be quite a bit of variation between them (for example, some options are offered through a university's business school and are far more business-oriented).

Top Tip

Many leisure courses are sandwich courses, meaning that students work for a year in the leisure and recreation industry at some point during their studies. Other courses might offer a year abroad option.

The most common type of degree in this area is leisure (and recreation) management. Typical units for such a course might include:

- foundations of leisure
- leisure analysis and information technology
- leisure business
- leisure facility management
- leisure policy
- sport industry
- sport tourism.

Combining leisure studies with other degree subjects

You may be able to study a degree in leisure alongside subjects such as business and management, accounting, nutrition, sports science or computing.

Leisure studies and your future career

Non-graduate jobs in leisure studies

There is a great demand for staff in this ever-changing sector and therefore it's possible for students with an A level in this subject to start working at junior supervisory levels in a variety of settings. As well as knowledge gained from the course, students need to emphasise their skills in teamwork, communication, customer service and using initiative. As their careers develop, students may want to consider moving up the career ladder by studying for a relevant on-the-job qualification.

Graduate jobs directly related to leisure studies

- **Betting shop manager:** responsible for running a betting shop profitably, organising, recruiting and training staff, security, and for ensuring fast and accurate payment of winnings.
- **Fitness centre manager:** responsible for the day-to-day running of the business, the design of activity programmes, budgeting, customer care, market research and marketing, membership sales and staff supervision, development and training.
- **Leisure centre manager:** promotes, organises and runs a leisure centre in either the public or private sector. He/she is effectively in charge of several small business operations: catering, personnel, customer relations, bars, promotions and financial planning.
- **Outdoor pursuits manager:** responsible for the provision of facilities and instruction in a range of outdoor activities. Duties include staff management, health and safety of clients, planning day and evening activities, and handling customers' complaints.
- **Personal trainer:** carries out fitness assessments and provides physical fitness and lifestyle health programmes, mainly in private sector health clubs or hotels but sometimes in organisations wishing to provide facilities for their employees.
- **Sports administrator:** works within a sport's governing body or the sports councils throughout the UK, dealing with financial, organisational and administrative aspects of their sport. This role may involve national travel to support events.
- **Sports development officer:** encourages people to take part in sport by promoting their sport to target groups. He/she usually works for a governing body or professional association.
- **Theme park manager.** This role involves recruiting staff, dealing with finances, ensuring high standards of presentation and service, marketing the park and liaising with other management staff.
- **Tourism officer:** plans and co-ordinates leisure activities, usually on a geographic basis for a local authority.

Other graduate jobs where a degree in leisure studies could be useful

- **Event organiser:** organises conferences, events or exhibitions, liaises with clients, is responsible for administration and manages staff and contractors.
- **Further education or higher education lecturer.** This role involves teaching classes on aspects of leisure and recreation by means of lectures, tutorials and practical skills.

- **Newspaper journalist:** responsible for news or information gathering and reporting. The role involves developing contacts, interviewing personalities, attending press conferences and producing copy to a deadline.
- **Public relations officer:** promotes events and sponsorship deals, and presents sport and leisure topics to the media.
- **Retail manager.** Specialist sports retail companies could offer management posts in buying, merchandising or store management.

Find out more about leisure studies

- Chartered Institute for the Management of Sport and Physical Activity: www.cimspa.co.uk
- Edexcel: www.edexcel.com
- Fitness Industry Association (FIA): www.fia.org.uk
- OCR: www.ocr.org.uk
- People 1st: www.people1st.co.uk
- Skills Active: www.skillsactive.com

MATHEMATICS AND FURTHER MATHEMATICS

Mathematics is at the core of many of the things we know about life, the world around us and even the movements of substances inside our bodies. What's the best way of predicting the likelihood of something happening? How fast is a particular planet spinning? How does the economy work in detail? How much profit will a company make? Trying to answer any of these questions involves the use of numbers and mathematics. This subject builds on the basics learned at GCSE or Standard level, as well as introducing new concepts and new ways to solve particular problems.

Is it right for me?

Maths has a reputation for being a well-recognised subject but also a tough one. You will need a good understanding of the basics (including algebra) from GCSE, so a grade B or higher is often required. If you found GCSE level maths challenging or you struggled with some of the concepts, then advanced level might not be the right choice for you.

Maths can be a very satisfying subject, when you start to get to grips with sophisticated techniques and can solve long, challenging problems. You will develop skills of analysis and logic that will provide a solid basis for further study in maths, physics (and other sciences), engineering, computing, geography and economics. These skills can also be applied to a range of jobs.

Top Tip

The AS level in Use of Maths is not seen to be an alternative to AS Maths by the country's top universities. The University of Sheffield features the subject on its non-preferred list. The University of Edinburgh considers it an approved subject but advises each applicant to check whether the subject is accepted for their chosen degree.

Subject options

Maths is offered through a number of different qualifications, including GCE A/AS level Maths and Further Maths. A/AS level Statistics is also offered by OCR, while AS Use of Maths from AQA offers a slightly more applied approach to the subject. Mathematical thinking can be tested further through the Advanced Extension Award (AEA) or the Sixth Term Exam Paper (STEP).

Maths is a compulsory component of the International Baccalaureate Diploma, with a higher level further maths option to be introduced in 2012. The subject can also be studied as a Cambridge Pre-U or at SQA Higher and Advanced Higher level.

Which maths options should I choose?   ?

- Mechanics covers forces and motion and is relevant to physics, engineering and PE.
- Statistics is the study of the collection, presentation and analysis of data and is used in psychology, geography, biology and economics.
- Decision maths is used in computer science, management and economics; decision algorithms can be put to use in solving many different problems.

You should talk to your maths tutors at school and at your chosen sixth form or college to discuss your mathematical strengths and interests; they will be able to help you decide on the most appropriate option for you.

A/AS level in Mathematics

Mathematics is really divided between pure maths and applied maths (where maths is applied to different contexts and uses). The qualification involves a lot of class work, with students learning new theories and then carrying out practice examples. You will spend a lot of your time using graphs and charts, equations and calculator work. Most units of the Maths A level are entirely exam-based, although coursework may be an option for one of the units in statistics.

The exam boards tend to give schools and colleges some choice about the options studied in the different mathematical areas. For an exact definition of the AS and A2 syllabus you will be studying, you should consult your school, college or the exam board itself. The main topics are given below.

Pure mathematics
All courses include pure maths, which develops some of your GCSE content to a more advanced level and introduces calculus. It is the foundation for what you do in other areas of maths and includes topics such as trigonometry, parametric equations, vectors and functions.

Mechanics
This aspect looks at physical forces and focuses on the way objects move. Topics studied include Newton's law of motion, linear momentum, centre of mass, equilibrium, energy, work and power, elasticity and inertia.

Statistics and probability
Collecting and presenting data; working out valid sample sizes from a group of data; probability; variables; mean value and spread; hypothesis testing.

Decision mathematics

Decision maths is part of the broader subject of discrete maths. It includes algorithms, networks, linear programming, game theory and dynamic programming.

Top Tip

The AS level in Maths requires students to take two compulsory core modules of pure maths alongside one optional applied module (chosen from mechanics, statistics or decision maths).

The full A level in Maths combines four core pure modules with two applied modules chosen from statistics, mechanics or decision maths.

A/AS level in Further Maths

If you are a strong mathematician intending to study maths (or a related subject such as engineering, computing or sciences) at university, then further maths will be a useful addition. It can only be taken alongside Maths A/AS level and you're likely to need a grade A at GCSE. The qualification introduces more complex theories and should deepen your understanding of A level Maths; students sometimes say that it makes A level Maths seem simpler.

A number of schools of mathematics at the top universities advise taking further maths if the subject is available to you; they may be more flexible in their offer if you have opted for this subject.

Top Tip

'Informed Choices' (the Russell Group guide to making decisions about post-16 education) indicates that both maths and further maths are facilitating subjects most often required by the leading universities.

The study of maths and further maths together has caused some issues in the past for applicants to medical schools. Most will now accept both A level Maths and AS Further Maths alongside one another, but you should research your options fully if taking both to full A level (see www.furthermaths.org.uk/files/Medical_Schools_entry_requirement_June_2011_1.1.pdf).

Higher and Advanced Higher in Mathematics

The Higher level qualification focuses on algebra, geometry, trigonometry and elementary calculus, and is assessed by closed book written exams. This knowledge is extended at Advanced Higher level, covering matrix algebra, complex numbers and vectors. An alternative option is available in the shape of the Advanced Higher in Applied Maths, with a choice of studying mechanics or statistics.

International Baccalaureate Diploma in Mathematics

Maths is available at Standard and Higher level; further maths is currently on offer at Standard level but is about to be introduced at Higher level. The IB includes an internally assessed coursework element alongside exams; this is designed to allow students to communicate mathematical ideas effectively and work outside the restrictions of written exams.

Cambridge Pre-U in Mathematics

Available in the Principal subjects of maths and further maths, the qualification is entirely exam-based at the end of the two-year course. The course comprises two components of pure maths and one of applied maths, which includes mechanics and statistics.

Alternatively, if you are looking to broaden your learning, you can study one-year Short Courses in maths (statistics with pure maths) and further maths through the Cambridge Pre-U curriculum. The Short Course in maths can introduce you to mathematical theories that would be useful for non-maths subjects at university, such as biology, geography or business. The Short Course in further maths extends learning beyond the Principal subject in maths but stops short of the further maths Principal subject.

Advanced Extension Award (AEA) and Sixth Term Exam Paper (STEP)

If you're looking for a way to develop your understanding of advanced level maths and to demonstrate a greater depth of mathematical knowledge, you might want to go for the AEA or STEP. Many of the leading universities value these papers and some (including the University of Warwick and the University of Cambridge) make them a requirement for maths and related degrees. Neither paper requires additional teaching, although you will need to prepare for the exams.

Aimed at the top 10% of students, the AEA in Maths allows you to apply the skills learned at Maths A level to solve a range of unfamiliar problems. Students answer a series of questions in examination conditions and will be assessed on the extent to which they can apply and communicate their understanding of mathematics; this might include problem solving and deductive reasoning, critical analysis, evaluation and synthesis. The paper is focused on core maths.

STEP was originally designed as an entry test for the University of Cambridge, but is now more widely used. It is aimed at the top 5% of A level Maths students. It can demonstrate potential, help to differentiate between strong candidates and also be a good preparation for the advanced mathematical thinking required at university. The questions include core, mechanics and statistics and probability.

You are advised to prepare by completing past papers. Your school may offer preparation sessions or you can get help through the Mathematics in Education and Industry (MEI) charity (see www.mei.org.uk/?page=stepandaea for details). For detailed information and examples of past papers for AEA, see Edexcel's website at www.edexcel.com/quals/gce/aea/9801/Pages/default.aspx. Find out more about STEP at www.admissionstests.cambridgeassessment.org.uk/adt.

Choosing other subjects to go with mathematics

Maths goes well with subjects such as physics, chemistry, computing or ICT, business, and biology. However, it can just as easily be combined with other subjects such as a modern foreign language, philosophy or music.

Mathematics at university

In order to study mathematics at a higher level, you will need to have achieved a good grade in the subject at A level. Degree courses can focus on different areas of maths, such as pure or applied mathematics, and may offer the opportunity to specialise in discrete maths or statistics. Examples of possible modules are listed below.

- Core modules:
  - calculus
  - geometry
  - introduction to dynamical systems
  - linear methods.

- Optional modules might include:
  - financial mathematics
  - quantum mechanics
  - space–time physics
  - thermodynamics and information theory.

Combining mathematics with other degree subjects

You can combine maths with plenty of other subjects at degree level; common joint degrees offered by universities include French and maths, maths and philosophy, maths and physics, maths and management, and maths with computer science.

Mathematics and your future career

Non-graduate jobs in mathematics

Mathematics is a very attractive subject to employers, as many organisations require some kind of mathematical work. It may be possible to get junior positions in retail, banking, insurance and many other areas straight after A levels. Alternatively, school-leaver training programmes are on the increase.

'I did not go to university in the end as I discovered Apprenticeships in accounting, which lead up to degree level qualifications. Maths particularly helped in the decision to go into accounting as I found it was the subject I was best at, so I wanted to use my skills as best I could.'

Abigail Tindall

Graduate jobs directly related to mathematics

- **Actuarial work.** An actuary studies past events to predict future outcomes. This often involves the application of probability and statistics to financial affairs, especially life assurance, pensions and social security.
- **Economic and statistical work.** A statistician collects, analyses and interprets quantitative information. This work is carried out in many organisations and research establishments, notably the Civil Service, the NHS and large industrial and commercial organisations.
- **Scientific research and development.** Most openings are for applied mathematicians with relevant higher degrees. Much of the work is carried out in multidisciplinary teams with other scientists.
- **Secondary school teacher.** You will normally have to undertake a PGCE before entering this field.

Other graduate jobs where a degree in mathematics could be useful

- **Accountancy.** Employers of trainee accountants rarely specify degree disciplines but all look for numeracy and literacy skills, and the capacity to establish interpersonal relationships rapidly.
- **Insurance and pensions.** Insurance companies offer many openings in addition to actuarial work, including investment analysis, systems technology and underwriting.
- **Management consultancy.** This covers a wide range of applications, with the type of work varying between sectors. Competition for posts is fierce.

- **Retail banking and personal financial services.** The growth in applications of information technology has led to an increase in careers for graduates in areas covering communications, data processing and funds transfer.
- **Software engineer:** specifies, develops, documents and maintains computer software programs to meet the needs of clients or an employer.

Find out more about mathematics

- AQA: www.aqa.org.uk
- Cambridge Pre-U: www.cie.org.uk/qualifications
- CCEA: www.rewardinglearning.org.uk
- Edexcel: www.edexcel.com
- Financial Skills Partnership: www.financialskillspartnership.org.uk
- Institute of Mathematics: www.ima.org.uk
- International Baccalaureate Diploma: www.ibo.org/diploma/curriculum/group5/
- Maths Careers: www.mathscareers.org.uk
- OCR: www.ocr.org.uk
- Royal Statistical Society: www.rss.org.uk
- SQA: www.sqa.org.uk
- WJEC: www.wjec.co.uk

MEDIA STUDIES

Do you want to know how the media works in this country and overseas? Do you have an interest in the film industry, print-based media and new media? Would you like to make your own media productions? Then read on.

If you study media, you can gain experience of both the theoretical and practical aspects of the subject. Whatever course you choose, there is usually a practical production element, but some courses are more vocationally oriented than others. In the more vocational courses, students will study the working methods of current practitioners in the media and gain an understanding of the job roles within the different areas. In the more theoretical or academic courses, students might focus more on the different genres of media, such as film, documentary, the press, and so on, and carry out a critical analysis of them.

Is it right for me?

The course will introduce you to the role of the media in everyday twenty-first-century life; you will learn about media regulation, the changing face of the media and the influence of the media today. Whether you choose a traditional or an applied qualification, the course is partially essay-based and you will need to research, interpret and evaluate. The practical element will depend on the facilities your chosen school or college can offer; options include print, radio, film and web design.

No prior knowledge is needed for this course but candidates must have a good standard of literacy, some creative flair and an interest in the sector.

Subject options

Media studies is available as a GCE A/AS level (by OCR, AQA and WJEC) and as an Applied A/AS level in Media: Communication and Production (by Edexcel). The SQA offers a Higher course in media studies. Alternatively, if you are more focused on film, see the information on *Film studies* on page 134.

A/AS level in Media Studies

The following outline is based on the AQA syllabus. Assessment is by a combination of written papers, coursework essays and media productions. At A2 level, you will be asked to research and write a 2,000-word essay linked to your own production.

Investigating media (AS)
Media texts, concepts and contexts; e-media, broadcasting and print; printed communications; broadcast fiction; film fiction; documentary; lifestyle; music, news and sport.

Creating media (AS)

Preparing a practical production; technical and creative skills; knowledge of relevant conventions; target audiences; production media; evaluation.

Critical perspectives (A2)

Representations in the media; impact of digital media; cross-media issues and debates; media theories.

Media: research and production (A2)

Research into a media text or theme; critical investigation; a linked production piece.

A/AS level (Applied) in Media: Communication and Production

The Applied A level still retains its theoretical content, although the main focus of the qualification is on practical activities. There is overlap with the mainstream A level in Media Studies, so you wouldn't study for both qualifications.

Teaching is by a combination of classroom work, talks by people in the media field, possible work experience opportunities and practical work. Students may also spend a lot of time working with different media (for example, print, TV, film, photography and so on). You will be assessed on the production of a media product (and the associated pre- and post-production evidence), on coursework and on written exams. The qualification is offered by Edexcel and covers the following.

Industries, texts and audience (AS)

Students learn different ways of looking at and analysing the media, considering aspects such as narrative, representation and ideology.

Skills development in media (AS)

Developing the practical skills needed to create your own video and your own printed publicity for a video.

Media production brief (AS)

Using the skills and knowledge learned in units 1 and 2 to prepare and create your own moving image product.

Researching for media production (A2)

Students develop an idea for a video product and research its viability from a professional and commercial point of view.

Media production project (A2)

Students make a film or video and are expected to show detailed evidence of how the production process was planned, using industry standard documentation techniques.

Professional practice in the media industries (A2)

Developing the knowledge of how media production works in different media industries, as well as the moral, legal and ethical context of those industries.

Higher in Media Studies

The Higher qualification in Media Studies includes units on 'media analysis (fiction)', 'media analysis (non-fiction)' and 'media production'. You will learn to interpret media texts and their underlying meaning and purpose. You will also get the opportunity to produce your own pieces of work, on which you will be assessed. The course also features exam-based assessment.

Top Tip

Media studies has a reputation for being a 'soft' subject and some of the leading universities will consider it only as a third or fourth choice, alongside more traditional subjects. For example, the University of Sheffield and University College London do not include media studies on their preferred subject lists.

Choosing other subjects to go with media studies

Subjects that might work well with media studies include communication and culture, English literature, drama and theatre studies, art and design, sociology or psychology. Considering media studies' poor reputation in some circles, make sure you choose your other A level subjects wisely if you intend to apply to a top university. You don't have to study media at advanced level to pick up the subject at university.

Media studies at university

At university level, degrees in media studies can come in many different forms. On the one hand, they can focus on a very specific area of media (digital media, media production, print media, television media or interactive media, for example); on the other hand they can relate to general media, such as media studies or media arts.

Examples of some media arts degree options are given below:

- French cinema
- Hollywood star performances
- media and history: Holocaust
- modernism
- postmodern film and television
- television genre
- women's cinema.

Media can be combined with subjects such as English, a modern foreign language, IT and many others.

Media studies and your future career

Non-graduate jobs in media studies

Advanced level media will give you good skills and an insight into the profession. The media profession is notoriously difficult to get into and you have to be prepared to make contacts and often work on an unpaid basis to build experience until you get your first break. Non-media careers are still open to you.

Graduate jobs directly related to media studies

Many students on these courses are interested in gaining employment in various aspects of the media industry. Careers in the media, however, are highly sought after and competition is likely to be fierce.

- **Broadcast assistant (radio):** assists with the production and presentation of programmes for local and national radio stations.
- **Broadcasting presenter:** fronts the programme; specific responsibilities vary depending on the programme.
- **Journalist:** reports on news and other areas of interest for newspapers, periodicals, radio and TV.
- **Multimedia programmer:** researches, develops and produces materials for new media-based company activities.
- **Programme researcher (broadcasting/film/video):** acts as an assistant producer with responsibility for the conception and implementation of a programme.
- **Radio producer:** responsible for initiating ideas, selling these to commissioning editors and managing the technical and creative team to produce the final programme.
- **Television/film/video producer:** undertakes the artistic interpretation of materials and directs the production of shows or films.
- **Television production assistant:** provides organisational and secretarial services for the programme director.

Other graduate jobs where a degree in media studies could be useful

- **Advertising account executive:** takes overall responsibility for co-ordination, planning and organisation of advertising campaigns.
- **Arts administrator:** acts as facilitator for the exhibition and preservation of cultural forms, including performing, visual and heritage arts.
- **Event organiser:** identifies potential business and researches, writes, plans and runs all types of conferences on behalf of a client or his/her own organisation.
- **Information officer/manager:** ensures effective communication of information relating to a particular field of interest.

- **Market research executive:** undertakes systematic research to determine the potential market for a product or service.
- **Public relations account executive:** works with clients in presenting their image to the public. He/she decides on strategies to be used and which media would be the most effective.

Find out more about media studies

- AQA: www.aqa.org.uk
- British Film Institute: www.bfi.org.uk/education-research
- Creative Skillset: www.creativeskillset.org
- Edexcel: www.edexcel.com
- OCR: www.ocr.org.uk
- SQA: www.sqa.org.uk
- WJEC: www.wjec.co.uk

MODERN LANGUAGES

Which modern language would you like to study? The list of languages on offer at advanced level is vast and includes French, German, Spanish, Italian, Portuguese, Gaelic, Welsh, Irish, Arabic, Modern Hebrew, Japanese, Urdu, Mandarin Chinese, Turkish, Russian, Dutch, Gujarati, Persian and many more.

The study of a modern language at A level not only allows you to communicate with people from other countries, but it also provides an insight into the cultures and histories of the countries where the language is spoken. If you studied French, for instance, you could also end up studying Impressionist paintings or other aspects of France's history or culture.

Is it right for me?

If you enjoy communicating and learning new words, and you have the talent (or the discipline) for remembering things, then studying a modern language could be for you. In today's global society, the ability to communicate in other languages and to understand other cultures is invaluable. A range of opportunities awaits language students – not just further study of the same subject.

A level (and equivalent) study builds upon the grammar and vocabulary you started at GCSE but extends your learning to cover current affairs, literature or the history of the society you are studying. In order to do well on an A level language course, you will often need a good grade (A or B) in the language at GCSE so that you will be able to build on your prior learning. A good grounding in English language is also helpful, so that you can understand the grammar. Some students experience a jump from GCSE to advanced level standard.

Some sixth forms offer the option to take a new language at A level, such as Russian or Italian; this might involve taking a GCSE in Year 12, followed by the full A level in Year 13. If you're considering this option, you'll need to be prepared for some hard work; it also helps if you have a good track record in another language at GCSE level.

Top Tip

You can choose to study a modern language, which will allow you to communicate with speakers of other languages, or an ancient language, which will give you an insight into the past. See page 90 for information on ancient languages such as Classical Greek, Latin or Biblical Hebrew.

Subject options

You can study a modern language at GCE A/AS level, Cambridge Pre-U Principal subject and Short Course, and SQA Higher and Advanced Higher. A language is a compulsory part of the International Baccalaureate Diploma.

Course content

Irrespective of the language you choose and the qualification or the exam board your school or college uses, your course will include some (or all) of the following elements.

- **Speaking.** You will be expected to converse regularly in the language, and learn new vocabulary and verbs. You may also take part in role plays and you may have to make a presentation as part of the oral exam.
- **Listening.** Students often find the listening part of learning a new language difficult. Throughout the course, you will listen to the language in different contexts, such as news reports, song lyrics and conversations.
- **Reading.** You will also have to do a lot of reading of different types of materials; this could be newspapers, literary texts, business letters, emails, and so on.
- **Writing.** The kind of writing skills you may need to develop as part of this A level include judging the right form and tone for a particular piece of written communication, as well as ensuring it is grammatically and linguistically sound. Tasks such as writing a reply to a letter, making a job application or writing a promotional leaflet may all be included.
- **Aspects of culture and society.** Some foreign language courses also include a separate element dealing with the culture and society of the country where the language is predominantly spoken. This could be related to literature, the environment, the media, health-care issues or many other topics.

Teaching is carried out via a combination of language conversations and listening, written exercises, and reading practice. Assessment is by a combination of written exams, oral exams, listening exams, reading comprehension and a small element of coursework.

Top Tip

If English isn't your first language, an A level in your native language (with the exception of some of the dedicated first language courses such as Welsh or Gaelic) might not be counted by the leading universities. You'll need to check any requirements carefully.

'We accept language A levels from all applicants, regardless of background or whether they might be a native speaker.'

Durham University, www.durham.ac.uk

'An A level (or equivalent) in your first/native language may not be counted.'

London School of Economics, www.lse.ac.uk

'We are unable to accept, from non-native speakers of English, an A level from your native language. If you are indeed taking a native language A level, you will be required to take a fourth A level in any subject except General Studies and Critical Thinking, and subsequently achieve a Grade A.'

Brighton and Sussex Medical School, www.bsms.ac.uk

Choosing other subjects to go with a modern language

You may choose to study more than one language at A level or you may wish to combine one language with contrasting subjects. Languages go well with almost anything, but popular subject combinations might include English literature, history, music, business, law or mathematics.

Modern languages at university

Languages are a popular option at university level. You may wish to study the language on its own, in combination with literature, or literature alone. You will need a good A level grade in the language you wish to pursue at university. Success in one language at advanced level often gives you the opportunity to study additional (unfamiliar) languages at university.

As well as degrees in specific languages or literature, many institutions offer a degree in combined modern languages. To get onto one of these courses, you often need to have studied two languages at A level.

On the whole, a degree in a modern language will develop a very high competence in the language and will be much broader in its scope than the subject at A level.

Modules on a French degree course might include:

- advanced French linguistics
- cinema in France
- French: the linguist's view
- landmarks: reading the classics of French literature
- language, communication and society
- textual revolutions: writing in nineteenth-century France.

Combining modern languages with other degree subjects

Studying a modern language jointly with another degree subject can be an attractive option. It's quite common to see combinations with English, politics, maths, history, classics, music, anthropology, travel and tourism, management, law and many others subjects.

Top Tip

Did you know that choosing a modern (or ancient) language might help to keep your options open if you are unsure what you will end up studying at university? Described as facilitating subjects (in 'Informed Choices', a Russell Group guide to making decisions about studies), languages are some of the subjects that are most often required as part of a university's entry requirements.

Modern languages and your future career

Non-graduate jobs in modern languages

Languages are a desirable asset at any level of employment. If you want to go into work straight after A levels, you could try approaching companies that do business with foreign countries, or you could target tourism industries, such as airlines, travel agencies and tour operators. You may only start at a junior level, but as there isn't so much of a graduate culture in these sectors, you should be able to progress quickly if you are good at your job.

Graduate jobs directly related to modern languages

There are a few roles where modern languages are central to the job. These include translation and interpreting work, teaching modern languages, some areas of journalism and some areas of work within the Diplomatic Service. In many cases, however, the languages you have learned become a secondary factor after the main skills and knowledge needed for the job. Having said that, they can often come in handy later on in your career, so it's important not to let your skills get too rusty.

Other graduate jobs where a degree in modern languages could be useful

- **Buyer/purchaser:** promotes and negotiates sales of products or services to customers worldwide.
- **Chartered accountant:** provides financial information, maintains general accounting systems and performs audits for clients on their UK and/or foreign operations.
- **Diplomatic Service.** Most posts abroad involve dealing with representatives of overseas governments, explaining British foreign policy and negotiating

over different issues or, in some cases, promoting exports and assisting trade.

- **Distribution/logistics manager:** co-ordinates the supply, movement and storage of goods and raw materials, including operational management.
- **English as a foreign language teacher:** teaching English to foreign students either in the UK or overseas.
- **Marketing.** This role involves analysing market information and promoting products worldwide with a view to achieving optimum market share and profitability.
- **Publishing and printing.** Initially you are likely to be recruited into sales, marketing, production, finance, editorial or administration. Over a third of the books published in the UK are sold overseas.
- **Solicitor.** Even in the UK, solicitors' services are offered in 22 languages and many big commercial firms have offices in trading nations worldwide.

Find out more about modern languages

- AQA: www.aqa.org.uk
- Cambridge Pre-U: www.cie.org.uk/qualifications
- CCEA: www.rewardinglearning.org.uk
- Chartered Institute of Linguists: www.iol.org.uk
- Edexcel: www.edexcel.com
- Institute of Translation and Interpreting: www.iti.org.uk
- International Baccalaureate Diploma: www.ibo.org/diploma/curriculum/group2
- National Centre for Languages (CILT): www.cilt.org.uk
- OCR: www.ocr.org.uk
- SQA: www.sqa.org.uk
- Why Study Languages?: www.whystudylanguages.ac.uk
- WJEC: www.wjec.co.uk

MUSIC AND MUSIC TECHNOLOGY

This subject will introduce you to a wide variety of music. You will be expected to do your own performing and composing, but you should be given a considerable amount of freedom in choosing the style, genre or repertoire. In essence, this course is for those who want to develop a career in music or simply deepen their musical knowledge and appreciation.

For those who choose to study music technology, the emphasis is much more on the study of music through technology and how to use technology to make music effectively. It also shows students what an incredible impact technology, and particularly digital technology, has had on music. While there is some overlap with A level Music, as students learn about musical traditions (for example, Western classical music and jazz), the emphasis is always on how technology is used in relation to those traditions or styles. There is also a greater emphasis on analysing modern popular music.

Is it right for me?

If you have studied music previously and have the talent to play an instrument or sing, then you might like to consider the subject. Entry requirements vary, but often you need to have reached Grade 5 in music or voice, or to have studied GCSE Music. It helps (and can often be a requirement) to be able to read music or music notation.

Part of the course will be theoretical and historical, looking at the way music has developed and evolved. You will spend your time listening to music as well as creating your own; learning about different genres and listening to new and different musicians or composers will help to extend your musical awareness and enhance your own musical style.

Although all music courses have an essential practical element, music technology is particularly reliant on coursework. The subject has more of a focus on popular music, including rock, reggae or hip hop.

Whether you intend to follow a career in music or not, the skills gained from this subject will be useful; self-discipline, dedication, creativity and logical thinking are all very relevant for further study and the workplace.

Top Tip

If your extended performance for A level Music exceeds Grade 6 difficulty then you can gain additional credit; however, if your performance falls below this level then your marks will be restricted.

Subject options

You can study music and music technology at GCE A/AS level. In Scotland, music can be studied up to Advanced Higher level, with the option to specialise in performing or performing with technology. Music is also an option offered by the International Baccalaureate Diploma and the Cambridge Pre-U.

A/AS level in Music

Whichever exam board your school uses, the course is likely to include performance, the history of music, listening, comprehension, composing and understanding the mechanics of music. For an exact definition of the AS and A2 syllabus you will be studying, you should start by consulting your chosen sixth form or college.

The following outline is based on the AQA specification. You will be assessed by a combination of written exams, coursework and observed performances. In the AQA course at AS level, 30% of your marks come from a written exam, 30% from composition and 40% from performance; at A level, the written paper carries 40% of the marks, with 30% each coming from composition and from performance.

- **Influences on music (AS).** The Western classical tradition; choral music in the baroque period; music theatre; British popular music (1960 to the present day).
- **Composing: creating musical ideas (AS).** Compositional techniques; free composition or pastiche in response to a given brief; arranging.
- **Performing: interpreting musical ideas (AS).** Solo and/or ensemble performances; technology-based performances.
- **Music in context (A2).** The Western classical tradition; English choral music in the twentieth century; chamber music; jazz and blues.
- **Composing: creating musical ideas (A2).** Compositional techniques; free composition or pastiche in response to a given brief; arranging.
- **Performing: a musical performance (A2).** A choice of solo, acoustic and/or technology-based performances.

A/AS level in Music Technology

You will learn by listening to musical works, reading about the history of music and through the practical work of composing and performing. It helps to be comfortable with technology, as you will spend plenty of time using it. Assessment is by written examination, performance and coursework; much of the course is based on practical and coursework activities, but some of this assessment will need to be taken under controlled exam conditions.

Edexcel is the only exam board currently offering this course. A brief outline of the syllabus is given below.

- **Music technology portfolio 1 (AS).** Using music and music technology skills, students prepare a sequenced-realised performance, multi-track recording and creative sequenced arrangement. The unit includes MIDI sequencing and multi-track recording and arrangement.
- **Listening and analysing (AS).** The development of popular music from 1910 onwards; you will gain an overview of the main styles and trends and an extended knowledge of two particular styles of music.
- **Music technology portfolio 2 (A2).** This unit builds on the AS unit but also includes composition and detailed study of the development of technology-based music.
- **Analysing and producing (A2).** The final unit allows you to develop and demonstrate your knowledge of music and music technology. Assessment of this unit is based on a combination of written work, manipulation of recorded music and practical production skills – all under exam conditions.

Higher and Advanced Higher in Music

The syllabus for both the Higher and the Advanced Higher includes units in 'music: composing', 'music: listening' and a choice between 'performing' or 'performing with technology'. Assessment takes the form of a written exam, along with live performance, composition, MIDI sequencing or sound engineering and production.

International Baccalaureate Diploma in Music

Options are available at Standard and Higher level, involving composition, performance, musical perception and critical analysis of a range of styles. At Standard level, students choose from creating, solo performing or group performing; at Higher level, you will be expected to create a solo performance. Assessment includes performance, a listening exam and an investigation into musical links.

Cambridge Pre-U in Music

The course includes musical interpretation, creation, analysis and history. You can choose your main area of specialism in which to complete a personal study; this could take the form of a dissertation, recital, composition or music technology project. Further assessment is based on written exams, performance and composition.

Choosing other subjects to go with music

Music goes well with a whole range of subjects, including the humanities, electronics, English literature, ICT or computing and mathematics. It also complements the more practical media or performance-related subjects.

Top Tip

Advanced level music tends to be well regarded by the leading UK universities and appears on preferred subject lists; music technology, on the other hand, is not given the same consideration. The University of Sheffield features music on its acceptable list, while music technology is accepted only as a third or fourth A level, in combination with more recognised subjects.

Music at university

You will need advanced level music to study it at a higher level. It is a subject which is not offered by every institution but, increasingly, universities are trying to position themselves as centres of excellence or specialist centres for music.

A degree in this subject will allow you to go into much greater depth than you did at A level and of course you will be able to further develop your skills in listening, composition and performance. A typical music degree might include the following modules:

- composition
- historical topics
- introduction to world music
- issues in theory and analysis
- musical techniques
- musicology
- notations of Western music
- performance
- practice and theory of performance
- principles of tonal music
- special study
- studies in contemporary music
- techniques of composition.

In addition, optional modules on a broad range of subjects can be selected, including 'film music', 'Mozart's piano concertos', 'music, politics, ideology', 'Viennese Modernism', and many more.

Top Tip

You can specialise at degree level by choosing to study BMus Vocal Teaching, BA Music Promotion or BA Contemporary World Jazz, for example.

Combining music with other degree subjects

Universities offer combinations with other subjects depending on the structure of their own academic departments, but typical combinations include music with a modern language, music with management, drama and music, history and music or mathematics and music.

'Music is a massive part of my life, and although the Music A level is difficult, it has formed a basis for my degree (BA Music and Theatre). I have applied to be a music teacher, and with that I need knowledge of music and music technology.'

Annabel Weeden

Music and your future career

Non-graduate jobs in music

It's hard to go into a musical career with A level Music alone but it could give you a head start by showing your interest and knowledge of music. As long as you are prepared to work your way up from the bottom, it's quite possible to find junior roles within a radio station, a music magazine or a record company.

Graduate jobs directly related to music

Even graduate jobs can be difficult to obtain because of the competitive nature of the industry and the relatively small number of openings. The jobs most closely related to music, either directly after graduating or after further training and work experience, comprise the following.

- **Composer:** writes original music, often commissioned by a third party. Very few musicians derive all their income from composition; an average income from composition would be 20% (with the remaining 80% usually made up from teaching or performing).
- **Editorial assistant:** assists in the production of manuscripts and textbooks for music teaching. All the music publishers in the UK are small employers, recruiting music graduates only occasionally and expecting them to start at the very bottom.
- **Magazine journalist.** There are many specialist publications covering all aspects of music. However, the field is extremely competitive and it may be necessary to work as a freelancer and undertake training in journalism.
- **Music librarian:** responsible for the acquisition and promotion of library music resources within the community, in education or within a private company. Graduates need to qualify as a professional librarian first, before being able to specialise in a field such as music.
- **Music therapist.** This role involves using music to treat, educate or rehabilitate people with emotional, physical or mental problems who are based in hospitals, schools, prisons, community centres or private practice.

- **Musician.** Most musicians are self-employed and accept a wide range of engagements. These can include not only orchestral, ensemble or solo work in the classical field, but also in clubs, on cruise liners and in cabaret in the popular music area.
- **Private music teacher:** teaches music in schools for all ages, in both the state and independent sectors. Some are employed as peripatetic teachers working in a number of schools in an area (and may be employed by the music service of the local authority).

Other graduate jobs where a degree in music could be useful

- **Community arts worker:** concerned with the promotion of the arts in the community, often through working with young people out of school hours.
- **Film/video production manager:** works on programmes in radio or television or for video production and post-production. This role is very popular but difficult to break into even if you are prepared to start at the bottom.
- **Museum/art gallery curator.** There are occasional openings for curators and assistants of musical collections in the major museums, following the appropriate postgraduate training.
- **Musical performance/festival organiser:** is employed on a small scale by orchestras, opera or ballet companies and concert halls but can also be employed by companies, conference centres and arenas to host and organise music festivals, such as Glastonbury, Reading and many others.

Find out more about music

- AQA: www.aqa.org.uk
- British Association for Music Therapy: www.bamt.org
- Cambridge Pre-U: www.cie.org.uk/qualifications
- CCEA: www.rewardinglearning.org.uk
- Creative and Cultural Skills: www.ccskills.org.uk
- Edexcel: www.edexcel.com
- International Baccalaureate Diploma: www.ibo.org/diploma/curriculum/group6
- OCR: www.ocr.org.uk
- Royal Academy of Music: www.ram.ac.uk
- SQA: www.sqa.org.uk
- WJEC: www.wjec.co.uk

PERFORMING ARTS (APPLIED)

Courses in performing arts give students an insight into the sector, equipping them with the skills and knowledge to progress to various different employment areas in the field or to apply for university. Students can explore aspects of the performing arts such as dance, drama, music, music technology, arts administration and marketing, as well as the technical and production aspects of performance.

Top Tip

The Applied A/AS level in Performing Arts is a broader and slightly more practical choice than the A/AS level Drama and Theatre Studies.

Is it right for me?

You need no prior knowledge of this subject to take the course, but an interest in performance or production, along with career motivation in this area, are beneficial. Good grades in English or English literature may also be required.

The focus of the course is on drama, dance and music (or musical theatre); you will normally concentrate on one specialist area from these three. If you are interested in becoming a musician, dancer, actor or even a music technologist or choreographer, you will focus on performance units; alternatively, if you prefer to be away from the limelight, you can choose production units with possibilities in lighting, sound or theatre design.

You'll need to work well in a team and be able to communicate your ideas and take direction, as well as demonstrating creativity and analytical thinking.

Subject options

This subject is available as an Applied GCE A/AS level.

Alternative options include A/AS level in Dance, which is offered by a limited number of schools and colleges. You may also be interested in the A/AS level in Drama and Theatre Studies (see page 111), which includes more theory (and written exams) and is more focused on drama, rather than on the broader study of performance.

Other academic qualifications with a focus on drama and theatre include Cambridge Pre-U in Drama and Theatre, IB Diploma in Theatre and SQA Higher or Advanced Higher in Drama (see page 112 for further details).

A/AS level (Applied) in Performing Arts

Classroom work might include analysing, discussing or devising performance or production. You will spend time in the drama studio, rehearsing and performing, and you will watch and evaluate performances viewed on screen and at the theatre. You should get the opportunity to visit different types of arts organisations and you will certainly need to carry out plenty of independent research into the sector. Assessment is mainly coursework-based but your performances (or productions) form a key part of your marks.

The outline below relates to the syllabus set out in the OCR guidelines. You should check the exact syllabus with your chosen sixth form or college, as their facilities may limit some options. There will also be some variation in relation to different exam boards, but the same content is more or less covered.

Investigating performing arts organisations (AS)

You will get an introduction to a range of performing arts organisations, from cinemas, theatres and dance halls to stage schools and arts centres. You will learn about the business side of the industry and the different job roles that are available.

Professional practice: skills development (AS)

Students produce a skills development plan for either performance (choosing from dance, acting or music) or production. You will choose one of the following two units.

- Professional practice: performance
  Students put into practice the skills that they have learned by performing a play, piece of music or dance for the public.
- Professional practice: production
  Students put into practice the skills they have learned by working on the production of a performance; this might cover costume, lighting, make-up, props, sets, sound or stage management.

Getting work (A2)

An introduction to the different careers within the sector, the main skills needed to succeed in the field and how to get work.

Exploring repertoire (A2)

Students from both the production and performance pathways get together to produce a piece of drama to enhance and develop their skills. You will choose one of the following two units.

- Producing a showcase
  A synoptic module requiring two contrasting pieces of performance, which students can use to show all the skills they've developed over the course.
- Production demonstration
  Students research, design, develop and realise the end result for their chosen production role.

Choosing other subjects to go with performing arts

A range of creative subjects go well with this one, including English, dance, art and design, media and music technology, as well as subjects such as business.

Performing arts at university

A few courses covering many aspects of performing arts are available at degree level, but the majority tend to specialise in one or two areas. Decide which part of performing arts you excel in and go for that.

Some of the areas that may be covered on a more general performing arts degree include:

- arts in the community
- dance in education
- international theatre since 1945
- music in education
- performance and text
- performance in virtual worlds
- performing arts: contemporary practice
- storytelling and poetry in performance
- the film industry.

At degree level, performing arts can be combined with music, a modern language, English, education, media and countless others subjects.

Top Tip

It is worth considering that many of the leading research-based universities in the UK prefer more academic study to Applied A levels. If you want to apply to one of these institutions, even for a degree in performing arts, then you will probably need to offer at least an additional two or even three preferred academic A level subjects.

Performing arts and your future career

Non-graduate jobs in performing arts

If you want a career in performance or in the technical side of performing arts, you will probably have to go and do further study. However, it may be possible to get your foot in the door straight after A levels by working, for example, in an administrative role within a theatre or in the box office of an opera house.

Graduate jobs directly related to performing arts

Some related jobs will require relevant postgraduate study; if you want to become a performer you may need further professional training.

- **Actor.** Using speech, body language and movement, an actor communicates a character and situations to an audience.
- **Dancer.** Working in a variety of genres, from classical ballet and West End musicals to contemporary dance and freestyle (disco), a dancer's role may also involve education or therapy, as well as entertainment.
- **Primary school teacher:** teaches younger children the full range of curriculum subjects.
- **Secondary school teacher:** teaches drama, music or other curriculum subjects in schools and colleges.

Other graduate jobs where a degree in performing arts could be useful

- **Arts administrator:** facilitates the planning and promotion of visual and performing arts activities, sometimes specialising in areas such as finance and marketing.
- **Community arts worker:** concerned with the promotion of the arts in the community, often through working with young people in schools and youth centres.
- **Drama therapist.** This role involves using drama to treat or educate people with health or emotional difficulties through therapeutic techniques.
- **Editorial assistant.** Degrees may enable entry to specialist publishing fields working with plays or new music.
- **Journalist.** There are many specialist publications covering the arts but entry is very competitive. Graduates might start in mainstream broadcast or print journalism and specialise or become freelancers later.
- **Programme researcher:** supports the producer by helping to organise and to plan the programme.
- **Television production assistant:** organises and co-ordinates programme activities, booking performers and facilities and providing administrative support.

Find out more about performing arts

- AQA: www.aqa.org.uk
- Cambridge Pre-U: www.cie.org.uk/qualifications
- CCEA: www.rewardinglearning.org.uk
- Council for Dance Education and Training (CDET): www.cdet.org.uk
- Creative and Cultural Skills: www.ccskills.org.uk
- Creative Skillset: www.creativeskillset.org

- Edexcel: www.edexcel.com
- Equity: www.equity.org.uk
- Incorporated Society of Musicians: www.ism.org
- International Baccalaureate Diploma: www.ibo.org/diploma/curriculum/group6/
- National Council for Drama Training: www.ncdt.co.uk
- OCR: www.ocr.org.uk
- SQA: www.sqa.org.uk
- WJEC: www.wjec.co.uk

PHILOSOPHY

Philosophy has been around for a very long time – as far back as the Greeks – and remains popular even today. Philosophy literally means 'the love of wisdom'; it touches on science, law, religion, history, literature, mathematics and politics. The subject includes questions about the meaning of life, the nature of reality, consciousness, how to live a good life, ethics, and much more.

Philosophers tackle questions such as the following ones.

- Do we really exist?
- Why are there wars?
- If we are controlled by genes and DNA, are we responsible for our choices?
- Can discrimination ever be justified?

Is it right for me?

The successful study of philosophy requires an analytical and logical mind, a curiosity about the world and the ability to look at things from different points of view. You'll be using logical thought and rational consideration to examine life's big questions.

You will develop strong reasoning skills and will learn how to apply abstract concepts to everyday issues. You will have to think for yourself and critically assess information before drawing conclusions; you should develop strong skills in articulating your argument. You will certainly need to absorb complex written information and write with clarity and precision.

Top Tip

Skills developed through the study of philosophy, such as the ability to question assumptions and the status quo, can be useful in many areas of work, such as journalism and the wider media, law, education, business and management, and also creative and scientific roles.

Although philosophy mostly focuses on questions and ideas rather than established answers and facts, there will be plenty of information to learn and digest. You will need to study and understand ancient and modern philosophers and their arguments. There is also plenty of new vocabulary to get to grips with.

Subject options

This subject is available at GCE A/AS level, as a Cambridge Pre-U in Philosophy and Theology, as part of the IB Diploma and as a Higher course in Scotland.

Studies relating to theology or religious studies may also include some philosophical content.

A/AS level in Philosophy

For an exact definition of the AS and A2 syllabus you will be studying, you should consult your school, college or the exam board itself. The main variations in philosophy are in terms of the particular philosophers and strands of philosophy that a school selects for its pupils to study. However, most exam boards stipulate that students should gain an appreciation of the major elements of philosophical thought.

Philosophy is taught by a mixture of classroom work and students' independent learning. In order to get the very top grades, students are encouraged to read around the subject to support the knowledge they gain in class. Class lessons may also include the discussion of philosophical concepts. The volume of reading and writing is high in this subject and students should be prepared for that before choosing it. Furthermore, becoming familiar with philosophical concepts and terms can be difficult at first.

Assessment is based entirely on written exams.

The AQA syllabus covers the following units.

- **Introduction to philosophy 1 (AS).** Reason and experience; the idea of God; why should I be governed?; why should I be moral?
- **Introduction to philosophy 2 (AS).** Knowledge of the external world; realism and idealism; tolerance; the value of art; God and the world; free will versus determinism.
- **Key themes in philosophy (A2).** Philosophy of mind; political philosophy; epistemology and metaphysics; moral philosophy; philosophy of religion.
- **Philosophical problems (A2).** You will develop an understanding of the issues considered by philosophers such as Hume, Plato, Mill, Descartes and Nietzsche.

At A2 level, you will be able to choose two themes in which to specialise.

Higher in Philosophy

Higher level philosophy includes four units: 'critical thinking in philosophy', 'philosophy: metaphysics', 'epistemology' and 'moral philosophy'. Applicants would normally be expected to have studied religious studies, philosophy or a social studies course at Intermediate 2. Assessment is based on closed book unit tests and a final written exam. The subject is not currently available as an Advanced Higher, although Religious, Moral and Philosophical Studies can be chosen as an alternative (see page 242).

International Baccalaureate Diploma in Philosophy

The subject can be studied at Standard and Higher level. The course is focused on clarity of understanding, which is developed through critical thinking, analysis and examination of texts, and the study of philosophical themes.

At both levels, you will study 'what is a human being?', along with a choice from 'grounds of epistemology', 'theories and problems of ethics', 'philosophy of religion', 'philosophy of art', 'political philosophy', 'non-Western traditions and perspectives', 'contemporary social issues' and 'people, nations and cultures'. Higher level students will examine the units in greater breadth and take an additional assessment reflecting on the nature, methodology and purpose of philosophy.

Cambridge Pre-U in Philosophy and Theology

This course has the following three components: 'introduction to philosophy and theology', 'topics and key texts in philosophy and theology I' and 'topics and key texts in philosophy and theology 2'.

All three units are assessed by written exam, taken at the end of year two. The topics covered include 'epistemology', 'New Testament: the four gospels', 'Old Testament: prophecy', 'philosophy of mind', 'philosophy of religion', 'ethics', and 'philosophy and language'.

Choosing other subjects to go with philosophy

Due to the breadth of philosophy, and its relevance to sciences, arts and humanities, many different subjects would complement it.

Top Tip

Philosophy tends to be well recognised by the Russell Group and other leading universities, but it is rarely listed as an entry requirement. The subject can be found on most universities' preferred lists, including University College London, University of Sheffield, London School of Economics and Trinity College, Cambridge (for arts degrees).

Philosophy at university

It's not necessary to have an A level in Philosophy to study it at a higher level; this is partly because the subject is not widely available through schools and colleges.

Although most philosophy courses at university level include an introduction to the main strands of the discipline, the content can vary widely. Some will focus on more traditional forms of philosophy, such as Plato and Aristotle, while others will place their emphasis on applying philosophy to contemporary issues in politics, law, religion and society in general.

Optional modules could include the study of particular philosophers, such as Wittgenstein or Hegel, the study of philosophy by country of origin, such as Indian philosophy and Greek philosophy, or the study of certain schools of philosophy, such as Marxism (named after Karl Marx) and Aesthetics (the study and appreciation of beauty and art).

Combining philosophy with other degree subjects

As the study of philosophy cuts across so many other disciplines, it is quite common to see this subject combined with both arts and sciences. A very well-known combination is politics, philosophy and economics (PPE), which is offered by some universities. However, combinations with history, modern languages, theology, mathematics, physics, literature and classics are pretty common, too.

Philosophy and your future career

Non-graduate jobs in philosophy

Philosophy is not a vocational subject and therefore it will not lead directly to a particular career. Undoubtedly, it does develop some very useful skills, such as critical thinking, the ability to create a persuasive argument, independent thinking, good judgement and logic. These could be useful for a range of jobs, including administration, some government work and some junior aspects of managerial work.

Other graduate jobs where a degree in philosophy could be useful

Careers include those which are open to graduates of any discipline and require strong analytical and communication skills.

- **Advertising account planner:** analyses the consumer response to advertisements and helps to integrate this into the advertising strategy. This role also involves evaluating the effectiveness of advertising.
- **Civil Service/local government administrator:** assists in the formulation of policies and procedures, in a government department or local authority, and co-ordinates their implementation.
- **Information technology consultant:** gives independent advice to clients on IT solutions to business problems, analyses problems, makes recommendations and develops and implements new systems.
- **Marketing executive, (consumer products):** assists in the development of brands and the promotion of fast-moving consumer goods and products to the public.
- **Newspaper journalist:** reports on news and other items of current interest for newspapers.

- **Personnel officer:** advises on all policies relating to human resources in an organisation, including employee planning, recruitment, pay and conditions of work, training and welfare.
- **Political party research officer:** employed in a variety of settings, including higher education, political parties and independent agencies. This role could involve working for Members of Parliament and Members of the European Parliament.
- **Public affairs consultant (lobbyist):** represents the client's case to those in government who make decisions that affect them. The client may be a large company, a trade association, a pressure group or a local authority.
- **Publishing copy-/sub-editor:** ensures for the publisher that a manuscript is accurate and appropriate for the intended readership, and also has a consistent style and a logical structure, before it goes to the production stage.
- **Solicitor:** advises individuals and organisations on legal problems; prepares wills, contracts and other legal documents; researches and advises on points of law.
- **TV programme researcher:** generates programme ideas, researches background material, and briefs production teams and presenters.

Find out more about philosophy

- AQA: www.aqa.org.uk
- British Philosophical Association: www.bpa.ac.uk/resources/careers-and-success-stories
- Cambridge Pre-U: www.cie.org.uk/qualifications
- International Baccalaureate Diploma: www.ibo.org/diploma/curriculum/group3/
- Royal Institute of Philosophy: www.royalinstitutephilosophy.org
- SQA: www.sqa.org.uk

PHYSICAL EDUCATION (PE)

As an A level PE student you will learn about specific physical activities and sports, and develop the skills of planning, performing and evaluating these activities. You will also get an insight into the historical and social contexts of sport, as well as learning more about the relationship between psychology and physiology in sport. This subject combines both academic and practical activities.

Is it right for me?

PE might be the right choice for you if have a love of sport and an interest in the body and its performance in sport. You will get a chance to consider performance from a physiological and psychological perspective. In addition to performance as a sports player, you will also study sports leadership and the role of the sports official.

The subject develops skills ranging from scientific research, discussion and evaluation to sports performance. It is a diverse course, offering a combination of academic study and physical activity. You don't have to have studied PE or sport to cope with the subject at A level; however, it can be helpful if you are strong in at least one sport.

Subject options

This subject is available as GCE A/AS level in Physical Education and as an SQA Higher and Advanced Higher. Alternative options include the Applied A level in Leisure Studies (see page 187), the International Baccalaureate in Sports, Exercise and Health Science (Standard level) and the Cambridge Pre-U in Sports Science.

A/AS level in Physical Education

By its very nature, PE is not a classroom-based subject. There will be the usual classroom note taking but you will also spend plenty of time engaging in various types of physical activities, games and sports. Assessment is by a combination of written exams, coursework and assessed practical activities.

For an exact definition of the AS and A2 syllabus you will be studying, you should consult your school, college or the exam board itself. A level exam boards offering PE include OCR, AQA, WJEC and Edexcel. The following outline is roughly based on the Edexcel syllabus.

Participation in sport and recreation (AS)

The unit introduces students to the component parts of a healthy and active lifestyle, including anatomy, physiology and nutrition, and how the body responds to exercise and different methods of fitness training. It also explores how competitive sport has changed over the years.

The critical sports performer (AS)
You will be assessed on your practical performance as player, leader or official; you will investigate all three roles from a local perspective and choose one role to study from a national aspect. Analysis of your own performance is also required.

Preparation for optimum sports performance (A2)
Students examine how elite athletes prepare physically, psychologically and technically (equipment, kit or training camps, for example).

The developing sports performer (A2)
Building on the foundation of 'the critical sports performer' at AS level, students learn how to improve practical performance and measure the improvement, while also researching the role of player, leader or official from an international viewpoint.

Higher and Advanced Higher in Physical Education
The Higher and Advanced Higher in PE cover units in 'perspectives on performance' and 'analysis and development of performance'. At Higher level, assessment is based on practical sports performance and a written exam; at Advanced Higher, practical performance activities are assessed along with a project report based on the work done in both units.

Top Tip

An advanced level qualification in biology can complement the study of PE. Take care, though, as some universities won't make offers based on both subjects because of the overlap in content.

Choosing other subjects to go with physical education
Subjects that may go well with PE include leisure studies, computing/ICT, biology and psychology. If you want to study sports science at degree level, you may want to choose one or two science subjects alongside PE.

How do universities view PE?

The most selective universities in the country might consider PE only as a third or fourth option; in fact, some would prefer you taking all traditional, academic subjects.

The University of Loughborough asks for at least one A level from a number of preferred subjects for its BSc (Hons) Sport and Exercise Science – biology, mathematics, physics, chemistry, psychology, sociology, history and English – but PE is not included on the list.

On the other hand, for BSc (Hons) Sport and Exercise Science at the University of Birmingham, PE is on a list of preferred subjects:

'AAB for applicants taking one of the following subjects: Psychology, Biology, Human Biology, Chemistry, Physics, Mathematics, Physical Education or Statistics. Applicants with more than one science subject at A level may receive a lower offer. AAA for applicants not taking one of these subjects.'

The best advice is to research your university options carefully.

Physical education at university

PE courses at university are often linked with teacher training courses, because PE is still seen as a school subject, to some extent. Degrees in sport science are widely available, although institutions sometimes express a preference for sciences at A level rather than PE, so always check in advance.

You will get the opportunity to explore this subject in greater depth at degree level, while also being able to specialise in a particular field. Degree modules could include the following:

- fitness and training
- IT for sport and exercise science
- nutrition
- physiology of exercise and health
- sociology of sport
- sport and exercise pedagogy
- structural kinesiology.

Sport science can be combined with almost any other subject, depending on your preferences and the flexibility of the academic departments. Here are some examples:

- chemistry and sport science
- English and sport science
- geography and sport science
- mathematics and sport science
- media arts and sport science
- applied criminology with sport science
- sport science with management.

Physical education and your future career

Non-graduate jobs in physical education

It's possible to get into a few sports-related areas without a degree. These include junior positions in sports clubs and gyms, as well as administrative roles within a hotel and leisure complex. It's even possible to become a personal trainer/coach with some further training, although not necessarily at degree level. Of course, other non-sports jobs are open to you, too.

Top Tip

Think PE teacher is the only job related to sport? Think again. How about coaching, sports rehabilitation, sports technology development, biomechanics or becoming a professional referee?

Graduate jobs directly related to physical education

- **Fitness centre manager:** employed mainly in commercial health clubs and gymnasia to manage the provision of physical fitness and lifestyle programmes.
- **Leisure centre manager.** There are opportunities in both the public and private sectors for promoting and running leisure and recreation centres.
- **Outdoor pursuits manager:** manages a centre offering instruction to a wide range of people in outdoor activities.
- **Personal trainer:** employed mainly in the private sector to provide physical fitness instruction and prescription of exercise/fitness programmes for individuals.
- **Secondary school teacher or higher education lecturer.** There are opportunities for teaching PE in tertiary and further education colleges, as well as in maintained and independent schools. Lecturing in HE is also available.
- **Sports administrator:** works within a governing body or the Sports Council (Sport England, Sport Scotland, Sport Wales and Sport NI). The role may be similar to that of the sports development officer (see below) but it is likely to have a greater emphasis on administrative and financial aspects.
- **Sports coach/instructor.** There are a few full-time posts in some sports. This work can also form part of the work of a sports development officer or a recreation assistant in a sports centre.
- **Sports development officer:** promotes various sports within the community, usually among particular target groups, or develops one sport on behalf of a local authority, governing body or professional association.
- **Sports therapist:** mainly concerned with the prevention and treatment of injury in sport, and with improving and maintaining physical performance.

Other graduate jobs where a degree in physical education could be useful

- **Armed Forces.** The active nature of many of the jobs and the leadership role of officers can suit sports people.
- **Health promotion specialist.** Understanding of nutrition and the relationship of fitness to health is a useful background for a health promotion specialist.
- **Journalist.** Familiarity with sports is obviously an asset if you want to be a journalist specialising in reporting and writing about sport.
- **Marketing.** The sports equipment and leisurewear industries could well value your knowledge of sport and exercise.
- **Physiotherapist.** This would be good preparation for a career in sports therapy. Many sports physiotherapists take relevant postgraduate study after a first degree in physiotherapy.
- **Police officer.** This challenging job could suit sport management or sport science graduates for reasons similar to those given for the Armed Forces roles.

Find out more about physical education

- AQA: www.aqa.org.uk
- British Association of Sport and Exercise Sciences (BASES): www.bases.org.uk
- Edexcel: www.edexcel.com
- Fitness Industry Association (FIA): www.fia.org.uk
- OCR: www.ocr.org.uk
- People 1st: www.people1st.co.uk
- Skills Active: www.skillsactive.com
- SQA: www.sqa.org.uk
- UK Sport: www.uksport.gov.uk
- WJEC: www.wjec.co.uk

PHYSICS

Physicists study the world, investigating the relationship between energy and matter in time and space and trying to discover why objects behave the way they do. Along the way, their scientific findings have also become the basis for many technological advances.

How is the universe changing? How can we predict earthquakes? How can we diagnose cancer through medical imaging? Physics is at the heart of the answers to these questions.

The study of physics will encourage you to understand how the physical world works, from particles to galaxies. You will explore the properties of motion, nuclear physics, energy transfer and electricity. You will develop your awareness of how advances in science and technology affect the world and learn how scientific work is evaluated, published and verified by the scientific community.

Is it right for me?

If you are interested in experimenting and considering the answers to fundamental questions about the universe, then physics might be a good choice for you. In order to study physics at this level, it helps if you like problem solving, using practical skills and investigating the way the world works.

Advanced level study builds upon what you already know about physics, but with a more mathematical focus. You will need a strong grasp of maths (particularly algebra) at GCSE or Standard level to cope with mathematical models and equations. While the study of advanced level maths enhances and complements physics, it is not a requirement.

This subject can demonstrate your analytical thinking, critical approach and mechanical understanding. It is highly relevant if you are considering a career in areas including engineering, electronics or computing.

Subject options

You can study physics through any of the qualifications explored in this book; it is available as a GCE A/AS level offered by all the major exam boards, as well as a Cambridge Pre-U, International Baccalaureate Diploma and SQA Higher and Advanced Higher.

Top Tip

If you're interested in the electronics element of physics, then bear in mind that some schools offer an A/AS level purely in this subject.

A/AS level in Physics

The A level is taught through classroom work as well as practical work in the lab, where you will carry out experiments. Assessment is by a combination of written exams and the assessed practical work. A level Physics tends not to have coursework, so think twice before choosing this subject if exams are not your strength.

For an exact definition of the AS and A2 syllabus you will be studying, you should consult your chosen sixth form, college or the exam board itself. The following outline is based on the Edexcel syllabus.

Physics on the go (AS)
This unit involves the study of mechanics (motion, forces, energy and power) and materials science (properties of materials, viscosity, Stokes' law, flow of liquids, elastic strain energy, and so on).

Physics at work (AS)
You will study waves, electricity and particles, including topics ranging from refraction and polarisation to Ohm's law and the nature of light.

Exploring physics (AS)
This unit requires you to carry out an assessed practical experiment (plus report) based either on a physics field trip or on a case study of an application of physics.

Physics on the move (A2)
You will study further mechanics, electric and magnetic fields, and particle physics, with the possibility of investigating contemporary experiments and research.

Physics from creation to collapse (A2)
In this unit, you will investigate thermal energy, nuclear decay, oscillations, astrophysics and cosmology.

Experimental physics (A2)
The final unit is based around planning and carrying out an experiment, and recording its results, before analysing the outcome and drawing conclusions. The practical activity will be supported by a written report.

Higher and Advanced Higher in Physics

The SQA course at Advanced level covers three units: 'mechanics and properties of matter', 'electricity and electrons' and 'radiation and matter'. All three units are assessed by written exam.

The Advanced Higher in Physics has units on 'mechanics', 'electrical phenomena' and 'wave phenomena', again assessed by a written exam. Students also carry out an assessed investigation report.

International Baccalaureate Diploma in Physics

At Higher level, core topics covered include 'physics and physical measurement', 'mechanics, oscillations and waves', 'atomic and nuclear physics' and 'energy, power and climate change'. In addition to further Higher level topics such as 'thermal physics' and 'quantum physics', you will also choose two topics from the following list:

- astrophysics
- communications
- electromagnetic waves
- medical physics
- particle physics
- relativity.

Assessment is based on three exams (76% of the marks), with 24% coming from practical work in the form of investigations and a multidisciplinary project.

Cambridge Pre-U in Physics

The Cambridge Pre-U in Physics combines classical physics with modern concepts such as quantum physics and astrophysics. The course offers a broad curriculum with some flexibility in teaching methods, while the personal investigation allows students to explore their own areas of interest in more detail. The rest of the assessment in based on three written exams taken at the end of the second year.

Choosing other subjects to go with physics

There is a lot of maths involved in advanced level physics, so studying maths at this level is a big help; you will often need advanced level maths to study physics at degree level. Other subjects that go well with physics include engineering, design and technology, chemistry and computing.

Top Tip

Physics is a safe choice, as it appears on all the preferred subject lists. The Russell Group guide to post-16 decisions, 'Informed Choices', classes it as a facilitating subject, which means that it is one of the subjects most often required by universities.

Physics at university

Physics at degree level is a well-established academic option. You can study the subject as pure or applied physics, or select something more specialist, such as astrophysics or molecular physics. Modules on a physics course could include:

- astrophysics
- computational physics
- classical mechanics and special relativity
- electromagnetism
- introductory quantum mechanics
- introduction to plasma physics
- nuclear physics
- radiation physics
- statistical mechanics.

Physics can also be combined with other subjects at degree level, for example physics and maths, physics and management, physics and computer science or physics and philosophy.

Physics and your future career

Non-graduate jobs in physics

Finding work in physics straight after A levels is a bit difficult, as most jobs in this field involve further study. A job as a trainee lab technician is a possibility. For non-science jobs, there will be opportunities in the commercial sector; you will need to demonstrate the skills you've developed from the course, such as problem solving, numeracy, manual dexterity and logical thinking.

Graduate jobs directly related to physics

- **Electronics engineer:** develops and designs an electronic product, process or device from initial brief through a tested prototype to manufacture.
- **Geoscientist:** collects, analyses and appraises physical data about the Earth in order to discover commercially exploitable mineral and hydrocarbon reserves.
- **Materials engineer:** works on the manufacture, development and use of a wide range of materials, such as glass, ceramics, metals and polymers.
- **Medical physicist:** provides scientific support to medical staff in the accurate, effective and safe diagnosis and treatment of patients.
- **Meteorologist:** interprets observations from the land surface, oceans and the upper atmosphere to forecast the weather both in the short and long term (for example, the results of global warming).
- **Research scientist:** organises and carries out systematic investigations into physical properties, behaviours and phenomena with the aim of introducing, developing or improving products or processes.
- **Scientific laboratory technician:** assists scientists and others who are engaged in research, development, analysis or scientific investigations by carrying out a variety of technical and experimental tasks.
- **Secondary school teacher:** teaches physics or science. A PGCE is necessary for teaching posts in state schools.

Other graduate jobs where a degree in physics could be useful

- **Forensic scientist:** investigates the scientific aspects of crime, fires and accidents.
- **Scientific journalist:** researches, writes and edits scientific news articles and features.
- **Systems analyst:** analyses the requirements of systems in both a business and technical context and determines the optimum solutions.
- **Technical author:** designs and writes documentation which communicates technical information.
- **Technical sales engineer:** provides the major link between the company producing technical goods and services and its customers, negotiating sales, orders, price and quality.

Find out more about physics

- AQA: www.aqa.org.uk
- Cambridge Pre-U: www.cie.org.uk/qualifications
- CCEA: www.rewardinglearning.org.uk
- Edexcel: www.edexcel.com
- Institute of Physics: www.iop.org
- International Baccalaureate Diploma: www.ibo.org/diploma/curriculum/group4/
- OCR: www.ocr.org.uk
- physics.org (Institute of Physics): www.physics.org
- Science Council: www.sciencecouncil.org
- SEMTA – Sector Skills Council for Science, Engineering and Manufacturing Technologies: www.semta.org.uk
- SQA: www.sqa.org.uk
- WJEC: www.wjec.co.uk

PSYCHOLOGY

Psychology is the scientific study of people, the mind and behaviour. It is an academic, essay-writing subject which uses scientific research methodology and the analysis of data to draw conclusions. Psychology is a popular A level choice and can be relevant to many aspects of life today, including education, health and crime.

The study of psychology will give you the opportunity to consider questions including:

- What is intelligence?
- How do we develop ideas about gender?
- What is normal behaviour?

You will look at topical issues, such as stress, eyewitness testimony and eating disorders, which can be better understood and managed using psychological methods. You will get to learn about different research methods and how to present results and theories.

Is it right for me?

Psychology isn't an easy option. You will need to be interested in people and what makes them tick. It helps if you are keen to read, research and discover new information. You'll also need an interest in science. There is no need to have any prior knowledge of this subject to take it at A/AS level.

Psychology will help you to develop skills relevant to many areas of work, including critical thinking, scientific investigation, effective communication and the evaluation of data and graphical information. This subject can be useful for a future in marketing, business, education or caring.

Top Tip

'Hard' or 'soft' A level? Psychology can be a challenging subject and appears on the preferred subject lists for the University of Sheffield, University College London and London School of Economics. Trinity College, Cambridge, includes psychology on its 'A levels of more limited suitability' list, which means it could be offered as a third or fourth A level in an application for arts courses, alongside two more favoured subjects.

Psychology is not classed as a facilitating subject by 'Informed Choices' (the Russell Group guide to choices post-16) because it is not widely specified as an entry requirement, even for psychology degrees.

Subject options

This subject is offered as a GCE A/AS level (by OCR, AQA, Edexcel and WJEC) and as a Cambridge Pre-U Principal subject, IB Diploma option and SQA Higher course in Scotland.

A/AS level in Psychology

A level Psychology is primarily taught in a classroom setting, through note taking and discussion about theories. You will also spend time learning how to carry out a psychological experiment and research effectively and correctly.

For an exact definition of the AS and A2 syllabus you will be studying, you should consult your selected sixth form, college or the exam board itself. The following outline is based on the AQA Psychology A level specification. AQA assessment is by written paper (two exams each year), although some courses may have an assessed project or practical element.

Cognitive psychology, developmental psychology and research methods (AS)
Cognitive psychology, including memory and eyewitness testimony; developmental psychology, including early social development, attachment and the effects of everyday care; research methods, in the context of the topic areas.

Biological psychology, social psychology and individual differences (AS)
Biological psychology, including stress, factors affecting stress, managing stress; social psychology, including majority and minority influence, obedience and independent behaviour; individual differences, including definitions of abnormality, approaches and therapies.

Topics in psychology (A2)
Biological rhythms and sleep; perception; relationships; aggression; eating behaviour; gender; intelligence and learning; cognition and development.

Psychopathology, psychology in action and research methods (A2)
Biological approaches; behaviourism; social learning theory; cognitive, psychodynamic and humanistic approaches; comparison of approaches; debates in psychology; methods in psychology; inferential statistics; issues in research.

Top Tip

Some university psychology departments ask for a grade B or above in GCSE Maths, alongside their advanced level requirements.

Higher in Psychology

The SQA Higher is made up of units on 'understanding the individual', 'investigating behaviour' and 'the individual in the social context'. The qualification covers aspects of developmental, cognitive (how we process information), physiological and social psychology, along with the psychology of individual differences. Students will be expected to learn about research methods and to develop practical research skills. Assessment takes the form of a written exam paper and a written investigation. The subject is not available at Advanced Higher level.

International Baccalaureate Diploma in Psychology

The syllabus is taught in an integrated way, which helps to allow the comparison and review of different theories. Ethical aspects of psychological research are also considered.

Psychology is available at Standard and Higher level; both levels include the same core topics: 'the biological level of analysis', 'the cognitive level of analysis' and 'the sociocultural level of analysis'. At Standard level, you choose one of the following options, while Higher level students get to choose two:

- abnormal psychology
- developmental psychology
- health psychology
- psychology of human relationships
- sport psychology.

All students are introduced to experimental research methodology and assessed on a related report they write. Higher level students will also be assessed on qualitative research in psychology. The rest of the assessment is exam-based, with two papers at Standard level and three at Higher level.

Cambridge Pre-U in Psychology

This qualification sets out to develop your understanding of human nature and your skills in thinking and communicating. The units are 'key studies and theories', 'methods, issues and applications' and 'key applications'; all of them are assessed by written exams at the end of the second year. In the 'key applications' unit, you will choose two options from sport, crime, abnormality, environment and health. You will also be assessed on the way you design, conduct and report a psychological investigation from any area of the syllabus.

Choosing other subjects to go with psychology

The study of psychology has some relevance to biology, computer science, sociology, philosophy, English literature and anthropology. It is a popular combination with subjects such as PE, law, health and social care, business or sociology, although this mix of subjects would cause problems if you wanted to get into the top universities.

If you want to do a degree in psychology then it doesn't usually matter which subjects you study. Psychology at advanced level is not normally a university entry requirement, but a science subject or two are required for certain courses; some universities (for example, the University of York) will accept Psychology A level as a science subject.

Top Tip

Some universities offer both the BA (Bachelor of Arts) and BSc (Bachelor of Science) in Psychology. So what is the difference between the BA and the BSc? In some cases, both courses are identical, including those on offer at the universities of Bangor, Exeter and Sheffield. Check your chosen university website for full details.

Psychology at university

Psychology is offered at many universities and colleges, where it is possible to specialise at degree level in, for example, development psychology or forensic psychology. A psychology degree might include modules in:

- biological psychology
- cognitive neuroscience
- psychology of religion
- sensation and perception
- statistical methods.

Combining psychology with other degree subjects

You could combine a psychology degree with maths, computing/IT, philosophy, physics, English or religious studies; there are plenty of combinations on offer. If you know you want to be a professional psychologist later on then make sure your undergraduate degree is accredited by the British Psychological Society (BPS).

Psychology and your future career

Non-graduate jobs in psychology

Psychology gives you many useful skills, such as the ability to research, analyse data, think logically and communicate effectively. These skills are sought after in most sectors, including health, business and other areas of the public sector. If you want to work in the field of psychology then further study is usually required.

Graduate jobs directly related to psychology

For the following careers – with the exception of counselling and HE lecturing – a first degree in psychology (or alternative graduate conversion qualification) accredited by the BPS is essential in order to enter further training and work.

- **Clinical psychologist:** applies psychology to the assessment and treatment of patients and clients in health-care settings, and conducts research in mental and physical illness.
- **Counsellor:** helps people solve problems, cope with distress and improve well-being. This role involves working with clients of all ages and in a variety of settings, including health, education and the workplace.
- **Educational psychologist:** applies psychology to the learning difficulties of children and young people, and advises parents, teachers and schools.
- **Forensic psychologist:** applies psychology to criminological and legal issues, including the assessment and treatment of offenders, and may have trained in criminological or clinical psychology.
- **Health psychologist:** applies knowledge and understanding of behaviour to finding ways of improving the quality of health care and the standard of health in the general population.
- **Higher education lecturer:** involved in teaching psychology in colleges and HE institutions.
- **Occupational psychologist:** applies psychology to people at work and organisations, including selection and assessment, training, work design and organisational change.

Other graduate jobs where a degree in psychology could be useful

- **Market research executive:** provides systematically acquired information on what people buy, want, do or think and explores the reasons why.
- **Personnel officer:** advises on and implements policies relating to the use of human resources, including employee planning, recruitment, training and welfare.
- **Psychotherapist:** develops a skilled relationship with clients in order to explore the underlying causes of their emotional conflicts or behavioural difficulties.
- **School teacher:** for teaching secondary level social science, science or another appropriate National Curriculum subject.
- **Social researcher:** analyses the impact and expenditure implications of proposed policy changes and monitors the effects of change.
- **Social worker:** assists and advises clients with social problems; this role offers the possibility to specialise as a mental health worker.

- **Speech and language therapist:** assesses, diagnoses and treats adults and children who suffer from disorders related to the voice, speech or language.

Find out more about psychology

- AQA: www.aqa.org.uk
- British Psychological Society: www.bps.org.uk
- Cambridge Pre-U: www.cie.org.uk/qualifications
- Edexcel: www.edexcel.com
- International Baccalaureate Diploma: www.ibo.org/diploma/curriculum/group3/
- OCR: www.ocr.org.uk
- SQA: www.sqa.org.uk
- WJEC: www.wjec.co.uk

RELIGIOUS STUDIES

You don't have to belong to a particular religion or even to have religious beliefs in order to study this subject; religious studies deals with developing an informed and logical approach to religion, exploring and sometimes challenging religious assertions. Students discuss and debate from a range of perspectives.

Religious studies allows students to consider the fundamental questions of human existence, examining issues such as the interaction between religion and science, as well as exploring religious experience and philosophical aspects of religious belief. The questions you will be asked are the big ones: who am I? What happens when I die? How do we decide what is right and wrong? You will develop your understanding of world religions and, on some courses, you will be able to practise textual criticism skills by studying religious texts.

Is it right for me?

You might not need religious beliefs, but you will need an interest in the issues covered to get the most out of this subject. Religious studies is an essay-writing subject so you will need strong skills in English. You will learn to use a variety of sources of information and evaluate what you have read before presenting a logical, well-organised response (whether verbally, in class discussions or in essay form).

You will strengthen your skills in analysis, critical thinking and communication. You will develop your own views and values, while taking a reflective approach. These skills can be vital for further study and for the world of work.

Subject options

This subject is available at GCE A/AS level through all the major exam boards. Some students might also be interested in A/AS level in Biblical Hebrew, offered by OCR.

The International Baccalaureate programme includes world religions at Standard level only. In Scotland, you can opt for the SQA Higher and Advanced Higher in Religious, Moral and Philosophical Studies.

Top Tip

The Cambridge Pre-U qualification includes philosophy and theology as a Principal subject; to find out more, see the outline under *Philosophy* on page 220.

A/AS level in Religious Studies

The content for religious studies is very similar among all the exam boards, although some specifications focus more heavily on the philosophy of religion or ethics, rather than on the in-depth study of a religion.

Teaching is mainly classroom-based learning and discussion but there may be visits to sites of religious interest. Assessment is based entirely on written exams, with two exams to be taken each year.

This outline is based on the OCR specification, where students choose two of the following units at both AS and A2 level:

- Buddhism
- developments in Christian theology
- Hinduism
- Jewish scriptures
- Judaism
- Islam
- New Testament
- philosophy of religion
- religious ethics.

It is recommended that you study the same units at both AS and A2, although this is not compulsory.

Higher and Advanced Higher in Religious, Moral and Philosophical Studies (RMPS)

At Higher level, you will study units on 'world religion', 'morality in the modern world' and 'Christianity: belief and science'. Assessment takes the form of a closed book test and a written exam.

On the Advanced Higher course, mandatory units in 'philosophy of religion' and 'personal research' are supplemented by either 'religious experience' or 'medical ethics'. At this level, 40% of the assessment is based on a 4,000-word dissertation, while 60% comes from a written exam.

International Baccalaureate Diploma in World Religions (Standard level)

This course introduces students to the analytical study of the practices of a range of world religions. You will explore five religions initially, including at least one from Hinduism, Buddhism and Sikhism, at least one from Judaism, Christianity and Islam, and at least one from Taoism, Jainism and the Baha'i Faith. You will later carry out a more in-depth study of two religions. A further investigative study allows deeper individual research into a chosen aspect of religion. Assessment consists of two written exams and a 1,500–1,800-word essay based on the investigative study; the essay forms 25% of the overall marks.

Choosing other subjects to go with religious studies

Religious studies is compatible with English literature, history, sociology, psychology and philosophy, as well as subjects such as archaeology, classical civilisation or history of art. It could contrast well with sciences and maths, offering a different style of teaching, learning and assessment.

How do leading universities see religious studies?

It isn't a facilitating subject, as it tends not to be an entry requirement for most university courses, yet it is well recognised by universities for the skills it develops. You can find religious studies on the preferred A level list for University College London, London School of Economics and the University of Sheffield. Trinity College, Cambridge, considers the subject generally suitable for arts degrees.

Religious studies at university

The skills gained from advanced level religious studies could be applied to many university courses, particularly humanities and social sciences. The subject is a good preparation for degrees in religious studies, theology or philosophy.

A degree directly related to this subject might be called religious studies, theology or divinity. Most degrees offer more depth and breadth in the kind of religions and religious sects than you will have experienced at sixth form or college. Units might include the following:

- does God exist?
- Islam's beginnings
- Islamic mysticism
- Jewish thought and practice
- moral theory and religion
- religion and the enlightenment
- the anthropology of religion
- theories of religion
- the problem of evil.

There are also more specialist degrees focusing on one religion, such as Christian theology or Islamic studies.

Combining religious studies with other degree subjects

A religious studies degree could be combined with most humanities subjects; possible combinations include theology and religious studies, history and religious studies, English literature and religious studies, and criminology and religious studies.

Religious studies and your future career

Non-graduate jobs in religious studies

This is a sound advanced level subject that will enable you, along with your other subjects, to get a junior position in many areas of business, the public sector and the not-for-profit sector. Jobs directly related to religious studies would be hard to find without a degree, but getting an administrative position in a religious-based non-governmental organisation (NGO) would be a possibility.

Graduate jobs directly related to religious studies

The most directly related job is minister of religion or religious leader, who teaches the religious beliefs specific to the faith, ministering to the spiritual and social needs of people in the local community. Information is usually available through the minister of your church or religious organisation. Other related jobs include the following.

- **Adult education lecturer/tutor:** plans and provides a programme of learning activities for adults of all ages, backgrounds and academic levels, in line with the tutor's own expertise.
- **Higher education lecturer.** This role involves teaching (undergraduate and postgraduate students), research (which may include work for agencies outside the university) and administration.
- **Secondary school teacher.** This role involves teaching religious studies and theology in schools or colleges.

Other graduate jobs where a degree in religious studies could be useful

- **Charity officer:** promotes the work of the charity and may be responsible for fundraising, arranging recruitment, training and supervision of paid and voluntary staff, and devising and managing the administrative systems, including the accounts.
- **Counsellor:** concerned with counselling people with personal problems. He/she helps the client to explore, discover and clarify more effective ways of living.
- **Housing adviser:** offers advice and support to people who have housing difficulties.
- **Journalist:** researches and writes features for broadcasting on television or radio, or publishing in periodicals and newspapers. As a theology student, you might be interested in the specialist field of religious publications.

Find out more about religious studies

- AQA: www.aqa.org.uk
- Board of Deputies of British Jews: www.bod.org.uk
- Buddhist Society: www.thebuddhistsociety.org
- Cambridge Pre-U: www.cie.org.uk/qualifications
- CCEA: www.rewardinglearning.org.uk
- Church of England Ministry: www.cofe-ministry.org.uk
- Council of Christians and Jews: www.ccj.org.uk
- Edexcel: www.edexcel.com
- Hindu Council UK: www.hinducounciluk.org
- Information Network on Religious Movements: www.inform.ac
- International Baccalaureate Diploma: www.ibo.org/diploma/curriculum/group3/
- Islamic Foundation: www.islamic-foundation.org.uk
- Network of Sikh Organisations UK: www.nsouk.co.uk
- OCR: www.ocr.org.uk
- SQA: www.sqa.org.uk
- WJEC: www.wjec.co.uk

SCIENCE

The sciences in this section are for students who want to learn how science is applied in a real, hands-on way. These courses concentrate on how science is used in the workplace and applied to many different industries. This may be in commerce, in industry, in research or any other way that is practical or that affects peoples' lives. General science is a versatile course, enhancing the study of other science subjects and complementing the study of arts and humanities.

Is it right for me?

You will need to have studied sciences before in order to build on your knowledge at advanced level. If you like coursework, then a qualification in science might offer fewer exams than individual sciences; however, you will need to be organised and able to meet deadlines. Perhaps you have taken a more applied course at GCSE level or maybe you're looking for one science subject to help you join a university course such as nursing, PE or psychology. This subject is also relevant for students who want to pursue specific scientific careers, such as laboratory work. General science courses like these tend to have more of a focus on biology, with some physics and chemistry studied alongside.

The Subject will help you to develop skills in research, practical investigations and deduction. You will also become stronger at making a case and putting forward your point of view. The study of science will also develop your skills in IT, numeracy, logical thinking and problem solving.

Top Tip

General science courses like these might not always be suitable to provide the National Curriculum requirement for teaching, nor are they widely accepted for some of the most competitive courses such as medicine, dentistry and veterinary science.

Subject options

Science in Society is available as an A/AS level through AQA, while AS level Science is offered by OCR. Several exam boards offer Applied Science from AS single award up to A level double award.

A/AS level in Science in Society

This subject allows students to learn about science, and how it affects our lives and the society in which we live. Assessment is carried out by a mixture of coursework and exams. Exams count for 60%, with one written paper to be taken at AS and one at A2; a further 40% is based on coursework and an assessed case study.

The following list is based on the AQA specification.

Exploring key scientific issues (AS)
The germ theory of disease; infectious diseases now; transport issues; medicines; radiation – risks and uses; evolution; ethical issues in medicine; reproductive choices; lifestyle and health; the universe; who we are and where we are.

Reading and writing about science (AS)
Review of scientific literature; the study of a topical scientific issue.

Exploring key scientific issues (A2)
Cells, chemicals and the mind; nature and nurture; watching the brain work; responding to global climate change; energy futures; sustaining the variety of life on Earth.

Case study of a scientific issue (A2)
Students have to evaluate a scientific or technological issue.

A/AS level (Applied) in Science
Students need to have reached a good standard in at least one GCSE science subject before taking this one. The course includes a lot of lab work, calculations and practical tasks. Sometimes visits are arranged to places of scientific interest (for example, a chemical plant). Assessment is carried out by a combination of written exams and portfolio of evidence. Around one-third of the assessment is based on written exams and the remaining two-thirds on coursework.

The various exam boards offering this subject (OCR, WJEC and AQA) include very similar content; your selected sixth form or college will be able to explain exactly what your course will cover. This example is based on the AQA syllabus, which offers the following modules.

- Investigating science at work (AS)
- Energy transfer systems (AS)
- Finding out about substances (AS)
- Food science and technology (AS double)
- Choosing and using materials (AS double)
- Synthesising organic compounds (AS double)
- Planning and carrying out a scientific investigation (A2)
- Medical physics (A2)
- Sports science (A2)

Students opting for the A level single award choose a further two units from the following list, while A level double award students select five optional units from:

- physics of performance effects
- controlling chemical processes
- the actions and development of medicines
- colour chemistry
- the healthy body
- the role of the pathology service
- ecology, conservation and recycling.

Top Tip

If you want to experience science outside the lab, alternative courses include SQA Higher in Biotechnology and Higher in Mechatronics, IB in Sports, Exercise and Health Science (Standard level), IB in Environmental Systems and Societies (Standard level) and the Cambridge Pre-U in Sports Science.

Choosing other subjects to go with science

Other advanced level science subjects would obviously go well but watch out for overlap; if the spread of your subjects is too narrow, this can cause problems with university offers. Your sixth form or college will be able to advise you further; university websites will also contain information on combinations that are acceptable (or not) for specific courses.

Other subjects that might go well include business, environmental science, psychology, computing/IT and maths. If you want to study a particular science at university, make sure you study that subject at A level (or equivalent).

Science at university

A level Science would count as a qualifying subject at some universities for certain science-based degrees, including environmental science, biomedical science, health science, food science, sports science and forensic science. The leading universities tend to favour pure science subjects in academic, rather than Applied, A levels.

Top Tip

Of the five leading universities that publish preferred subject lists for general entry to their courses, three class general science as being suitable only in combination with a number of more favoured subjects. London School of Economics and University of Edinburgh are the exceptions, but you would still need to check specific entry requirements for the course you intend to study there.

It is rare to find an undergraduate degree in science alone, although you may discover Foundation degrees in Applied Sciences and bachelor's degrees in Science and the Media or Natural Science. It is far more common to specialise in one of the main branches of science, such as physics or chemistry. However, many courses are even narrower than this, focusing on the study of cell biochemistry or astrophysics.

Science-related degrees can be combined with a whole range of subjects at university level, including maths, IT or computing, philosophy, business or management and sometimes a modern language.

Science and your future career

Applied science can set you up for particular career pathways in science, such as working in scientific analysis, the environment, manufacturing, health care and electronics. In many cases, further study is required to work in scientific roles. Nevertheless, science is still a good subject to prepare you for entry level jobs in many sectors of work, including non-science areas such as commerce and parts of the public sector.

Employment options for science graduates really depend on the particular course studied. For career options, look under the jobs sections for *Biology* (page 76), *Chemistry* (page 87), *Physics* (page 233) and *Environmental studies* (page 131) in this guide and you will see that there are many possible opportunities for science graduates.

Find out more about science

- AQA: www.aqa.org.uk
- Chemsoc: www.rsc.org/chemsoc
- Cogent – Skills for Science Based Industries: www.cogent-ssc.com
- Forensic Science Society: www.forensic-science-society.org.uk
- Institute of Biomedical Science: www.ibms.org
- Institute of Physics: www.iop.org
- NHS Careers: www.nhscareers.nhs.uk
- OCR: www.ocr.org.uk
- SEMTA – Sector Skills Council for Science, Engineering and Manufacturing Technologies: www.semta.org.uk
- Society of Biology: www.iob.org
- WJEC: www.wjec.co.uk

SOCIOLOGY

Sociology is the scientific study of society and helps us to make sense of the world in which we live. It looks at the different social relationships that people share with each other: in their families, their schools, their communities and their work. Sociology looks at how people behave and the influence that society has on determining who we are and who we become.

Sociologists might ask questions such as:

- What determines our beliefs and values?
- Why do girls do better than boys at school?
- What is culture and how does it affect us?

The course concentrates on the sociology of the family, the mass media, health and welfare policy, education, work and training, and law and crime. As sociological theories are based on research and evidence, you will learn some of the methods sociologists use and how to apply them.

Is it right for me?

If you have an interest in human nature and human behaviour, then you will almost certainly be interested in sociology. You will get the chance to consider various perspectives and to use your critical thinking skills.

You don't need any prior knowledge in order to study sociology successfully, but an interest in the issues is important and strong skills in English are helpful. There is a lot of reading and writing in this subject and much consideration of contemporary political and social issues.

You will learn how to investigate, evaluate the limits of information and use evidence to back up your argument. You will almost certainly improve your ability to communicate your point of view and work well with others, which are great skills for university and for work.

The skills and knowledge gained from this course can be relevant if you are interested in nursing, social work and teaching, but also marketing, PR or law.

Subject options

This subject can be taken at GCE A/AS level and as an SQA Higher in Scotland.

Alternatives to sociology include A/AS level in Anthropology and the International Baccalaureate in Social and Cultural Anthropology; these subjects take a broader perspective on society and culture. Find out more about the IB diploma option at www. ibo.org/diploma/curriculum/group3/socialandculturalanthropology.cfm. Information on A level Anthropology is available at www.aqa.org.uk/qual/gce/humanities/anthropology_ overview.php.

A/AS level in Sociology

For an exact definition of the AS and A2 syllabus you will be studying, you should consult your chosen school, college or the exam board itself. This outline is based on the AQA syllabus.

You will primarily learn through classroom-based methods. You may look at government policies, newspaper reports, films and social documentaries to bolster your knowledge. Assessment is carried out by two written exams each year.

At AS level, you will develop your own social awareness and learn about contemporary social changes. The AS level is made up of two units covering the following topics:

1. culture and identity; families and households; wealth, poverty and welfare
2. education with research methods; health with research methods.

At A level, you will develop a deeper and broader knowledge and show enhanced skills in analysing, interpreting and evaluating. The A2 level is made up of a further two units covering the following topics:

1. beliefs in society; global development; mass media; power and politics
2. crime and deviance with theory and methods; stratification and differentiation with theory and methods.

Higher in Sociology

You will cover units on the sociological approach to studying human society, along with two units on understanding human society. You will study topics that include the sociology of class, education, family, welfare and poverty, crime and deviance, and mass media. Assessment for the Higher course is by written exam and closed book assessments. The subject is no longer available at Advanced Higher level.

Choosing other subjects to go with sociology

This subject could be combined with arts or science subjects. English, history, psychology, government and politics, communication and culture, health and social care, and economics would all go well. Sociology could provide some balance alongside science subjects.

Top Tip

Sociology is sometimes perceived as a 'soft' subject, yet the universities that produce preferred subject lists for general entry all include it as an accepted subject. Trinity College, Cambridge, indicates that sociology is an A level of more limited suitability, as it is considered only for arts courses. Remember that you should check individual course requirements, too.

In spite of this, it appears that some top universities still accept fewer students with subjects such as sociology. In research carried out by the Policy Exchange, it was revealed that Nottingham University took three times more students with Economics A level than Sociology, even though A level Sociology is studied by a far higher proportion of pupils (see *The Hard Truth about 'Soft' Subjects*, www.policyexchange.org.uk).

Sociology at university

At university level, sociology is studied in far greater depth and you will develop many more critical approaches with which to analyse the issues.

Institutions do not normally require A level Sociology to study it at degree level; in many cases, universities ask only for particular grades or UCAS tariff points, rather than any specific subjects.

There are many different kinds of degrees in this area.

What is the difference between sociology and social policy?

The two disciplines are closely linked, looking at the same kinds of issues but taking a different approach. Sociology concentrates on how society works, while social policy is focused on people's welfare.

As well as social policy and sociology, universities sometimes offer a social science degree which covers both of these subjects and more (for example, social research). Some of the modules you might find on a three-year Sociology BA include:

- deviance, crime and social control
- identity, difference and inequalities

- introduction to race and ethnicity
- key debates in sociology
- research methods
- sociological thinking
- sociological analysis of contemporary society
- stigma, deviance and society.

This subject obviously goes well with social policy but can also be combined with subjects such as politics, economics, philosophy, geography, English and history.

Sociology and your future career

Non-graduate jobs in sociology

Sociology will enable you, along with your other subjects, to get a junior position in many areas of business, the public sector and the not-for-profit sector. Jobs in sociology might be hard to find without a degree but getting an administrative position in social services, the prison service or a non-governmental organisation (NGO) could be a possibility.

Graduate jobs directly related to sociology

- **Education, teaching and lecturing.** This can be at secondary level, where a PGCE is required, or in further or higher education.
- **Probation officer:** provides a social work service to all the courts. Work involves the supervision of offenders in the community, the care of offenders in custody and the aftercare of released offenders.
- **Social/community work.** This includes social work and community work, careers and educational guidance, and counselling roles.
- **Social research.** This could mean working for a local authority, charity or campaign organisation, trade union, political party or as a parliamentary research assistant at Westminster.
- **Social worker:** supports people who need help or protection. Work is done with children and families but also with those coping with issues such as homelessness, addiction or mental health problems.

Other graduate jobs where a degree in sociology could be useful

- **Counsellor:** works with individuals and sometimes with groups, in confidence, to explore dissatisfaction or distress. A counsellor will aim to enable someone to overcome personal difficulties and facilitate change.
- **Housing manager:** develops, supplies and manages housing for local authorities and housing associations.
- **Prison governor:** plans, organises and co-ordinates the activities and resources necessary for the efficient running of a prison in accordance with Home Office policies.

- **Welfare rights adviser:** concerned with giving information and advice to members of the public on matters which are usually of a legal or financial nature and affecting the individual's rights and basic welfare.

Find out more about sociology

- AQA: www.aqa.org.uk
- British Sociological Association: www.britsoc.co.uk/WhatIsSociology/
- OCR: www.ocr.org.uk
- Skills for Care (Social Work Careers): www.skillsforcare.org.uk
- Skills for Care and Development: www.skillsforcareanddevelopment.org.uk
- Skills for Justice: www.skillsforjustice.com
- SQA: www.sqa.org.uk
- WJEC: www.wjec.co.uk

TRAVEL AND TOURISM (APPLIED)

The global travel and tourism industry is big business, which means that the demand for well-qualified staff is high. As a student of this course, you will essentially learn how the travel and tourism business operates; you will find out about tourist destinations, and how the industry works and learn more about customer service, managing events or marketing.

As well as giving you a good background in this area, you can also choose to focus on particular career areas, such as marketing, customer service, worldwide travel, events management or tourism development.

Is it right for me?

If you are interested in a career in this industry and want a course that applies your learning in a slightly more practical way, then travel and tourism might be right for you. The subject is predominantly based on coursework, with some exams alongside. You do not need to have studied the subject beforehand to succeed on the course at advanced level.

You should develop plenty of skills that will make you more employable, including ICT, teamwork, communication, time management and customer service, along with an understanding of the way businesses operate.

Subject options

This subject is available as an Applied A/AS level, both single and double award. It can be studied as a Higher course in travel and tourism in Scotland.

Alternative options include the SQA Higher PBNC (Project-based National Course) in Travel and Tourism. Find out more at www.sqa.org.uk/sqa/41175.html.

A/AS level (Applied) in Travel and Tourism

As AQA is withdrawing this qualification, OCR is the only exam board continuing to offer the course. The details below are based on the OCR syllabus. As options taught will vary between institutions, your selected sixth form or college will be able to give you the most reliable information.

As well as classroom work, students may visit different types of travel and tourism organisations and do lots of independent research about the sector. Assessment is carried out by a combination of externally set and marked written exams and internally assessed portfolios of evidence. About two-thirds of the marks are based on coursework, with one-third coming from written exams.

AS level options include the following.

- **Introducing travel and tourism (AS).** The nature, scale, structure and development of the industry.
- **Customer service in travel and tourism (AS).** Principles of customer service; the needs of customers; customer service skills; assessing the quality of customer service.
- **Travel destinations (AS).** Key features and geographical locations of major destinations; the appeal of different destinations; how destinations change in popularity; research skills.
- **International travel (AS double award).** Transport to and from the UK; consumer issues and factors influencing international travel; additional products and services for international travellers.

AS double award students also choose two additional subjects from:

- tourist attractions
- organising travel
- hospitality
- working overseas.

A2 level options include the following subjects.

- **Tourism development (A2).** Objectives, impacts and agents of tourism development.
- **Event management (A2).** Feasibility planning; teamwork; financing and marketing the event; occasion management; evaluation of the project.
- **Marketing in travel and tourism (A2 double award).** Market research; marketing communications; the marketing mix.
- **Human resources in travel and tourism (A2 double award).** Recruitment and selection; induction, training and development; staff motivation; performance management and appraisal; termination of employment.

A level students choose a further subject from the list below, while A level double award students choose an additional two subjects:

- the guided tour
- ecotourism
- adventure tourism
- culture tourism.

Higher in Travel and Tourism

This course should develop a detailed knowledge of the travel and tourism industry, together with an understanding of travel and tourism marketing and customer service required by the industry. Standard Grade English, history or geography at Grade 3 tends to be required.

All students study 'structure of the travel and tourism industry' and 'marketing in travel and tourism: an introduction'. Students can then choose to focus on domestic or international tourism by choosing between 'the Scottish tourism product: an introduction' and 'tourist destinations'.

Assessment takes the form of a written exam paper, along with a unit report and closed book assessments. The subject is not available at Advanced Higher level.

Choosing other subjects to go with travel and tourism

This subject goes well with other applied subjects such as leisure studies and applied business; just watch out for any overlap in content (your sixth form or college will be able to tell you more). Equally, it would go well with advanced level study in languages, geography or PE.

Top Tip

Remember that Applied A levels are not welcomed by all universities. If you want to get into a top university, this subject might need to be taken in combination with more traditional, academic subjects.

Travel and tourism at university

If you decide to continue with travel and tourism at university, you can choose from degrees in travel and tourism management, international tourism management or airline and airport management.

Modules might include:

- adventure tourism
- e-tourism
- global tourism issues
- incoming and domestic tourism
- marketing and accounting
- organisational studies
- tourism today
- travel agency operations
- travel trade and IATA studies
- visitor attraction studies
- world geography
- a language (French, German or Spanish).

Some degree courses are sandwich courses, meaning that students get to work for a year in the travel and tourism industry during their course (some courses might offer a year abroad option). You don't necessarily need to have studied this subject previously to be accepted onto a degree course.

Combining travel and tourism with other degree subjects

Travel and tourism can be studied in combination with other subjects. It goes very well with a modern foreign language but can also be studied alongside subjects such as accounting, geography or even dance.

Travel and tourism and your future career

Non-graduate jobs in travel and tourism

There are opportunities in this sector for students to get jobs straight after A levels. Trainee positions exist with travel companies, agencies and tour operators, as well as with some airlines.

Graduate jobs directly related to travel and tourism

- **Holiday rep:** employed in resorts to look after holidaymakers; this role includes children's reps and administrators. Work is hard and demanding, and usually based on a rota system.
- **Tour manager:** travels with groups of holidaymakers on package tours at home and overseas.
- **Tourism officer:** develops and promotes a quality tourism product which will attract visitors and produce significant economic benefits for a country or region.
- **Tourist information centre manager:** provides information to visitors to the area and sells guidebooks, maps and products.
- **Travel agent:** acts as a link between the client and tour operator. They are responsible for advising customers and selling travel services.

Other graduate jobs where a degree in travel and tourism could be useful

- **Arts administrator:** responsible for managing a theatre, gallery or other arts venue, managing financial resources, marketing and attracting sponsorship to support the arts.
- **Event organiser:** identifies potential business and researches, writes, plans and runs all aspects of conferences or exhibitions on behalf of a client or his/her own organisation.

- **Hotel manager:** manages a hotel or restaurant, whilst promoting facilities and services, organising special events and recruiting staff.
- **Public relations officer:** writes press releases, produces publicity brochures and promotional literature (perhaps in conjunction with a marketing department), and produces customer or staff newspapers and magazines.

Find out more about travel and tourism

- Association of British Travel Agents (ABTA): www.abta.com
- Institute of Travel and Tourism: www.itt.co.uk
- OCR: www.ocr.org.uk
- People 1st: www.people1st.co.uk
- SQA: www.sqa.org.uk
- Travel Industry Jobs: www.travelindustryjobs.co.uk

ENDNOTE

Now that you have an understanding of what matters when choosing your qualification and subjects, you can start to make the decision. Getting this right first time will take some thought and research, but you should find yourself rewarded with interesting studies and a wealth of possibilities.

'I have really enjoyed learning more about myself, what I am good at and enjoy the most in order to decide what path to take after A levels, as well as meeting new friends for life along the way.'

Abigail Tindall

'My A levels got me into university to study history, which has helped me towards my overall goal of becoming a history teacher.'

Sian Burke

'The best things for me have been experiencing a different place to study, having more freedom than at school, being more independent in my learning and knowing I would have the capability to go to university afterwards.'

Annabel Weeden

'They were very challenging subjects, but it was very rewarding when I achieved a good exam result.'

Andrew Burnage

'I am proud to say I have achieved the A levels I have in maths, physics and geography.'

Melissa Handley

'I get to study for a qualification in something which I am very passionate about and thoroughly enjoy.'

Rachel Etherington

Glossary of terms and abbreviations

Term/abbreviation	Definition
AQA	Assessment and Qualifications Alliance. One of the five main exam boards in the UK.
A levels	Advanced levels.
Advanced Highers	Scottish qualifications available after Higher courses.
AEA	Advanced Extension Award. These are for candidates who want to show an exceptional standard in maths.
AS levels	Advanced Subsidiary levels, forming half of a full A level, but also a qualification in their own right.
A2	The second half of a full A level.
BA	Bachelor of Arts undergraduate degree.
BMus	Bachelor of Music undergraduate degree.
BSc	Bachelor of Science undergraduate degree.
CAD/CAM	Computer-aided design/computer-aided manufacturing.
Cambridge Pre-U	New advanced level qualification offered as a route to university.
CCEA	Council for the Curriculum, Examinations and Assessment – exam board in Northern Ireland.
Diploma	Usually lasts one or two years and is often related to a specific area of work. It can be taken at a variety of levels, including advanced level.
Edexcel	One of the three main exam boards in England.
EP	Extended Project – an independent piece of work, of up to 5,000 words, produced alongside your level 3 courses.
Fieldwork/field trip	Practical activities related to a subject of study that happen away from school or college, often outdoors; for example, a visit to a site of archaeological importance.
Foundation degree	A higher education qualification below Bachelor's degree level, offering vocational education. It can be converted to an honours degree or used to go on to specific areas of employment.

GCE	General Certificate of Education.
GPR	Global Perspectives and Research – a core component of the International Baccalaureate.
HE	Higher education.
Highers	Scottish advanced level study which can be taken as a standalone qualification or continued to Advanced Higher.
HL	Higher level of the International Baccalaureate.
IB	International Baccalaureate Diploma. Two-year advanced level curriculum offering a broad and balanced combination of subjects.
IGCSE	International GCSE. It is comparable to GCSE level and taught in over 100 countries, as well as in schools in the UK.
NVQ Diploma	A qualification which assesses students' ability to carry out work-related activities.
OCR	Oxford, Cambridge and Royal Society of Arts Examining Board.
PGCE	Postgraduate Certificate in Education – a requirement for most trainee teachers.
Sandwich course	A degree course which includes a year of paid work.
SL	Standard level of the International Baccalaureate.
Specification	Exam boards produce a specification for each course, giving details of course content, assessment, and so on; it is also known as a syllabus.
SQA	Scottish Qualifications Authority.
UCAS	Universities and Colleges Admissions Service. This is the central body for handling applications to universities. You can search for courses on their website.
UMS	Uniform mark scale – used in grading AS and A levels.
Viva (or viva voce)	A short presentation or discussion with an examiner about your work.
WB	Welsh Baccalaureate.
WJEC	Welsh Joint Education Committee – the examining board for Wales.